LET'S FACE IT

MEMOIRS, SPEECHES AND WRITINGS OF A CAREER MARINE
AND TWO-TIME PRISONER OF WAR

FELIX J. McCOOL

Felix J. McCool

To Karen,
Thanks for your interest
and support in this project.
I hope you enjoy the stories
we've put together.
My best wishes,
Aileen

PROLOGUE

by SCOTT MARCKMANN

Along the course of life there are people you truly want to meet. As a child, many want to meet sports or movie stars. As you grow older, those choices may change to famous authors, or still movie stars. I was no exception, but as an adult (and military officer), I wished I could have met my great-uncle Chief Warrant Officer Felix McCool. He lived an exceptional life, filled with adventure and love, but also extraordinary hardship. He is in a small club, as a two-time Prisoner of War, living through the worst of man's inhumanity to man. He experienced some personal despair in his life with the dissolution of his first marriage and finding great joy in his second.

As a military officer, history buff and family member to Felix, I wish I could have learned more, first hand, about his life. From Pre-World War II in Shanghai, both periods as a POW, his appearance on television as well as his perspective on the world today based on his experiences. There are so many questions and details untold.

His body of work shows a man of great character, a hardened career Marine, sensitive poet, passionate teacher and mostly a patriotic American. Living through the indoctrination of the Chinese Communists during the Korean War certainly shaped his life post-captivity and became a driving force upon his return to America to tell the story not only of enduring the prisoner of war experience but also the truth behind the Communists attempts to brainwash the POWs and disparage America. It seems fitting his birthday is Flag Day.

This book was a labor of love by my mother and me. It is dedicated to his widow, Marion, the extended McCool family, the Marine Corps, and Felix's fellow prisoners.

The first part of the book is some of Felix's early recollections of his childhood, followed by the book called "Let's Face It," he intended to publish upon his return from being a Prisoner of War held by the Chinese. He felt a burning desire to reveal to Americans the true nature of Communism. He worried that people would be fooled by the notion of communist ideals and forget about the freedoms we hold dear.

The next section is a collection of his letters from his Korean Prisoner of War camps. This is a short selection of letters to the family from North Korea. The third annex is a collection of speeches and writings concerning the time spent as a POW during the Korean War. This includes some statements of others regarding Felix and his comments about a few other POWs. . The third annex contains some information about his captivity during World War II and includes an article from the Saturday Evening Post from 1946 about a portion of his captivity during World War II. The final annex includes a speech to a middle school, military citations and a recollection from my mother.

This journey to publish Felix's words and works has led me and my family on a great journey. We have met men who shared the Prisoner of War experience with Felix, Veterans of multiple conflicts, many historical stories and even a trip to the White House to attend the Medal of Honor ceremony for a POW interred with Felix during the Korean Conflict- Capt (Father) Emil Kapaun. There is the story of a dog that survived the capture of Corregidor and was repatriated at the end of WWII (Soochow and the 4th Marines). We learned about the battle of Chosin from those who survived and those captured with Felix. There are so many stories behind each veteran, battle and family member behind those who serve.

TABLE OF CONTENTS:

Prologue by Scott Marckmann... i

Unknown Bio v

Timeline xi

Early Recollections:..xiii

Purpose of the book xix

Chapter One Capture.. 1

Chapter Two Comrades.. 13

Chapter Three 14 Day Camp 21

Chapter Four Along the way to Kanggye 25

Chapter Five Arrival at Kanggye... 31

Chapter Six Kanggye 41

Chapter Seven Futile Escape... 57

Chapter Eight Guards and Lies Our Indoctrinations 59

Chapter Nine Camp Activities 73

Chapter Ten Humor and Incidents 85

Chapter Eleven Letters Home... 93

Chapter Twelve Stolen Chow.. 97

Chapter Thirteen In the Can.. 103

Chapter Fourteen The March To Nowhere 107

Conclusion..113

Prayer...115

Annex 1 – POW Letters Home..119

Annex 2 – Korea 179

    Code of Conduct Speech 235

    Evening of Inspiration 261

Annex 3 – JAPAN/WW II..271

    From the Saturday Evening Post 293

    Felix Letter Home 301

Annex 4 – MISC...303

Acknowledgements 331

UNKNOWN BIO

It would be easy to compose a riddle about Marine Chief Warrant Officer Felix James McCool.

Of himself, he says" "Twice I was born and twice I have died," and he goes on to relate how he once survived death by escaping into a Japanese concentration camp.

In a 24 year career in the Corps spanning a period of history when America fought her toughest war, the 41 year old veteran has survived the last ditch stand on Corregidor, the infamous Bataan death march, 3 ½ years as a Japanese prisoner of war and another 2 ½ years as a Chinese prisoner of war during the Korean Campaign.

But strangely – or possibly not so strange if you know McCool – one of the most unique facets of his action-packed career has to do with a subject as far removed from the horrors of concentration camps as a classroom in a quiet American school.

For Felix McCool entered the Marine Corps in 1934 with one goal in mind – to get an education. "Of course the travel and adventure and the snappy uniforms had something to do with it," he admits, "but those were tough times back there and I'd learned to appreciate the value of the education I didn't have, "he recalls. McCool quit high school in the 10th grade.

The first mistake McCool made was joining the Reserve instead of the regular arm of the Corps. The fledgling gyrene was told he would have to be a regular before he could really take advantage of the Corps program in education. That meant waiting for reenlistment into the regulars in 1938.

The second mistake, if it can be called that, was joining the Corps at a time when the world was teetering on the brink of chaos. And just about the time McCool finally got his studies underway, the world took the plunge into the Second World War.

McCool was with the Corps in Shanghai in 1940, taking high school courses through the Marine Corps Institute. In 1941, he had to drop two courses in American history and chemistry when his unit was transferred to a Pacific island that was soon to become a household word synonymous with bravery and raw courage: Corregidor.

When the bullets started flying, the books were put aside. McCool was a sergeant in charge of a machine gun unit on the beach defenses of the island. Before Corregidor fell, surrendered by General Jonathan Wainwright, McCool was wounded seriously, his leg shattered by bullets and body riddled with shrapnel.

In that condition he was herded with other survivors onto the tail end of the infamous Bataan death march. But his wounds prevented him from keeping up. He fell out of the column, was taken for dead and transported to a mass grave. But he crawled out, took refuge in a sugar cane field for four days and from there "escaped from death into a Jap POW camp" – Bilibid Prison, Cabanatuan.

He was a prisoner of the Japs for 3 ½ years –the last year at Futase City, Kyoshu, Japan, where he worked in a coal mine.

The books were gone, temporarily, but education and learning hadn't stopped. His experiences mastering the art of survival in the camps and in a Jap "hell ship" packing 1600 prisoners into a small, dark hold, taught him "how to survive on a few grains of rice, the art of cleanliness necessary to keep alive – the qualities of simplicity."

Returning to the States in 1945, McCool kept reaching for his own particular star – a star that had guided and sustained him through the dark, depressing hours of his imprisonment. He took an Armed Forces Institute General Education Test and earned a high school equivalency diploma. The diploma was granted by the principal of his old school in Oklahoma City, Okla.

By 1948 he was back in the Philippines and hard at work through the MCI on college courses. He passed another exam giving him the equivalent of one year's college credits.

But his work was interrupted by another war – the bitter Korean campaign. In July, McCool's outfit was sent to Korea. The places where he served read like rallying calls in the Corp's history" Pusan perimeter, Naktong, Inchon-Seoul, Hungnam and Hamhung.

On his second trip to the Chosen Reservoir, McCool was caught in a column of British soldiers heading for battle and surrounded by thousands of Communist Chinese troops. After a day and night of bitter fighting at point-blank range, the survivors were surrendered by the officer in command in order to save the lives of the wounded.

McCool was taken to a place called Pyockdong where he was to remain a prisoner until 1953.

But in that camp McCool continued his education. "The men started educating themselves, partly to offset the stuff the Commies were forcing on us," McCool says. Religious groups such as those formed by the martyred Father Emil Kapaun of Kansas, sprouted up.

The men began organizing and teaching each other French, English, math, geography and other subjects. McCool taught a course in bookkeeping. Those who taught the course spent a year of painstaking work preparing textbooks made from rice paper issued to the prisoners by the Chinese.

But the activities aroused suspicion and at the end of the year, a surprise shakedown was ordered. The prisoners were stripped, their barracks ransacked, and the work of a year confiscated. A committee of protest confronted the camp officers. They pointed out the men were not "politicking" but merely engaged in a process of self-improvement. The Chinese "magnanimously" issued notebooks and told the men they could have the privilege of starting all over. That consumed another year's work.

"While I was there I studied such things as American history, literature, languages – including Spanish (at which he became fluent) – poetry and even dancing."

Then he began to write, mostly poetry in open verse. His collection of poems has since been published under the title of "The Exile."

In it is a poem, "The Drums of Death," from which the lines, "Twice I was born and twice I have died" are taken, recalling his experiences on Corregidor.

"When I fell wounded there, I thought I was dead. And later they told us we would all be left for dead," he says.

His experiences as a prisoner taught him "it is the simple things that count: air, sleep, kindness. I learned if you didn't help your fellow man like Christ taught, you didn't survive. I saw men fight over the butts of cigarettes with 10 good puffs left in them. The butts were worth 10 lives. And I learned a man needs a luxury – more than the simple routine to sustain life."

"Men tend to compromise and rationalize the truth away when they are prisoners in order to be able to stay alive. But I learned that when the time came that a man could welcome death, he no longer was compelled to compromise or rationalize. Only then could he accept the truth. And life isn't worth living as a lie."

McCool is stationed at Camp LeJeune, N.C., where he teaches transportation and traffic management in Marine Corps supply. He will complete his final year for a bachelor's degree at the University of Miami after his retirement from the Corps later this year. Then he wants to get a master's degree – and maybe a doctorate.

His goal to teach American history and government.

Why? "It's like this, : he says, "I learned something else, too, in those Chinese POW camps where they brainwashed the kids. I learned a man needs real knowledge of his own government and the history of his country if his beliefs are to be made strong enough to carry him through the ordeals of war."

Unable to forget his own experiences, struggling for an education, McCool has one aim as a teacher.

"I want to lift people," he says. "Maybe all these things I've been through can make sense that way – if they help me to help others because of the insight they've given me."

He is also contemplating a book about his experiences.

"I've thought a lot about the war," he says, "trying to figure out how one group of men could possibly be as inhuman to another as the Japs were to us. I think I've found part of the answer, and I think that's helped me find myself, too."

Over the years he has continued the habit picked up in the POW camps of scribbling thoughts that come to him on scraps of paper. He saves these and the collection will one day become the core of his book.

One thing McCool promises: It won't be a surface thought of thing. It will go deep, and, I hope, penetrate the reasons why.

Writing about the "reasons why" might come easier to McCool than most people. Not only is he an accomplished writer –as his poetry indicates (his verse contains lucid word pictures and reflects a real talent based on his ability to feel compassion, a well-developed imagination and a feeling for prose rhythms) – but his life has followed in the wake of the whys.

If McCool ever does reach up and grab his own star – the star he's been following out of the depression days of his youth – chances are it will have a big "why" engraved on it.

And maybe when he does –say in publishing his book – McCool will be given the world his own big answer.

TIMELINE

June 14, 1912 – Born in Pawhuska, OK

1934 - Joined the Oklahoma National Guard

1935 - Worked odd jobs in Miami, Florida and Los Angeles, California

1938 - Infantryman, U. S. Marine Corps. -Assistant squad leader and promoted from Private to Private First Class.

1940 - Shipboard duty as Squad Leader headed to Shanghai, China for Asiatic-Pacific duty.

1941 - China duty as a Corporal and Sergeant with the 4th U. S. Marines, squad leader and gun captain. The 4th Marines left China for the Philippine Islands and disembarked at Subic Bay, Philippines two days prior to World War II. Embarked for Corregidor with the 4th Marines Machine Gun Company

1942- Corregidor surrendered to the Japanese on 6 May with survivors taken prisoner and attached to the "Death March." Imprisoned at Bilibad and Cabanatuan.

1943 – Imprisoned at Camp Lipa in the Batangas Province. Shipped to Japan on the ship Isha Maru then sent to Futase City, Camp Number 10. See Saturday Evening Post "WE WERE SABOTEURS" by Felix J. McCool 1946.

1945 - The surrender of Japan, repatriated to San Francisco and then to Long Beach Naval Hospital for treatment of injuries sustained as a POW.

1946 - Transferred to duty at the Department of Pacific USMC, San Francisco, California as Post Exchange Officer and made rank of Warrant Officer.

1948 - Transferred to Subic Bay, Philippines as Post Exchange Steward and Platoon Sergeant of the Headquarters Platoon.

1950 - Transferred to duty at Oahu, Hawaiian Islands and to Camp Pendleton, CA. The Korean War began June of 1950 and Felix volunteered for duty with the 1st Marines. In September, the Marines land at Inchon. In November, the Battle of Chosin and Felix captured.

1953 – Ceasefire reached in July and Prisoner exchange in September. Felix released from captivity September 1953 and stationed in the San Francisco Transportation Branch of the USMC.

1956 - Transferred to Camp Lejeune, North Carolina and took various Marine courses. Wrote courses to be taught to other Marines. Served as a lecturer for various organizations on the "Code of Conduct" and Liaison Officer in various Public Relations matters.

1957- Felix appears on the Ralph Edwards television show "This is Your Life" (2 April 1958).

1960 - Retired for United States Marine Corps as Chief Warrant Officer. Completed a Bachelor's Degree in Business Administration (Management) at the University of Miami and began teaching at a Miami High School.

December 27, 1972 – Passed away Miami Fl

In The Words of Felix J. McCool

EARLY RECOLLECTIONS:

Pawhuska, Oklahoma, Osage county seat. Born June 14, 1912

Pawhuska was a dirty little town with a paved downtown street and as I remember it snowed one day. A single car rode over the street in front of our house on 6th St. When I awoke I called my sister's, Aileen and Antoinette, and told them we had 'street cars' in Pawhuska – just look at the tracks. However, that also could have been accomplished on a smooth dirt road!

I remember Uncle John Lynn's place on the outskirts of town where the pecan and walnut trees were in thick clusters. There was a ball park on the place, too. One day I was sliding down a wooden slide when I ran a splinter into my thigh. I hurt and I cried. Two girl friends of my sister Mary took me home (theirs or mine), undressed me and took the splinter out. I was then given a delightful warm bath. This always comes to me when I'm tired or something.

There are three places I recall living in Pawhuska – one on or about 6th and Main St where Dad had a brick building. Upstairs were flats and rooms for rent and downstairs was McCool's department store and Fry's Plumbing Shop. Fry's rented from Dad. It was in Dad's store that I called my sister, Aileen, a bad name, Dad sent me upstairs to Mamma and I got a whipping. It was a name I had heard Dad use often and I felt terribly abused and unjustly treated.

Dad's mother lived in a part of the red brick building and she was always a fearsome person to me. Mamma didn't like her either which had transferred to me. Mamma was the strong personality, or at least that feeling that the Lynn side was the side to be on generated to me.

There were some trips to Kansas, Mamma's home, where I had lots of fun playing on the farm. My half sister, Clara McCool Cole, lived on a farm in Hydro, Ok where the true nature of a boy comes out – riding, playing on the haystacks and the multiple things that a farm has on it.

Another place we lived was a low house on a dirt road and Dad had a grocery store with a meat counter adjacent. We kids would help in the store. The closest sisters to me were Antoinette and Aileen. Mary, Cecelia and Patricia were teenagers and in my childish mind were far removed from me. Patricia had gone away and married Ernest Cone who died a short time later. Her two children, Ernest Lynn and Patsy came to live with us.

I think I remember the home I was born in from the description given by Mamma. The night I was born there was a terrible thunder and lightning storm. The electricity was playing and crackling on the lines outside according to Mamma's description.

Another place we lived in was the Eddlemon House named after the man who owned it. The happy and rich part of Pawhuska seems to emerge from this place. I remember coming home from school walking into the warm rooms rich with cooking pastries and cakes. Mamma was baking bread, pumpkin pies and there was closeness to Uncle John's place down the road a piece. We seemed to be more prosperous at that time.

That was where I remember losing a good tricycle. My half-brother, John McCool, ran over it with a car and I never did forgive him. John had lost a leg and he would play hide and seek with us kids. He could leap prodigious distances on his crutch and his wooden leg fascinated me.

There was another half-brother, Frank McCool and his wife Lena who are very vague in my mind. It seems I saw them once and then half-brother, Bill McCool lived in Oklahoma City but owned property in Pawhuska. Bill had married an Osage Indian, Clara McCool.

Uncle John Lynn's wife, Clara Rogers, was a cousin of Mamie Rogers who was Will Rogers sister. Will Rogers was the famous cowboy star of movies and also a poet. Uncle John had a family of boys and one girl – John, Willie, Pat, Joe and Teresa. Teresa was like the "Lady in the Lake" to me. She was like a shadow which emerged occasionally. I would see her at home, always leaving the room or in the pecan groves as though going away. She had been hurt but I never knew what had happened. She looked to me like a wispy angel.

I went to St. Joseph's School and the kids all sat two to a seat. It was great fun. One day a girl had to go and she kept putting her hand up. The teacher disregarded her and called her to the blackboard to write. She piddled on the floor and then she cried. I felt terrible for her and ducked my head. When I got home my mamma told me that she thought I was a good little boy to be so sensitive as all the other kids had laughed. I learned then that if I cared for others pains that I would be rewarded.

I remember serving as an altar boy for Bishop Meershart, the first Bishop of Oklahoma. When he dedicated St. Joseph's church, which had been built by Father Edward Von Vasberg, I couldn't hold the water sprinkler up to him so he leaned over and took it and patted my head. I heard a woman say to her boy, 'stand up straight like he does'. I learned people like to see you stand up straight. From then on, when in church especially, I stood very straight and stiff hoping someone would complement me and say 'my how straight he stands'.

The kids I first knew in school came on wagons, ponies and some in cars. They were mainly Indians, such as Homer Buffalo Hide, Marcella Buffalo Hide, Ben Running Deer, Kenneth Strikeax and many more too vague by name for me to remember. One of the boys died and I attended the funeral. We all sat in a room and wailers (crying women) came through with food in bowls. Some of it was un-Indian, like sandwiches and coffee. It seems to me that the wake lasted for days.

There was a mythical person called John Stink, an Indian who had been buried alive and woke. Since he came back the Indians ignored and banished him. He was very wealthy but became a hermit. Whenever we kids would come around he would 'sic' his dogs on us, a pack of about

25. He would run at us with a knife in his hand screaming an Indian curse. We'd dare him out of bravado when we were actually terrified.

A convent where my mother had attended was adjacent and I'd visit my little cousin, Gertrude Hayes. I idealized her and her sister Anna Catherine Hayes. They lived in Pawhuska off of Bird Creek. My time in the warm days was spent walking the banks of Bird Creek holding Gertrude's hand as though I'd lose her.

Mamma was so dogmatically definite in her likes and dislikes that I formed many an opinion which could possibly be erroneous. People she knew were good or bad and she would tell you right off about them. No compromise, no weakness. If you associated with bad boys or girls, you were bad. Soap in the mouth helped. If you used a bad word, confession for the sins of the soul was go to church. If there was a blizzard up to your ears, you must go anyway.

I remember the O'Sullivans as being good Irish. Charles was about my age and we used to pal around. We fished, swam, smoked corn cobs and talked about girls. He had a pretty sister whom I thought wonderful and I think he was sweet on one of my sisters. We never got around to going with either.

I remember 'Sand Creek' which was an Alladin's dream of a place for a kid. It was shady and sun lit, with a sandy bottom and pool clear water which was not over your head. I discovered that when I was forcibly thrown into it and thought that I'd drown. I saw a girl for the first time there. I went behind some bushes and there she was on the ground where she had fallen, trying to put on her bathing suit. She was so pretty and so startled that we just stood there looking at each other. I carried that picture in my mind for a long time.

My sister Antoinette was being hounded by a girl name Vina. I guessed it was a girls rivalry but it upset me when they would quarrel. The other kids would try to antagonize them in an actual fight.

There was a bully who made life miserable for me. He would kick me, run after me, tear my books and in general cause life to be unbearable. A boy about half again my size took up for me, his father kidded me about fighting back which I hadn't the courage to do. So I made up my mind if the bully picked on me again I'd fight. Sure enough a lead car was pushing it on the street and running after it. This character got it in his hands, threw it into the path of an oncoming car and my little car was smashed. All the other kids began laughing at me because I had said I'd fight if this bully ever hurt me again. There he stood on the curb, hands on his hips daring me. So I called another boy over to be my second, took off my coat and started to roll up my sleeves very deliberately. The man who owned the store we were in front of – Smiths Racket Store at 6th and Main in Pawhuska – told us to run off. We decided to go to the alley. When we got there my second stood behind me holding my coat. I deliberately rolled my sleeves real high, hitched up my belt and started after the bully. He broke then, cried and ran. I learned to face your troubles even if you can't lick them. Sometimes they vanish.

I remember Mamma wanted me to learn the piano so she hired a professional teacher who had a studio in the top of one of Pawhuska's hills. I had to go each Saturday and learn the key board, then the scales. The teacher was big breasted and inclined to nervous sweat. She was a pretty woman as I recall but when she would reach over to correct something I'd get a face full of slightly rancid cloth under which was something firmly soft and nearly asphyxiated me. I didn't want to say anything as I was afraid she would be offended or would tell Mamma that I was a bad little boy. It always seemed that she sat too close to me, leaned on me too much and I finally went on strike. I hid out. She came looking for me and I hid in a culvert. I could see her legs from my spot. She waited until school was empty and after about 20 minutes she said, 'come out Felix McCool. I know you're in there'. I came out and cried and had another music lesson. Incidentally I never learned to really play.

We moved to Oklahoma City soon after that. I remember Mamma used to say to Dad, 'the children do not have the right environment here in Pawhuska. We should move'. Then they would quarrel and discuss into the night. I was just beginning the 6th grade so I couldn't have been very old when we left for Oklahoma City.

Still in Pawhuska I remember visiting half-brother Bill McCool who was going to France. It was WW I and he was at Ft Sill, Ok. He would send me letters and cards from France and pictures of bears and animals which always delighted me. In Pawhuska one night, all the folks were down in front of the store and the talk was about the 'terrible huns' and how they were so tricky and deceitful. So I took a quarter back to the druggist who had given me too much change for something I had purchased for Mamma. I was thinking to myself, 'I'm not like those huns' but thought of all the good candy I could have bought with that quarter. I wanted to tell Mamma how noble I was but knew she would see through the fact that I was going to keep the quarter in the first place. So much for nobility.

PURPOSE OF THE BOOK

- To show the reactions, personal observations, and inner philosophy of one man to the immediate events leading up to and through the Korean situation.

- To report authentic events pertaining to this sequence and the deadly routine of POW life.

- To report the heroism, suffering, humanism, weaknesses and strength of the POWs.

- To show through actual events, the techniques of torture, mental and physical, inflicted by the Chinese Commies.

- To pay tribute to the Marines and all armed services personnel, of all nations, who stood up to the common enemy and placed love of God above love of person.

- To pay homage to the ideals and the revered memories of home which were part of the souls of the men.

- To underscore and point out, by the day by day living account, the strength and weakness of men, their ideologies and their countries.

- To leave with the readers an image of returned POWs possessing a faith activated in the horrors of war that now turns in a positive manner to, not living with, but living FOR God, Man and Country.

PROLOGUE

Somewhere in the velvet blackness of the room a telephone jingled shrilly.

The woman stirred uneasily in her bed and came awake at the second ring. The man beside her didn't stir. She threw back the covers and groped with her feet for slippers. They were cold with the thin chill of early morning.

She picked up the receiver in the middle of the fourth ring.

"Hello?" Her voice was helpless and full of sleep.

"Mrs. Anhalt?" The voice was feminine, yet sexless, without expression.

"Yes, this is Mrs. Anhalt, who is this?"

"I am a friend of your brother, Felix. You have been told that he is missing in action in Korea, haven't you?"

"Felix, why yes"

"I have word from him that he is alive and well. He is a prisoner of the Chinese Communists. He is being treated kindly and is happy. He wanted you to know that."

"Who is this speaking," her voice was awake now and taut with apprehension? Like the string of a violin that sounds just before it breaks.

"Felix wants me to ask you not to do or say anything that will make it-difficult—, for him."

"Felix!" The room was suddenly crowded with memories. They flowed through the shadows and became a remembered and loved voice-the comforting words of a big brother who never lost his tenderness for his sisters as adulthood claimed the family. The brother who made his home with her whenever he had leave from his career with the Marine Corps. The brother who had spent more than three years in the miserable hell-holes of the Japanese prison camps. The big brother who went back again, to Korea this time, and was officially listed as missing-inaction. This was Felix.

But the blackness was charged with something else now. Tentacles of terror crept along the changing patches of shadow and an alien horror reached out through the night, using a fragile wire as a catalyst through which to manifest into her heart.

"How can you know about Felix?" Her voice stood on fearful tiptoe, "Who are you?"

"I will call again. Don't forget that he is depending on you."

Silence! The call was disconnected.

Slowly, she dropped the telephone onto the hook. Her fingers were cold and cramped and she rubbed them as she went into the living room. Crossing over to the window, she looked out at the rain-swept night that flurried by under the pale aura of the street light.

Rain. Gentle tears from heaven falling on the sleeping city. Mysteriously it swirled down through the lonely hours of the night. She seemed suddenly to stand alone in the center of time. There was no one else, anywhere, in the world. Her husband and children sleeping in the rooms behind her were gone.

There were only she and the everlasting rain that whispered a strange song against her ears, I am a friend of your brother, I am a friend of your brother, I am a friend of your brother.

Then, the rains changed again, just rain. The familiar wall of the room merged back into existence and the bulky patches of furniture were restored to their proper places. It was her house. This was the city of Glendale, California and this was the United States of America. This was home!

Her step was sure again as she returned to the bedroom. The shadows had lessened somehow. Her husband's unbroken breathing filled the room and the murmur of rain humming on the roof was once more reassuring.

She kicked off her slippers and slid gently back under the warm covers. The silver crucifix on the wall opposite the bed caught and reflected a vagrant ray of light from somewhere and glowed briefly in the gloom.

She smiled to herself. Felix was all right. He would be all right. There was no room for fear within her, either for him or herself.

She would tell Louis about the phone call in the morning. She would tell him that Terror had called in the night, but had found nobody at home.

DEDICATION TO CHAPTER ONE

"… by the Lunga's side our comrades died
In the fight to keep us free.
In the crawling mud they spilled their blood,
Rising wounded out of fox holes,
In sleepless, grim routine;
To alien sky they gave reply as to "why is a Marine."

—Halls of Montezuma

CHAPTER ONE

CAPTURE

Snow flurries shivered across Northern Korea from the Yalu River to the Pacific Ocean, adding a soft white covering to the ice frozen fast for the winter. It was late November 1950.

The First Marine Division was positioned out in companies and units along the road from Hamhung to Hagaru-ri and the surrounding area, fighting shoulder to shoulder along with other United States and United Nations forces against the Chinese Communists, who preferred to be officially identified as the Chinese Peoples' Volunteers.

Capt. Bill Barher's Fox Company was defending Toktong Pass to the west of Hagaru-ri against an enemy outnumbering it twenty to one. It was so cold in this sector that wounded men died because the blood plasma couldn't be thawed for use.

Major General Oliver P. Smith, Marine division commander, helicoptered into Hagaru-ri to set up an operational CP and await orders from Corps top level. His men at Yudan-ni had caught holy hell and were torn by heavy losses and fatigue. The Eighth Army was falling back from the west.

In the absence of an order, he decided to consolidate troop positions at Yudam-ni, and ordered Lt. Col. Ray Murray, Fifth Regiment, to dig in and hold. Col. Homer L. Litzerberg, Jr., Seventh Regiment was directed to keep the road open between Hagaru and Yudam-ni.

Troops and supply units were going north from Hamhung through Koto-ri and Pusong-ni toward Hagaru-ri and the Chosen Reservoir. That area was under constant harassment and attack from enemy groups in the surrounding mountains. The enemy was employing a sort of "now you see us-now you don't" technique, which was most effective.

Col. Lewis "Chesty" Puller had his First Regiment billeted in Koto-ri and had strengthened the perimeter there with personnel from various U.S. Army and British Marine groups located there.

After an unusually quiet night, newsmen cornered Puller in his HQ hut, "We hear you gyrenes had it easy here. What happened to the enemy?"

Puller grinned.

"We've been looking for several days now and have finally found him. He has us surrounded!"

That summed up the situation pretty well.

To the rest of us the whole UN operational effort at Koto-ri had the appearance like a jig saw puzzle tossed into the air and permitted to land helter-skelter around the countryside.

The road from Koto north was jammed with traffic of all nature. Jeeps, Tanks, trucks, and troops from the Army, Marines, Aussies, Royal Marines were collected in a hodgepodge of white-breathed men clad in bulky winter issue. Loaded down with gear and weapons, they plodded onward or rode grimly through the frozen hills.

The Chinese had mortars registered on the road and just kept lobbing them in. Sooner or later somebody or something drove into a burst and casualties became common element of our troops headway. Whenever a hit on a truck or other large equipment was made, a temporary road block was affected and the enemy would run in machine guns and other small arms fire to make it hot for those forced to stop.

Something needed to be done, so Col. Puller organized a group which he designated "Task Force Drysdale" to push north toward

Hagaru-ri and try to clear the road. It was named for a Royal Marine Commando, Lt. Col. Douglas Drysdale, who was put in command of the unit, and was composed of men from Capt. Charles Peckham's Baker Company of the 31st Army RCT, the British 41st Independent Commandos, Royal Marines, and Capt. Carl Sitter's George Company. In addition to the combat units, a truck convoy under the command of Major Henry Seele, was also added. The command was now fully set for the breakout of this Chinese trap.

I had returned from the Chosen Reservoir to Hamhung on November 27. My platoon was scattered along the lines as elements of the First Division Service Battalion, trying to provide laundry service to the combat troops. Part of my duties were to coordinate activities of these units and see that we maintained a maximum efficiency from the equipment. I also tried to keep my men housed as well as conditions would permit, but conditions were best described as lousy.

Battalion had set up a command post in Hamhung in an ancient temple of some sort. Seeing that there was no other suitable building in the town for our purposes, Major John Stone, Battalion Executive Officer, acting for our CO, Col. Gus Banks, looked up the old man who acted as caretaker and asked permission to set up in the temple yards. Such polite consideration nearly overcame that worthy gentleman, and after agreeing to the proposition with alacrity, he treated us with utmost respect.

On November 28, it was blustery and cold with a chill gray mist clinging to the roofs of the huts. I was fixing my own breakfast over the small stove in my quarters when someone banged at the door.

"Come in, it's open," I said.

Shaking snow from his coat collar about the room like a huge dog, a Marine corporal stepped inside and kicked the door shut again with one foot while stripping the heavy gloves from his hands.

"It's a bitch out," he announced disinterestedly, backing up to the fire and cupping his hands over the flame.

"So what else is new," I asked pointedly. "It's always a bitch in this country."

3

He sighed deeply and added in a brisker tone, "Warrant Officer Felix McCool is directed to report immediately to the Battalion Commander."

I zipped into a parka and slung my carbine over my shoulder. Grunting a farewell, I stepped out into the brittle, frosty air.

At headquarters, Major Stone motioned me over to his field desk.

"I've got a mission for you to run, McCool," he said, "It will take you up to Hagaru-ri. I realize that you just returned from there a few days ago, but the lieutenant I was going to send is sick. As you know, things are rough north of Koto-ri. The Chinese had three road blocks running at the last report. Do you want to go?"

"Yes sir."

"Fine, then it's settled." He leafed through some papers on the desk before him and selecting several, folded them together. Sealing them into an envelope, he handed them to me.

"These must be delivered to Col. Banks at Hagaru-ri. By the way, on the way up there stop by the ration dump and drop off the mail, will you?"

As I was leaving, Capt. Segar, my company commander, waved me down and when he learned that I was going back up, he told me to drop by the mobile laundry and hitch on a trailer load of heavy underwear and woolen socks. "They'll need them up there," he said, "It's twenty degrees colder at Chosen."

As I stepped out into the compound, one of my old drivers, Corporal Leon Roebuck gave me the high sign. "If you're going somewhere sir, I've got the Battalion Exec.'s jeep and it's all buttoned up." He had rigged strips of canvas over parts of the vehicle to act as a windbreak.

We made three quick stops before pulling out. Once to pick up my personal gear, then to hitch up the trailer, and lastly to pick up a Marine gunnery sergeant to serve as the "shotgun" for the trip.

Traffic was congested almost immediately after we left the city outskirts and got worse as we traveled northward. Twice we were halted by military police turning back unnecessary vehicular movement, but each time we were permitted to proceed. Occasional snipers took a few shots at us from some of the bluffs but things weren't any worse than usual until after we passed through Koto-ri.

We happened along at about the same time "Task Force Drysdale" was leaving Koto-ri and became more or less permanently fixed at about the center of the column, which was headed by eight Sherman Tanks commanded by Capt. Bruce Clarke. Marine and Navy Corsairs had given air support in the morning and were still attacking in spite of weather conditions, but the snow flurries were minimizing their effectiveness. We came under increasingly heavy enemy fire, which indicated a much heavier grouping of Chinese soldiers than anyone had anticipated.

It was early afternoon when the column began to move out from Koto-ri. We were under constant fire from that time on. Casualties mounted steadily. As the tanks met the roadblocks set up by the Chinese, we were forced to stop and take whatever cover was afforded by the shallow ditches alongside the road.

At one spot my group had perhaps an eighth of a mile of clear road ahead of us and I shouted to Roebuck, "Let's get across this open space, fast! We'll keep you covered."

With the trailer careening wildly behind us, we slithered and skidded down the rut-choked roadway while bullets stitched crazy patterns in the snow about us. The sergeant and I blazed away at the enemy concentrated on the slopes and we had covered about half the distance before concentrated fire forced us to dive headlong from the jeep into a ditch, Roebuck included. We lay there trying to dig right down into the ice and rock while whining lead scattered fragments of both over our heads.

We were less than a mile from a collection of huts known as Pusong-ni and knew we were in serious trouble. The road at this particular site twists through a narrow gorge commanded on one side by a high bluff. It was a typical site for an old-fashioned ambush, and the Chinese had one going. There was debris blocking the road and their mortars and machine guns on the bluff were raising hell on our positions.

Radio contact in the column was shot out and the lack of communication was beginning to seriously affect our combat effectiveness. At this point I was standing by a Lt. H. Barrow Turner, attached to the tanks, who was spotting and giving them enemy locations from the radio telephone control on his jeep. As I stood there listening to him give firing directions, a burst of machine gun fire rattled between us and literally blew the receiver from his hand. He stood there frozen into immobility for a second, then hurling the useless phone to the ground. He shook his uninjured fist toward the bluff.

"Damn you filthy bastards!" he shouted. Turning to me he explained bitterly, "There goes our last radio contact!"

To make matters worse, it was now getting dark. At the head of the column, casualties were becoming heavy. Drysdale was hit. His adjutant, Lt. Dennis Goodchild was wounded. Sitter's machine gun officer, Lt. James Crutchfield, fell. The Chinese there were close enough to lob hand grenades into the ranks of the trapped column.

The tanks finally blasted past the road block and fought on toward Haggaru-ri. Sitters' men managed to squeeze in behind the tanks. They were the last men destined to get through.

As soon as the fire power of our tanks was removed, the enemy closed in on the commandos. An ammo truck was blown up at the tail-end of the commando column and completely blocked any possible forward motion. Other trucks were hit at the end of Seeley's convoy to the rear and all movement stopped.

It was a maniacal scene, one out of the madness of "Dante." The burning trucks gave off the only light, which reflected redly, like blood, from the snow and ice. It was too cold for the blood of the wounded to show. That froze on their bodies.

Confusion was now rampant. Those cut off in our group were a representative cross section of almost everything. Mail clerks, MP's, liaison groups, specialized units, and what not. We were unorganized and pinned down in the best, or worst, military manner by a withering enemy fire.

My jeep was stopped in the center of the road. A shallow ditch bordered the road on the west, and from there on rice paddies reached to the frozen Changjin River. On the east, the road was bordered by a waist-high ditch and a level stretch of ground which covered some hundred yards to the abandoned Sinhung railroad tracks. Behind this was a plateau occupied by Chinese guns. More mountains rose abruptly behind the plateau.

I took what ammo I had and ran across the road to the shallow ditch where I could get in better shots up the hill. A burst of machine gun fire tore up rock under my elbow as I bellied down into shelter and someone groaned beside me. It was a young Marine-just a kid. I started to pull him down out of the line of fire, but it was no use. He was dead.

A line of defense had been set up at the head of the column by Lt. Col Aurthur Chidester and Major John McLaughlin but their casualties were mounting swiftly in the Chinese crossfire. Major James Eagan took a group of men to the railroad embankment to try to create a diversion enough to make our fire more effective but we learned later that his group was overwhelmed and captured almost immediately.

Chidester was wounded and McLaughlin assumed command of all the troops in our segment of the convoy, including Peckham's Army unit. Warrant Officer Lloyd Dirst had organized a line facing the plateau and they cut down the little men in the padded clothes like chaff in the wind until ammunition ran low.

At the columns to the rear, Seeley had formed his men into a compact unit along the river bank and though able to defend his own position, but he was cut off from McLaughlin's group by enemy troops infiltrating between the lines.

Dirst and I were carrying ammo along the road to the men in the ditch, when he staggered and fell. I turned back and knelt beside him.

"Are you hit, Mac?"

He tried to answer, but couldn't. I ran on up the road, carrying his load with mine. Another Marine pulled him down into the ditch. Frank Noel, Associated Press correspondent and photographer, and a Marine corporal got hold of an operative jeep, turned it around and tried to break through the Chinese at the rear of the column to get back to Koto-ri to bring help and ammunition, but were captured.

Our wounded men occupied most of the deeper ditches now and the situation had progressed from critical to desperate. Groups of the swarming Chinese had worked close enough to lob hand grenades into our positions and they contributed greatly to the horror. One Marine, less than ten feet from me, was hit on the chest by a phosphorus-grenade which exploded up into his face. He ran screaming across the rice paddies, blindly tearing at his face with his hands trying to dig the fire from his eyes. He died out there somewhere.

A persistent shout from the east side of the road caught our attention and after identifying himself, Sgt. Guillermo Tovar, USMC, approached our lines accompanied by three Chinese soldiers. He had been captured with Eagan's group.

"They want to talk to you about surrendering," he called to McLaughlin.

"Tell them to come to the railroad for a parley, then," Mac shouted back.

The foursome went into a brief huddle. Then, one of the Chinese, evidently an interpreter, called out for McLaughlin to surrender and lay down all arms. "If you do, we will permit your wounded to go back to Koto-ri," he promised.

McLaughlin stalled them off temporarily and went back to the ditch where Chidester lay.

"They want us to surrender. They promise to let the wounded be returned to Koto."

"Can we trust them?"

"What else can we do, Art? We've got to do what we can for the wounded- it's their only chance."

Chidester stirred uneasily. "OK Mac. That's it then." "I'll have to contact Seeley, first," McLaughlin said, and wearily climbed back onto the road.

After a lot of shouting back and forth, a sort of dubious peace settled over the sector as Seeley got his men to stop firing long enough for Tovar to approach and brief them in on what was happening. Seeley came out and joined Tovar in a visit to Eagan behind the Chinese line. We learned later they got out as they were closer to Koto-ri.

Seeley was able to work his men and wounded back out over the mountain to the rear of his position and make it safely back into Koto-ri.

The rest of us weren't that fortunate. Official reports later showed that of the combat units which started for Hagaru during that operation, Drysdale's had 90 casualties, Sitter's 63. Forty-four Marines were reported missing in action, and 22 Royal Marines, and an untold number from the Army's 31st Regiment.

It was just turning dawn and milling Chinese troops covered the bluff on the east and the level stretch below it like a swarm of white grotesque toads. There was no fighting now and all hope for escape was gone.

The road was covered by a sprawled crazy-quilt of scattered gear including canteens, guns, ammo belts, and blankets. Bodies of the dead lay frozen where they had fallen. Acrid smoke from the still burning vehicles hung motionlessly in the freezing air. Suddenly, the only sounds were the muffled moans of the wounded.

I stepped up on the bumper of a still burning truck and taking my papers and the orders for Col. Banks from my pocket, and I fed them carefully into the flames. The Chinese watched and being worn out or stupid, let me continue, they probably thought I was warming my hands. The driver of the truck was still sitting in the front seat, his burned away face twisted into a caricature of laughter. He had the last laugh on some of us still living, at that.

After the nightlong battle in the freezing weather, climaxed by the utter confusion and uncertainty attending the final surrender, most of us wandered around in a state of exhaustion and shock. The lesser wounded stumbled aimlessly up and down the road, staring with blank eyes at their captors. Those of us who were unwounded tried to do what we could for those wounded laying helplessly in the ditches. We loaded some of them into the stalled trucks where they would have at least partial shelter from the cold. There is no way of knowing what actually happened to those poor devils. It is probable that most of them froze or died of their wounds. One thing is for sure, they never got to Koto-ri or any other place, as the Chinese had promised. This was the first great lie, which we experienced personally at the hands of the Communists.

I hadn't seen Cpl. Roebuck or the "shotgun" sergeant since we had hit the ditch for the last time. Later I heard that the sergeant had been killed during the melee. I was to bump into Roebuck again that same day.

Just before I was herded into a column along with the rest of the prisoners, someone clasped my shoulder. I turned around to face a Marine master sergeant.

"Remember me, Mac?" he asked.

I shook my head, dumbly. His face was familiar but I suddenly seemed to lack the capacity to think or remember anything.

"My name's Pettit, The last time I saw you was at Corregidor. We were captured by the Japs that time. You, Freddy Stumpges and I took that long hike over the hills. Freddy's here too. He was captured about 50 yards down the road."

My emotions had no resiliency left to register either surprise or amazement. The whole thing was like rerunning the tail end of a stinking movie over and over again. Script, lines, they were all the same only the characters had been changed, and they were worse than the original cast.

I draped an arm over Pettit's shoulders as we walked toward the forming lines of prisoners.

"This is going to be a replay of that time all over again-only worse. Let's face it."

DEDICATION TO CHAPTER TWO

"The morning wind began to moan,
But still the night went on:
Through its giant loom the web of gloom
Crept till each tread was spun:
And as we prayed we grew afraid
Of the justice of the sun."

Oscar Wilde

CHAPTER TWO
COMRADES

The Chinese were more interested in looting our supplies and gear than they were in us, at first, any ways. Little brown faced men with squinted slant eye and padded clothing that made them look like miniature Frankenstein monsters; they quickly searched through every pack and vehicle, taking everything they could use for themselves. The woolens on my trailer were particularly a welcome find that was immediately confiscated by the Chinese officers. Articles that were of no use to them or that they did not recognize or understand, they purposely destroyed or trampled beneath their feet.

I nudged Frank Noel who was standing beside me. "Let's get what we can. Everything we can pick up now will be a help to us later."

We managed to find a few packs of cigarettes, Old Golds and Kools, some C rations and a couple of sleeping bags. That was all that was left, except for one thing that I was to remember vividly in the months and years to come. As they marched us over a small hill to a scattering of mud huts, I saw a box of Whitman Sampler chocolates lying unbroken in the road. For some reason I didn't have enough sense to pick it up.

We were separated into small groups and put into the huts, under heavy guard. The dwellings were small, with mud packed floors, and held the cold in like an icebox. We had been in our prison for a very few minutes when a Chinese put his head in the door.

"Are their truck drivers here?" he asked.

Frank Noel and I stepped forward simultaneously and at a gesture, followed the interpreter back down the pathway, tailed by a dozen guards, to the scene of our capture. The Chinese wanted to pick up the less seriously wounded for reasons of their own. Several other captives joined us, among them my driver of the ill-fated trip, Cpl. Roebuck. We nodded in silent acknowledgment.

As we worked futilely trying to start one of the frozen vehicles, Noel whispered under his breath, "Let's try one of the jeeps and see if we can't crash the gates - out."

We tried to act nonchalant as we worked our way past several trucks and with what we hoped was a casual manner, bent over the engine of a jeep. After a few critical sputters, the engine caught and roared into life.

A guard who had attached himself to us climbed into the front seat and sat there impassively, motioning for us to get in.

Buttoning down the hood, I said quickly to Noel, "There isn't another guard within twenty yards of us. Let's knock that gook out of there. You drive. I'll grab his gun; put it in compound till we get through this mess back to the clear part. OK?"

He nodded. I looked around, and it might really be carried off! No one was paying the least attention to us, even our personal guard was relaxed and lighting a cigarette behind cupped hands, the rifle placed casually across his knees!

I took one step toward him, and stopped. All of the wounded had not yet been cleared from the ditch and at this particular moment, a tall giant figure clad in Marine green staggered up toward our jeep and stood swaying directly in front of the vehicle. His parka was ripped open and a dark stain covered one whole shoulder. He was bareheaded and without gloves. I remember having met him once just outside of Seoul with the Seventh Regiment. His name was Meeks.

14

Frank and I looked at each other for a long moment across the vibrating hood.

"We better get him and cover him up," I said finally.

"Yes," Frank answered, "He's probably suffering from shock."

That is all we said. We bundled him up as best we could and helped him into the back of the jeep.

At this our guard started raising hell. He blew up such a stink that in no time at all we were surrounded by curious Chinese. By many gestures, we were informed that a badly wounded man was expendable.

Noel exploded in anger.

"Frig yourselves, you Commie sonabitches," he ranted, "One kid like this is worth a thousand bastards like you ... "Fortunately, they didn't understand any of what he said, but they got the meaning all right. Things were tense for a minute.

I tried some of my poor Chinese on them, hoping to calm things down a little. I don't know what I said, but I used the word "pungyo" frequently. In old school Chinese, it means something like "friend or comrade." Then I gestured up the road toward the interpreter, trying to indicate that he was friendly with us. It must have worked, for they let the wounded man stay put.

We drove around, now under a heavy, watchful guard, picking up other wounded men who might recover. One of them was a boy, not yet twenty, sitting with the patience of old age by the side of the road, waiting for death by freezing. He had a compound fracture of the leg.

"This is going to hurt like hell," we told him.

He nodded in understanding, but couldn't restrain the screams as he was moved into the jeep.

Frank turned to me and grinned a tired sort of grin, "Mac there just isn't any room left -for us."

With that we gave them a push to get started. Meeks turned just before they left and gave me a slight hand wave.

"Thanks, Mac," he said.

They disappeared over a rise and were gone.

Back at the huts I ran into McLaughlin who informed me that he had been to visit Chidester and Eagan. "I saw them both," he said, "They are seriously wounded and things look quite grim for them. However, they are receiving something to eat."

Barrow Turner and Noel joined us and Mac told them the same thing.

"Do you think the Chinese will let me go see them," I asked?

"No, gunner, Mac shook his head, "They won't. They understand that the Colonel was in direct contact with you in the Division. They wouldn't let you for a minute." I had met Chidester during the Inchon-Seoul landing. Eagan had been his assistant at that time.

I didn't get to see them before we were marched out and I heard that they died down by the river somewhere.

In the afternoon they arranged us into single file columns and under a constant guard, we started on the long walk which would eventually end at Kanggye, near Manchuria. The march became a frozen nightmare after a few hours. Those who fell from exhaustion were doomed to death by freezing unless helped by fellow prisoners.

Nights were nightmares within nightmares. The cold was a deadly, insidious enemy that never relaxed its attempts to woo us into death. We were allowed to rest on the trail that first night on some straw conveniently strewn along for some yards.

"We can get some warmth out of it, anyway," Noel remarked.

I noticed that he kept squirming about. Finally he sat up and began to peer about him.

He looked over at me. "Do you smell something peculiar?" he asked.

I started to say no and then I did get a whiff of something unpleasant. A brief investigation disclosed the cause, and explained the presence of the straw. We had made our beds on a spot used by the Chinese troops to relieve themselves! Luckily, the excrement was frozen. Needless to say, we moved to a different location.

The days and nights became an endless monotony of fatigue, pain, and wracking hunger and thirst. We were fed only twice a day and then our diet consisted of thin rice gruel.

While on the march, we would see men pass out while still on their feet. We knew we must help them or they would freeze to death if left alone on the ground. The Chinese ignored it and provided no assistance. Now and then a prisoner would slide from the arms of the man supporting him and when there was no effort made to pick him up again, we didn't need to ask why. He had escaped, in the only escape left. I remember one day Capt. Peckham, who had a bad case of the flu, was walking in a daze and passed out on his feet. Capt. Robert Messman grabbed ahold of him and walked along side of him, but was having to struggle to keep him upright and balanced. I pushed up to them and got ahold of his other arm. We walked on that way for several miles. I didn't think I could do it , but found an inner strength that invigorated me as I helped others. Peckham finally came around, still on his feet and smiled his thanks, so we pushed on. Allan Lloyd was with us, kept his head down, never giving in, never complaining. I thought he must be made of steel. Over the next couple of years I got to know Allan better, he was made of stern stuff, had a wonderful mathematical brain and taught us math at our last camp.

Noel and I worked out a system of falling down to slow up the march and sometimes we'd manage a five minute rest. Other times, Chinese boots urged us to stand again and the march would continue uninterrupted.

We weren't allowed to drink any water, so we scooped up snow with our caps, and used a mouthful of snow to quench our thirst. Do you know how much snow it takes to quench a thirst when on a forced march? It takes all you can eat constantly. Thirst was a relentless thing and we could not get enough water.

We were beginning to meet donkey pack trains corning in from Manchuria now. The roads were mere trails, covered with ice and snow.

The ice would form and reform across our path -at spots where springs fed out from the mountains and we were forced to clamor over miniature ice bergs. Sometimes we would meet the pack trains where the trail had thinned out over a precipice and we would press back into the mountainside as they passed so as to not be swept off into the chasm.

Major McLaughlin did things for us and when he did them you knew it was as if he had a spring in his step and a smile on his face through those dark days. He was always there helping with those who could be helped, giving of his strength and courage which never failed him even in the bleaker months to come. I remember in particular when Capt. "Curly" Reid picked up dysentery and would have been forced to drop by the wayside to die, it was McLaughlin who carried Curly's load and helped him keep up with the march.

We were able to deduct from the behavior of our captors that we were nearing our objective now and we prisoners looked forward to the event with even greater interest than they, for it would mean the end of the brutal forced march and possibly food and shelter.

That last night we cleared a high pass in the mountains and after a brief snow flurry, the sky became partially clear. I remember looking off to the left, a needle point mountaintop was silhouetted blackly against the canopy of heaven, and its tip seemed to point out a distinct clear blue star which hung like a diamond just over the ragged horizon. Perhaps I had never noticed the beauty of the sky before but it seemed especially beautiful that night. It might have been the same bright star that shone long ago over a warm desert country in a faraway land. I believed it to be the exact same one and it lent enchantment to that night that not even the miserable cold or Communist guards could take away. Everyone seemed to be able to walk a little straighter and think a little clearer. I prayed, literally, that this star might be an omen of hope and I drew strength from remembering others, who nearly two thousand years before, had suffered, lived and died in the fight for decency.

I looked to heaven that night and found new faith. It was Christmas Eve, 1950, somewhere in North Korea.

DEDICATION TO CHAPTER THREE

They went with songs to the battle, they were young
Straight of limb, true of eye, and aglow
They were staunch to the end against odds uncounted,
They fell with their faces to the foe.
They shall not grow old, as we that are left grow old;
Age shall not weary them, nor the years condemn.
At the going down of the sun and in the morning
We will remember them.

From for the Fallen

CHAPTER THREE

14 DAY CAMP

There was one stop over on that long march from where we were captured to Kanggye. It here that we received our initial indoctrination talks with the Communists.

It was called the "fourteen day" spa because we were there for that length of time. It wasn't any Palm Springs vacation in any sense of the word. There was just a large Korean mud hut with an outhouse.

The Chinese herded us onto the frozen roadway and then separated the officers from the enlisted men. Other United Nation prisoners had been marched into the compound that same day and our worn dirty tattered ranks were increased by more dirty tattered men just like us. Next we were quickly placed into a small room of the hut, about ten feet square.

In my group from the capture near Koto-ri there were McLaughlin, Reed, Lloyd, Turner, Noel, Peckham and myself. The new arrivals included Capt Rudy De Sylva, Lt. Fred D. Soiano, Lt. G.P. Shedd, Lt. George Snipan, Capt R.E. Alley, Lt. Hector Cordero, all of the Army; and Lt. Robert Messman, USMC.

After an exchange of names and discussion of events leading up to our present situation, we settled down more or less patiently to wait whatever fate was in store for us.

I crowded into a corner where Frank Noel sat with his legs drawn up under his chin, industriously engaged in scratching lice from his thinning hair.

"How do you like traveling with the First Marine Division?" I asked.

Noel grunted, "My mother wanted me to be a minister.

Just shows you, kids should listen to their folks." Things were silent for a little while.

"What happened to the family who lived here?" someone asked.

"They are still here - in one room," McLaughlin answered, "there are seven of them, including kids."

"There's thirteen of us!"

"Why in the hell did you have to bring that up?" "My feet are killing me," groaned George Snipan.

"He's not kidding," Messman explained, "They're frozen."

"So are De Sylva's."

"Mine stink as badly as they hurt," de Sylva complained. It was silent again. The door to the room banged open and a Chinese with a face the texture and color of an old prune stood at the entrance.

"Welcome to our little community, comrades," he began in a high-toned voice. "We will continue on our march in a few days, but we have something to do before we go on. In our usual humane fashion we are going to permit you to all write letter home. No doubt you are all beset with worries about what your families think, so in our extreme lenient way, we are going to permit you to write."

With that the door banged shut and we were alone again.

"You were through this with the Japs, McCool, and" McLaughlin said, "Any ideas on this letter writing business?"

I answered "that it is like having an insurance policy, to have your name known in the States as a captive. If you come up missing, someone would have to explain."

That seemed to make a point with everyone, and we decided in favor of writing. We got a chance the next day.

After a breakfast of purple-pink rice slops, we were given paper and pencil and told to write.

We wrote letters home. Just simple notes saying that we were alive and how much we missed everyone. They were collected but within five minutes the door burst open again and there stood a whole delegation of Commie officers. They were angry. One of them threw our letters violently to the floor.

"Comrades," he said coldly, "You have not written the truth to your families at home. You have not told them of how well we are treating you, how well you are fed, how warm you are. We must, evidently, reeducate you before we can send you back to fight for the peace-loving people of the world."

"These capitalistic lies will not be mailed. As you have violated our trust in you and have repaid our kindness with such misrepresentation, you will be permitted one letter only for the entire group. The rest of you may sign it."

"However," he added grimly, and it must contain only the truths of our kindness and our magnanimity."

It became obvious that if we were to get any word of our plight out to the world it would have to be couched in the language dictated by our captors.

That was how we came to write the letters which were later published in American newspapers, described by the commies as a "voluntary" message from prisoners who approached them with the request that their signed statement be publicized. It purportedly came from an unnamed special correspondent of the Hsin Hua News agency, official Red China new organization.

We finally left the "fourteen day place" with George Snipan and his frozen feet on the sled pulled by a cow. I gave him my sleeping bag. The temperature was somewhere below zero and the air was so cold it hurt your lungs to breathe it. Occasionally we would march past a hut with gray smoke spiraling from the chimney and the desire to obtain some of the warmth from its source would become so great that we would literally have to hold one another back from breaking for the house.

One night we stopped at a cow barn. It had a roof, partly open slat sides and a little straw on the ground. McLaughlin, Noel and I laid down in one corner of the shed. Allan Lloyd, Messman, Curly Reid, and Peckham were in another. Our fingers frozen to the zipper on our torn parka. Some groups of ROK prisoners had joined our party at the last stop and were being marched with us toward Kanggye, which we had overheard was our objective. That night, the ROK's were forced to stand outside in the deadly cold-all night. One of them in particular, I will never forget. He was wrapped only in light cotton pantaloons and a shirt. He had no head covering and his ears were black, frozen shapeless lumps. The stubs of his frozen feet were wrapped in rags. He stood there, sort of rocking back and forth, endlessly, throughout the night. The silver frost on his hair and clothing gave back the light of the snow and ice with an eerie glow that enshrouded him in a sort of giant halo. We couldn't help him or even speak to him. It was forbidden by the guards, but we who lay in the comparative warmth and security of the shed and straw were suddenly ashamed of our comfort.

McLaughlin awakened me in the morning and handed me a steaming bowl of kaoliang.

"Where did you get this? " I mumbled, hardly conscious I was awake, numb and aching from the contact of the ground.

"Eat it Mac," he whispered, "Never mind where I got it." Later I heard a Commie Chinese screaming out about thieving capitalist warmongering Americans. Guess he was the one who lost the slop. But even that simple and necessary task of eating was rendered impossible by the terrible cold. I managed to spill it down over the front of my clothing, where it froze. That was my breakfast.

We continued to march, I remember Chuck Peckham gave me a rosary that his wife had sent to him and was addressed "do not open till Xmas." He managed it to evade the search, so I gained a rosary and a friend.

By nightfall we had reached our destination - Kanggye.

CHAPTER FOUR
ALONG THE WAY TO KANGGYE

Generally, upon entering a town, we approached it from a hill by way of a winding mountain road. We look down on it. Very seldom do you look up to it. Water is there and there are flat surfaces for planting rice. A river generally runs through the town or is nearby.

They use the stream for everything, for washing and drinking. Approaching town I see over on the right by the river, three to ten women pounding clothes on the rocks.

As I approach, I see native women picking up their water. Whenever they pick up a water jug, they never bend over, they squat, and when they balanced it, they lift the jug with both hands and lift it straight up. This gives them leverage. Looking over into a field, maybe fifty to seventy five yards beyond the village, I see a flat green color; this is probably a rice paddy. I see men bare footed, arms exposed, a small white towel wrapped around their heads. The Chinese wear colorful towels: The colors that they use denote the local town that they come from. Right on the border line the colors are mingled and it is made to denote which village they represent. There may be a bunch of naked kids running around from two to six years old. The only difference in the women in the winter and in the summer is that in the summer time the women wander around slowly; in the winter time they have a little snap in their step. In a small town everybody is interested in everybody else. The older folks will be sitting in the sun. Actually, this is a very stupid thing to do, that is, to stop work, because, they are then taken off to some little houses outside of the village and just left to die. This is a very ancient custom but the people can't be bothered with the old ones anymore and so they are just left there to die a slow death without care or food.

When I first came into the village the first thing I see is an archway. I see this upon entering and leaving the village. I might look to the left and see a group of gnarled trees that are all twisted. They remind me of our cypress trees. Then on the left of the village will be a small ancient prayer temple. I don't know what faith they practice though. As I enter the main part of town, I see a small store and in the window see bottles of all shapes, sizes and colors. There probably is some kind of candy or liquid in the bottles. The bottles look as though they are home made to me. The little mud huts on either side of the road are crowded closely together. All the houses have red tile roof. They add the red coloring from the color in the terrain. On either side of the street are the slop gutters with a stream to wash it out. This is used as a form of sewage system. In the villages the toilets are always outside of the house.

The buildings are un- interesting; they are mostly one story mud huts. Very seldom do I see one worthwhile. If the man was the Mayor or the Honcho of the city, he may have a very nice home. A man of town would have a three front building. The first wall would be the storm wall to keep the extreme cold out. The second wall would be the corridor front. The third wall takes you into the living room. They use sliding paper doors. The first two doors may be removed and that gives you a porch-like effect in the summer time.

In the winter time they'll put them in again, and that gives protection. The floors are raised two feet off the ground level and underneath that they have rocks to give a channel for heating. You step down into the kitchen. There is a little sliding door that they use to drop down into the kitchen. It has an outside door at ground level also. To get to the kitchen from the rest of the house you lay on the floor and slide down into the kitchen. Everyone is so small that they scamper around like mice. You go into the kitchen and they have these iron pots and a fire is built which lay under the rocks and this forms a draft for the fire; this is their crude way of a heating system which goes under the house. It warms the floor until about 10 o'clock and the house stays cold until four o'clock. If he is a rich man he uses wood and keeps the house warmed all day. The houses are drafty. The draft comes through the floor through the separated rocks. When the fire is lit, you have to leave the house because of the smoke. There is a room where everybody sleeps. When they eat everybody sits on the floor. They use a charcoal brazier. When they pull the fires from the kitchen they take the coals and put them in the brazier. In some big shot's house he has three rooms and a room for the garden tools. They are arranged in a "C" shape. Draft animals are kept in sheds that are on either side. Each room has a sliding door on it. Korean animals consist of big bulls. They have a tawny golden fur.

A servant or person, who works for someone else, might have a little one room shack with doors four feet high.

Dogs are treated extremely cruelly, they are usually eaten. After a dog has reached its maximum potential, that is, if it has had as many pups as it is going to have, it is put into the cooking pot. They also eat a great deal of rice, which is considered to be the highest quality of food you can get in Korea. They also eat Kaoliang which is a blue grain. This blue grain is similar to the food we feed cattle called "high gear." They grow cabbage that is very similar to Chinese cabbage. This cabbage is called Pichie. This type of cabbage is also grown in the Philippines, China, and Japan. It is considered one of the staple foods. Corn is merely saved for animals. The only time that corn is eaten by the people is in the summer time when just a little bit is given to the children. Most of the better foods are saved for the animals that is the grain food.

The biggest impediment to food supply is the lack of space. Usually, right in back of a house is a hill and the people must farm on a little space on the hill.

Another food that they eat is Kimche. This is made from Pichie which is fermented with garlic and pimento. It is considered a fine delicacy.

There are few stream fish, and if there are any, they are usually very small.

If a man raises more than one pig, he is considered very wealthy. They raise pigs for food and also to sell. There are a few sheep, quite a few ducks and also a few chickens and goats. They eat the chicken and also raise them for the eggs. They might take a little piece of pork, take grease and fry rice with green onions, garlic and peppers.

Houses are made out of mud and straw. You can build a house in a couple of days. Space is of the essence. Everything is crowded in a little valley. The streets are never paved. In the winter they are ice; in the summer they are dust; and when it rains, they are mud. The most popular mode of transportation is by foot. There are no carts and there are only a few Siberian horses. The Korean people have an extreme politeness toward each other. One of their sayings is "Omn Na Sam De Da?" meaning, "Good morning, how are you?" When we would be walking down to the river to get some water, if we would stand aside and give a woman a hand with picking up water, they would say "Omn Na Sam Ne Da?" One lady even cried when we helped her.

The Commies were completely indifferent to human attitude and human feelings. One old woman was crossing the ice and had a big load on her back. We helped the old woman with her load and helped her across the ice. The Commies looked at us as though we were crazy. They thought we were crazy because we helped an old woman.

They bury a person on a hill overlooking the town. There usually isn't much grass on the hill but you could see large rounded mounds covered with grass-these were the graves. I have been told that the dead people are planted sitting up. They made us turn our backs when a burial was taking place.

We were marched through two villages, then were isolated into groups and spread out. Our captors would go into a house and tell the Korean women and children to go into one room and then they would pack us 25 to 30 men into one small room. There was nothing to keep us warm except the warmth of our bodies. For a while we had little bowls to eat from but most of the time we used our hands to eat. We were under communist guard all the time. They were well dressed. A typical communist soldier dressed in rubber soled shoes canvassed with horse hair about an inch thick. The sergeants and above wore better clothing, they had padded trousers. They also had Russian rifles about 27 caliber bolt action. Later on they got some modern rifles. The First Class troops had Russian automatic weapons. They changed guards often, but we had to keep on going. There was no possible way of telling how many men dropped off.

They never kept us together. If our men did drop off ahead of us, we never saw them. The commies must have hidden their bodies.

Then they would march us in small groups, done in a confusing manner, so that we couldn't keep track of the other men. They were doing this for some purpose, so that we wouldn't know who fell out. When we marched, we never saw any paws lying on the roadside. We guessed that they must have buried the bodies, because we saw fires up in the hills during the night. We wondered what the fires were for a long time, but finally we found out that they used the fires for softening the ground to bury the dead. Major Mac and I were talking about it one time. Frank Noel and Curly Reed were in an open shelter one night and were just sitting there wondering what all the fires were for. Some Koreans had told one of them that they did this so that they could bury the dead.

I was pretty well dressed before the march. The day before I left Hamhung I saw the supply sergeant and told him that I would need equipment for trips up into the mountains. You never can tell what may happen. When the Commies needed clothes, they took it off us. If they didn't need any clothes, they let us alone. If a Korean needed something, they would get it from you. The Chinese commies would let the militant Koreans get our clothing, i.e. The Korean Civil Police and the PRK.

I only knew the few people in our group. I heard that a prisoner was dead but I didn't know him-but the fires-they indicated that there was death. I felt it, the finger of death.

Imagine yourself in a vast space of white, nothing else, all you can see is white and it's icy and you hear a constant 'whoo-whoo', a terrible wind and the snow all around you and you march mile after mile and you look down and there are miles and miles of nothingness and you hear the faint sound of the water miles below. During the falling of the snow, it is very windy and after the fall of the snow it is quiet and the snow's brightness is blinding because it is so white. We would take a little piece of cloth and make a slit in it. The entire march was in the winter. We were starting to cross a river, we called it "the unnamed river', when the guards ordered us to stop, saying, "The weather is changing and the ice is breaking up." The march stopped.

CHAPTER FIVE
ARRIVAL AT KANGGYE

Kanggye was in a valley about twenty kilometers from the Manchurian border at the Yalu River. The column was broken into small groups, and stopped about a mile or so from where we were finally housed. Six of us flopped in a little pig shack, too tired to move our blistered, aching feet from the all-night march. Muscles so tired and aching that each breath was a sharpened agony. After we had been laying there about twenty minutes, a guard stuck his head into the door with a small slop bucket of cold rice. We all dug our grimy hands down into the bucket and started sucking the frozen particles through our beards.

Peck said, "For heaven's sake! We're just like pigs." He sat down and began counting his rosary through his fingers.

Reed was so beat he just lay over in a corner of the pig trough with his head down. A pig came in and rooted against him, searching for the little warmth coming out of his steaming mouth. He turned over in a half-hearted way and pushed his hand into the hog's face and said, "Get out of here, you hog!" The pig lunged backward and landed square in the balance of the food in the bucket.

About that time a couple of the guards came in with fixed bayonets and poked at us, shoving us outside. I reached over and scooped up what little rice was left and ran out into the road, filthy and bleary eyed.

The column was strung down the road. Little kids were lined up hooting and hollering at us throwing rocks and cow dung in our faces, saying, "Me gook, me gook. Nomba ten, Me gook. Numba ten."

One old woman grabbed up a bunch of burning branches and poked them into Frank Noel's face, gouging at his eyes. He just pulled his grizzled face in and gave sort of a half-smile to me. We put our heads down and plodded down the road again.

We got into some little village. There was nothing but utmost confusion. The Koreans didn't know how to take us.

Some were smiling and some were ferocious. They watched the guards. If the guards were decent, then they were decent. A bunch of the officers was crowded over into a corner of the yard and pushed down.

Bob Messman started singing "God Bless America." That went along until one of the guards who spoke a little English screamed out, "Stop! You American Capitalistic are tools of the War Mongers." That expression got about as common as "I've got to go to the head." And we went to the head fifteen or twenty times a day. With the change from a protein diet to a soppy wet rice substance, it seemed like all the water we drank ran right through. I must have pissed thirty times a day.

A gold tooth son of Cathay came over to us with an obsequious bow and facial grin and said, "Me Chen." He motioned some of us to follow him but when we were slow about moving the grin meant nothing, because the slowest man got a kick in the ass.

They put fifteen of us in a room. We had to sit on the floor, feet facing out. The feet on the man opposite you faced yours. For an hour it was damn comfortable. Three hours later it was an aching, screaming jumble of the tissues and muscles of my out stretched legs and back.

Bob Messman was made the squad leader of all of us. It was his duty to see that we were at roll call and did what they called exercise. A form which was designed to torture weak bodies and minds and it would work.

They would then start out in a torment at least to us, of Chinese songs with all of its cacophony and resonance which is found in the Oriental style of music. Which disregards western rules of our tones.

Using all of the sound that emits from a reed or stringed instrument, it gives a banshee wail as a group of Toms on a spree and it continues for what seems to be hours of horrible discord.

Discord, it was to us, it will always be. We just don't see or hear alike. We were then asked if we did not know something to sing to amuse ourselves with so we did, choosing the song, "Some one's in the kitchen with Dinah." It was liked very much; we then had to sing it for about three months. By the time it was over we wished that we were in the kitchen with Dinah, as the chow became more lousy as it went along.

We were getting a little piece of pickled daikon (a long radish) and two small bowls about two ounces of kaoliang (rice slop) twice a day. Once in a while there would be a little boiled dog meat or hog.

The Chinese Major Wei would come in at these times and say, "Your food is good?" We would look at him and give a sickly smile, because we knew if we complained it would get worse. Then he'd say, "The dog meat that you have received was the best that you could receive under the circumstances. I realize it is garbage but what else do you have. You have been nothing but animals to invade this peaceful country and threaten our China with your invasion. We know that you had intended to come into Manchuria after you had taken Korea. That is why we glorious volunteers are here."

He would go into his act which was boring and he knew it was to us, as we showed it, so he would just sit there while we ate and would have a smile on his face. Some of his stooges would come in often and sit with him to watch us.

They never stopped and we would get hysterical with laughter, at the fact that we were the prisoners and they had watch and listen to such absurdities was just more than our intellects could absorb.

We'd doze or make signals to each other while we were sitting in the squalor of the room, with all of its smoky oil lamp, just a little broken dish or pottery with some oil in it. We'd weave a wick of sorts to burn in it. Freddie was the custodian of the match hoard. The only way that we could get a match was to beg for it. Begging didn't go well with us, so we didn't make out too well.

We established a friendship with the Korean's who lived with us in the other room. They stood by for us, and gave useful things to us many times, when it would have been impossible for us to get them from the Chinese.

How this got by the Chinese is beyond me.

Sometimes I think that they knew and just gave in to it. This attitude by the Korean peasants' was common, whenever they could get away with it.

One time when Major Wei came in and he held us from 7:00 A.M. to 9:00 P.M., before we were given food. The food was fish heads and sort of steamed doughy bread, only two pieces per man and one fish head.

I got sore. Curly was dishing it up on our little bowls. Allen Lloyd was sitting next to us, and I pushed my way into a Chinaman hoping that he would leave. He didn't so I put my tail up in his face when I received my portion of food and let it stay there. The Chinaman took this for as long as he could, then left. This was about 11 P.M.

He returned in a few minutes with an indoctrination lesson. Our work began in a room full of lice, rats, and fleas. Our interrogation and indoctrination started in earnest there.

The people who lived in the balance of the house were an old woman, her mother, and a young Korean male who claimed to be a student and UN sympathizer. Separated by one room were an old crone, two ragged little boys, mean as sin, and an old man. He used to gather twigs in the mountains for heating the house. Another room contained Gold Tooth, the Platoon leader, and two of his henchmen. Outside were the inevitable guards. The interrogators and indoctrinators lived in another hut.

The entire valley was guarded and prisoners were in every hut. Our seriously wounded men died there and we could see the fires in the hills where they thawed the grounds in order to dig graves, gave me a comforting thought that fire warm earth reaching out for her own. Much better than a lonely ditch where the men who died on the march were thrown. Well we were there as I say from day after Christmas, 1950 to March 1951. The indoctrination started hot and heavy. In the rooms, all day and all night, we weren't allowed to pick and squash lice during class, so they just ate on you. All together it was a hell made up by the communists and nature.

Incidentally, George Snipan came into the camp a few days later and said that he had seen Korea through the ass end of a cow and she had dysentery.

Rudy Desylva was coming along with his frozen foot. They had plied off some of its' putrefied flesh. The blood blisters on my foot had broken and were healing. Life began to brighten up just a little in that respect. We always knew that things would get worse, and they did.

A typical day of indoctrination, we'd have breakfasts that were the two small bowls of kaoliang. Then three of the stooges would come in. They would start: "You Officer's and men are the victims of a big plot in America by the Capitalist of mordant Imperialism. They are the aggressors here. Your 'Dulles' said he wanted to take over the People's Republic of Korea just a few short days before the war started. So you can see that you are the aggressor. This logic is irrefutable. You are dupes. You can never become a millionaire in America."

"Only a few moneybags hold the control of the U.S. Now if you will just sign our papers telling how you feel about your warmongering leaders, I can submit it to headquarters and your situation will improve, even though your Bombers are hitting our supply lines."

"We will take care of our friends. Just as we will take care of our enemies. They are mad dogs and we will dig a big pit where we may put them so they will rot and not stink up the place with their putrefied flesh."

This veiled threat was a constant reminder and made one think. We'd discuss what had been said, after first making sure that no one was

35

listening to us. Major Mac then would say a prayer (The Our Father) for guidance as we knew that the thing was bigger than we were.

No one dissented. We stuck together throughout. Some showed more strength than others but all in all they were Americans throughout.

The Chinese would call us out one at a time for interrogation, to find out about the size of our outfit and what equipment we used. We gave them garbled accounts. There was no getting away with just giving the name, rank and serial number. Nothing like that. So we had to lie and salt the lie with enough of the truth so that the next time we were called for interrogation, we'd remember what was had said and give a creditable report.

If not, punishment was the snow. In order that you might appreciate what I mean by the snow, just open a deep freezer and place your hand in it for an hour or more.

Well, the rooms which we lived in were like that. At night Frank Noel, Major McLaughlin, Hector Cordero, Rudy DeSylva, Chuck Peckham and I lived in a room which had a half inch of rime, frost on the mud walls. We had a blanket between two men and that was all except what we had scrounged and had on our backs. The only time we took off our clothes was to delouse.

I called a vote in our room one day, "Gentlemen," I said. "We are all aware of the difficulty of going out in the cold, and we also realize the uncomfort of lice and how much easier it is to pull them off our clothes and smash them in the room letting them fall on the floor. Well, I'm against doing it that way because sometimes the lice live. I propose that whenever you must delouse, let's do it outside, and not drop them on the floor."

There was much discussion about this by all. We finally put it to a vote. To go out of doors won by a close margin.

We also voted on when we would have a smoke. The way that got started was this; I had been in Hamhung just before capture and had picked up a bag of Bull Durham tobacco as a gag to pull on one of the Officers of our Battalion. He had asked me when I was at the Chosen Reservoir, to pick up a carton of Camels when I returned to the Battalion rear. So I did but I also picked up a bag of Bull so that 1 could kid him when I got there. I was going to say, "Listen, Fellow, I couldn't get any Camels but I did get this."

Well, the joke turned on me as I was captured and ended up with the bull Durham in my pocket. I lost the Camels because they were in my jeep.

I found the bag of bull at the fourteen-day place and everyone elected me to be the official cigarette roller. I would roll two cigarettes for the 15 of us and we'd call them: Two Draggers," meaning that only two drags were allowed for everyone in order that everyone would get a smoke.

It worked but I was stuck with the job from then on. And when anyone felt that we should have a smoke he would suggest it to the group. Anyone who was asleep would be awakened and if a quorum was reached, we smoked. Sometimes we'd light up "Big Bertha." This was a pipe that Major Mac had given to Capt. Freddy Speer, USA, who had joined us later. I finally talked Capt. Ronny Alley to help on the rolling of the cigarettes. Some liked my brand and some liked Alley's.

One day a group was called out by the Koreans who insisted that every man present would write 30 pages on military matters. We sat there dumbly. So they made us kneel on the floor, then they came up and placed pistols at our heads. They did that to Capt. Peckham and the atmosphere became tense. We knelt there all afternoon until late at night with no food or water or toilet relief.

The Chinese came up to see what was going on and the Korean's released us to them with the promise that tomorrow they would be back. Sure enough they did! They tried to soft soap us then with hot chocolate, and cigarettes. We still stood dumb. The third day they broke and told us that we could write about anything. Some wrote on skiing, some on boating. I gave them a descriptive account of a 'fifty' in one box. It is a Post Exchange ration box containing many articles of candy, soap, shaving gear, etc. Their mouths were drooling after reading this, as I added many types of Chocolate with nuts and cherries. This was too much for their feeble brains so they let me go.

I do not want to create the impression that I or any of us always got away with such things, 3S that isn't so. We sometimes hit rock bottom and would realize that we had let our stomach overrule our heads and might have said something that we'd have given our left nut to retract.

There was a big barn where they held lectures. The place was surrounded by mountains. There was a snow-covered valley. You could hear the water running under the ice into the valley. Our hut was about eight hundred yards from the barn and the kitchen was about five hundred yards at a left angle. There were guards around the perimeter and by each hut. The civilian defenders were armed with spears.

After suffering that miserable lice ridden winter, spring came. Thoughts of home, family, kept dipping into our brains 'til we were nearly mad.

The girl who lived in the house started sneaking small bowls of food through a slit in the crack of the door. This girl was a woman in stature but a child of nature, emerging from adolescence into maturity, enjoying an emergence from the chill spring of youth into the warmth of womanhood.

Seeing us Americans, she watched our manners, and what we had been through in our environment, then compared us to the brutal bestiality of the men in her own life. She chose us to look at, admire, and began to use the subtle charm that a woman has and can dominate the hearts of men wherever she might be, by a look, a quirk of the lip, a small smile, a softening of the eyes. It was there and to us famished and loved starved prisoners, she was there a stimulus to think, to do, to act, to keep up a semblance of respectability. She was WOMAN and we loved it.

Whenever we were allowed to go out of the room would think up ways to be allowed to stay out longer. To see and to breathe in spring's emergence both in a new season and in a woman. It was there, an angel around us and each in his own way reveled in the fact. I remember one day when I had been out to carry some water. I came back to the hut and noticed that the guard was gone. I stepped out into the tiny courtyard. Her door slid back and she came out. She was carrying a large canning knife. She looked at me and the barest semblance of a smile hovered over her mouth. She approached me. The path was narrow and we met. I looked into her liquid eyes and remembered all that I had known in the past. It was heady and good. It was life! The moment passed, but it had lived and it will always live in the heart of man. She was on the way to feed the work animals by cutting up the old stalks of last summer corn stalks into shreds, then cooking it down into a mushy substance.

Animals had her care, while we men, fifteen in a room, lived in squalor, filth hunger, longing for life's call. We sat there reflectively, lost in our private thoughts.

It looked like we get a break.

Gold Tooth came in with an interpreter and said, "You are to get ready. Tomorrow we will leave." And he threw some cigarettes to us and some dough balls to carry on the march. They left and the room buzzed. "What do you think, Mac?" "Are we gonna leave?" "Maybe this is it. Maybe the damn war is over. Haven't heard any planes lately?"

"No". I said. "They couldn't be releasing us. We wouldn't sign their Goddamn peace pamphlets."

Noel and I went down to the river to get some water. He was telling me about New York City and I was telling him about Glendale. We ate a vicarious meal with imagination for the entree. We looked down that quiet hidden frozen valley for the last time. Dipped the gourd through a hole in the thick ice, through its thin skin, into the crystal blue depth of the river and drank deeply of the diamond droplets. Our excitement was consuming us in anticipation.

We walked on the narrow ledge of the dike back to the hut, feeling that never ceasing eye of the perimeter guard fingering the trigger on his rifle.

The next day we split up what little tobacco we had and toilet paper for rolling cigarettes and started out for the bombed out city of Kanggye.

CHAPTER SIX

KANGGYE

We arrived in Kanggye, had sat in one room for four months without water to wash with, two bowls of Kaoliang per meal, and two meals per day. The room was full of lice, rats, and fleas. The fleas are the most miserable.

The people who lived in the balance of the house were two Korean women, one about 22 who had a small son, an old woman (her mother), and a young Korean male who claimed to be a student and UN sympathizer.

Separated by one room was an old crone, two ragged little boys (mean as sin) and an old man. He used to gather twigs in the mountains for heating the house.

Another room contained Gold Tooth: a Platoon leader and two of his henchmen. Outside were the inevitable guards. The Interrogators and indoctrinations lived in another hut. The entire valley was guarded and UN prisoners were in each hut.

The balance of the seriously wounded died there and we could see the fires in the hills where they thawed the grounds in order to dig graves. It gave me a consoling thought that fire-warm earth was reaching out for her own. Maybe it was better than the lonely ditches where the men who died on the march were thrown.

Well, we were there from the day after Xmas 50 to March 1951.

The indoctrination started hot and heavy. In tile rooms, all day and part of the night, we weren't allowed to pick and squash lice during class. They both, the lecture and the lice, just ate on us. All together it was a hell made up by the communists and by nature.

Incidentally, George Snipan came into the camp a few days later and said that he had seen Korea through "the ass end of a cow, and she had dysentery". He was a coarse looking sight. Rudy DeSylva was coming along with his frozen foot and he had peeled off some of its putrefied flesh.

The blood blisters on my foot had broken and were healing. These little things began to lift up our spirits. We found out through the months that things can always become worse, and they did.

The day would begin with a breakfast of two small bowls of kaoliang. Then three Chinese goons would come in, and would begin: "You Officers and men are the victims of a big plot in America by the Capitalist of mordant Imperialism. They were the aggressors here. Dulles looked over at communist held Korea, just a few short days before the war started. So you can see that you are the aggressors. This logic is irrefutable. You are dupes, you can never become a millionaire in America, only a few moneybags hold the control of the U.S. Now if you will just write how you feel about these people, to me, I can submit it to headquarters and the situation will improve here even though your Bombers are hitting our supply lines, we will take care of our friends. Just as we will take care of our enemies—they are mad dogs and we will dig a big pit where we may put them so they will rot and not stink up the place with their putrefied flesh".

This threat was a constant theme, and made one think. We'd discuss what had been said, after first making sure that no one was listening to us, Major Mac then would say a prayer, the "Our Father," for guidance as we knew that this business was bigger than we were. No one dissented.

We stuck together throughout. Some showed more strength than others but all in all they were 'Americans' throughout.

The Chinese would call us out one at a time for interrogation, to find out about the size of our outfit and what equipment we used. We gave them garbled accounts. There was no getting away with just name, rank and serial number, nothing like that, so we had to lie and salt the lie with enough of the truth so that the next time we were called for interrogation, we'd remember what we had said and give a credible account. If not, our punishment was the snow, in order that you might appreciate what I mean by the snow, just open a deep freezer, place your hand in it for an hour of more.

Frank Noel, Major McLaughlin, Hector Cordero, Rudy DeSylva, Chuck Peckham and I lived in a room which had a half inch of rime frost on its mud walls. We shared one blanket between two men and that was the warmth we had except what we had scrounged and were wearing. The only time we took off your clothes was to delouse.

I called a vote in our room one day thus: "Gentlemen, we are all aware of the difficulty of going out in the cold, and we also realize the uncomfort of lice and how much easier it is to pull them off your clothes and smash them in the room letting them fall on The floor. Well I'm against that method, because sometimes they live. I propose that whenever we must delouse lets go outside, and not drop them on the floor."

There was much discussion about this by all, and we finally put it to a vote. To go out of doors won by a close margin.

We also voted on when we would smoke. The way that got started was this. I had been in Hamhung just before capture and had picked up a bag of Bull Durham tobacco as a gag to pull on one of the Officers of our Battalion. He had asked me when I was at The Chosen reservoir to pick up a carton of Camels when I returned to the Battalion rear, so I did but I also picked up the bag of Bull so that I could kid him when I got there. I was going to say listen fellow, I couldn't get any Camels when I returned but I did get this."

Well the joke turned on me as I was captured and ended up with the Bull Durham in my pocket. I lost the Camels because they were in my Jeep.

I found the bag of Bull at the 14-day place and everyone elected me to be the official cigarette roller. I would roll two cigarettes for the 15 of us and we'd call them "Two Draggers" meaning that only two drags were allowed for everyone in order that everyone would get a smoke. It worked but I was stuck with the job from then on. When anyone felt that we should have a smoke, he would suggest it to the group, anyone who was asleep would be awakened and if a quorum was reached we smoked.

Sometimes we'd light up "Big Bertha" this was a pipe that Major Mac had given to Capt. Freddy Speer. I finally talked to Capt. Ron Alley to help out with the rolling of the cigarettes. So from then on some liked my brand and some likes' Alleys'.

One day some groups were called out by the Korean's who insisted that every man present would write 30 pages on military matters. We sat dumbly, so they made us kneel on the floor, then they carne up to us and placed pistols at each head. They did that to Capt. Peckham and the atmosphere became tense. We sat all afternoon until late at night no food or water or toilet relief.

The Chinese carne up to see what was going on, then the Korean's released us to the Chinese with the promise that tomorrow they would be back, and sure enough they did.

They tried to soft soap us then, had hot chocolate and cigarettes for us, we still stood dumb. The third day they broke and told us that we could write about anything; some wrote on skiing, some on boating.

I gave them a descriptive account of a 'fifty' in one box. It is a Post Exchange ration box containing many articles of candy, soap, shaving gear, etc. Their mouths were drooling after reading this—as I added many types of chocolate with nuts and cherries; this was too much for their feeble brains so they let me go.

I do not want to create the impression that I or any of us always got away with things, as that isn't so. We sometimes hit rock bottom and would realize that we had let our stomach overrule our heads—and would have said something that I or any of us would have given our left nut to retract.

Colonel Guy Thrash took over when Major Mac was sent to jail for fighting the commies underground. Colonel Thrash was a man who had a calm courage that couldn't be shaken by The Chinks or slopes as we used to call them in China.

He (Thrash) was a Marine aviator and had been with Lt. Dick Still on a flack control mission trying to see where the heavy anti-air guns were located.

They tried to get him to admit to 'Bug Warfare', then tried to get him to sign some documents, and finally took him out of camp claiming that he was a belligerent and kept him for 11 months in solitary confinement.

The next Marine Officer to take over was Major Jerry Fink, he was a giant of a man in stature, hard as nails physically, but a gentle nature could do sculpture, and carving. He was knowledgeable in the Humanities and conducted a school on it for us. He helped along with 1st Lt. Ralph Nardella, to carve a cross like the Crucifix which became a Christian symbol and it was used in by all, Protestants and Catholics alike.

They also fashioned a wooden leg for Major Harrison USAF, and inside of the leg was placed the death list which was later reported in the newspapers.

An Army Officer by the name of Chet Osborne also got out of camp with a list which was turned over to our authorities. Many men tried in any way they could to sabotage the routine of the Communists and many succeeded.

There were some, and I'll say they were in the minority, who were playing The Chinese for all they could get. We were quite sick of them and I believe if any of them read this they will know what I mean. After all, a man has to shave and in order to shave he has to look at himself in a mirror, enough said!

A man one night spoke to me a truism, his name is Bo. He said, "Mac, point your finger at an object, now look down your arm at your fingers, your index finger is pointed at an object isn't it, but where are the other three fingers pointing, yes they are pointing at you aren't they, so take heed cause you can't win when you point a man out, you are pointing three fingers at yourself."

Well that is a factual observation however, Winston Churchill once said, "Never judge a man unless you have experienced the same thing that he has, under the same circumstances."

We had a Puerto Rican Officer in our camp; he was one of the gutsiest men I have ever met. Some criticized his actions at the time, but he had a great loyalty to the USA.

He used to steal chickens from the Koreans and Chinese. The way that he would do it was to borrow a little rice from the kitchen then he would get a long piece of string, attach the rice, place a little of the rice behind the outhouse, push a hole in the mud wall and wait. When a chicken would go after the rice, he would pull the string and reach out, grab the chicken, get it inside, pull off its head, and let it bleed into the hole, then skin it.

He would wrap it in a piece of cloth, bring it into our hut and if we had a fire going, he would pack mud around it, put it in the coals and bake it. I got a piece of that chicken and it was good. The trick endangered a lot of us, but the good that he did offset the harm that we might have had in discovery.

He was finally caught and spent two months in jail. Whenever I say jail, I mean a wooden, barred small room where you couldn't lie down, just room enough to sit up.

The hole was another place where we could neither sit up nor lie down, it was just plain misery. Carved into the ground, about four feet deep, it would take on the natural dampness of the ground.

There were plenty of rats for company. A Korean gray rat is as big as a tomcat, and much more vicious.

Solitary confinement was a cross between the hole and the jail, and the most brutal part of it was the darkness and lack of communion with any human being. Some men spent two years in solitary before they cracked.

I believe that someone named 'Portia' from the Merchant of Venice said that "The quality of mercy is not strained; it falleth as the gentle rain from heaven."

Well the Chinese Communists said, "we will teach you that black is white and white is black" and sometimes I began to wonder if the two colors didn't merge, after a few days of starvation and the hole*.

*-The following is a description of "the hole" by Felix and his time spent there.

THE HOLE – FELIX J. MC COOL

This happened in the camp at Pingchong ni where, for quite a while, I had been causing friction and disruption about the study program. During a lecture I would ask: "Where did that pamphlet come from"? The lecturer would say: "This pamphlet came from your America". I would respond: "Did I hear you right, that we in America do not have freedom of expression and of the press, that our press is controlled by Wall Street?" He would always answer, "It is true what you say". I would then remark, "If we have no freedom of expression in America and no freedom of the press how do you account for the fact that the pamphlet which you are reading from, which reviles America, and belittles our government, was printed in America. How can you say America has no freedom of expression?"

The pamphlet or magazine which I am referring to is called 'Masses and Mainstream' which was some of the propaganda the Communists used and we were forced to listen to was indeed printed in America.

The lecturer would invariably pull out his little 'black book' which had many things in it. One time I told off Comrade Sun in front of a group of his comrades which made him lose face. I was made to stand at attention before the enlisted and officers for an hour as humiliation. This happened at the same time they had Frank Noel on trial for his life for trying to escape.

I used to harass the guards at night when they would come for bed check by cat calls, hisses or walking my shoes behind them in the dark. I slept on the floor and I would pat the canvas shoes behind the guards when they had bed check. They would turn and try to see who it was. By being on the floor I could take my hands out of the shoes and they wouldn't find the culprit who was supposedly following them. They had a hunch that I was not too good with their propaganda as I would ridicule the talks after they were over. This was taboo but most of the men indulged in it.

I knew my number was almost up as one night about midnight a Chinese man entered the room making quite a bit of noise waking me up. I watched him check all of the men with his flashlight, putting the light directly in their faces. When he came to me, putting the light in my face, I said: "you SOB, get that damn light out of my face". The light immediately flicked away, then he turned to me again saying: "who sleeps there, speak to me, I am a comrade in the noble Chinese Peoples Volunteer Army and you cannot speak to a volunteer that way. We shall punish you for mocking a CPV". I said: "Yes, I know you will punish me, but you woke me from a sound sleep and it made me angry. You always try to make us angry so that we will commit some infraction and then you can punish us. It's just a form of torture that you inflict on us to make us soft. Now get the hell out of here and let me sleep or call the guards, whichever you please. My name is MC COOL!"

I turned over and he stood there for a long time before he left. I waited but nothing happened. A few nights later, just after bed check, I got up to clear my throat, went to the window and spit. There was a Chinese man standing just outside of the window with a flashlight in his hand. He said "Who are you?" I drew back and hopped into bed calling over to Doctor Anderson and Allan Lloyd to let them know I may have some trouble. I think one of those bastards thinks I tried to spit on him. About 11:30 pm, two guards came to the room armed and a Chinese man flashed the light of his flashlight in my face saying: "McCool, take all and come with me." I said to him: "Can't it wait for morning?" and he replied: "Silence, obey me." I knew that there was no use to argue further so I got up, rolled up what I could find in the dark and followed.

We walked to the Honcho's House and there in the gleam of the candles sat 'Shoestring under the neck Wong', the 'Hatchet Man', the platoon leader and the interpreter. They stood me in the middle of the room and as I leaned over for a cigarette, the Hatchet Man kicked me on the leg and the interpreter said: "Stand at attention." I came into a half way attention glaring at the platoon leader. The company Commander walked into the room and said something in Chinese. The interpreter said: "What have you been doing wrong in the past?" I answered: "Nothing, I have been a paragon of virtue." He then said: "What is this paragon of virtue?" To which I replied: "I have been a good boy." He said or rather screamed after he had given my answer to the company Commander "You lie." They all seemed to be trying to work themselves into a rage, so I stayed cool, watching them, as the Hatchet Man kept jabbing at my feet. That just increased my hatred of them.

Sun walked in for a minute and I asked him what the hell they were doing as, after four hours, it began to take on the semblance of a nightmare. I was made to reflect and they finally came down to that very night accusing me "You called one of our noble CPV a SOB tonight, did you not?" I said: "No"! and he responded: "You lie, you lie, you lie" with a slobber effect. I knew whatever I said I had had it and might as well face it.

They came in with a big sheet of paper and marched me out of the room. It was coming close to dawn as I was taken out of camp and marched down the road past solitary confinement. I could hear the groans coming from those poor devils in 'solitary'. I was then taken past the wooden jail, a place that was made out of heavy timbers put into a slat like upright position, similar to bars in a modern jail. I heard someone say: "Who is it?" and I whispered: "McCool" at which time the guard jabbed at me with a bayonet. I kept quiet. I believe the voice was Bob Howell, an Army Lieutenant. He said: "Keep your chin up, it isn't so bad in here once you get used to it". He then said something to another officer who was in stir with him, "Its McCool, Bruner", then I heard Riley Bruner's voice say: "Keep your chin up". This statement became slightly off center a few hours later as I was in a hole in the ground where you couldn't get your head off your knees. The guard grunted something and they took me across the street, pulled a heavy log off of a small aperture in the bottom of a building, made me get on my hands and knees and crawl in. I hollered for a flashlight as I seemed to be going into a bottomless pit or a cesspool. I thought it was outright murder and I was being buried alive. They put the light into the hole and I wished that they hadn't. It was slimy, full of large grey rats and about 3 feet wide by 3 feet and about 3 ½ feet high. The floor and up the wall was covered by a sticky ooze. Lice were so thick that you could see them in the gleam of the light, along with the fleas.

There were some bamboo frames to make the hole a little smaller. I was kicked and jabbed into the hole head first and I wanted to kill. There wasn't anything to kill but the rats and they were plenty. I killed two of them with my bare hands, broke their necks and squashed them. The other rats began to eat on them instead of me, fortunately. As dawn broke and that part of the nightmare receded, the light, even though slight, was pushing its way into the hole through the cracks scared those slimy rats into their smaller holes. I thought: "Rats in a trap and I'm one of them".

I had heard of the 'hole' before as that was where they put you to extract a confession, have you sign some peace pamphlet or 'rat out' one of your brothers in arms. I sat up and took stock of the situation; if I had a smoke I thought it wouldn't be so bad. But no smoking and worse than that there was no match. Nature calls began to force themselves upon me and I started calling for a guard: "Benjo, Benjo" which means that you have to go. The guard came over and poked a bayonet into one of the holes and said: "Buduey, no speak". I called a few more times and nearly lost an eye on the point of the bayonet. I heard some American voices and looked out of the crack. This group of grizzled Americans trooped by going to the head and they kept saying: "Keep your chin up". I recognized Carol Wright and Paul O'Dowd's voices, and then I heard Mike Lorenzo. I laughed to myself, "Yes, keep your head up and if I do I'll lose it on the top where there were spikes pointing down. The hole was designed to make a quick break down.

I felt some water splash on me, it was warm and I peered out of the crack. There were some women up above using the hole as a public urinal. Pretty soon a Korean man walked by and dropped some to-bacco and a match down to me. It was a scene from the 'Pit and the Pendulum', kindness amongst brutality. I took the smoke and let the devil take the hindsight.

I stayed in the hole for twenty four hours before any one came to me. At that time a guard poked his head into the hole after rolling the heavy log away. (I discovered it was an old pig trough.) I was told to climb out and I was taken to a toilet. My needs had long since been satisfied in the hole but I went anyway for the breath of fresh air and to see the place in the daylight. I was directly across the street from the jail and could see the prisoners in it. There were a few mud huts scattered along the road and the river ran behind the shack about fifty yards back.

The guard hurried me and I had to climb into the hole again – dirty, unshaven, hungry and thirsty - I climbed in. They came with a gallon bucket with some slop that looked like hog slop and gave me a bowl of it. I drank it down and ate the grain that had been placed on a board by it. I did all of this by reaching out of the hole onto the walk leading to it. The stench was terrific in the place, but I had reached the point where it didn't matter. Little things like cleanliness, fresh air, a shave and food faded into the things that angels deserve. The driving urge in my mind was to keep my sanity and to stay alive so that someday I could tell of the 'lenient' policy of the Communists.

The next day was torture; I was fed again about dark. When I would ask for relief, I was denied. The guards would come around and peer in at me and laugh, like fiends from hell. Then the rats started. There was a little ledge just about the height of my ear where I was sitting. I'd see the rats either coming or going by, they didn't seem to be too bothered when I kept active, such as moving my hands or feet back and forth. But when I stopped I could feel a tentative nibble on my hand or along my neck. I'd shudder or draw back or hit out, I really didn't want to hit them again because the first few hours of squeezing them had made an impression on me. I could still feel the crawly skin and the crunch of the bone with a warm spurt of blood on my hands from the two I had killed before. I didn't want to kill any more of them and I was trying to keep them off me by placing little bits of my food on the ledges and around the floor where I sat.

The lice started up and I could feel them skitter on my body along my belly or around my belt and shoe tops. They go where the clothes fit tight and then a little sting and I knew that I was being drained alive. It was like a thousand miniature vampires drawing my life's blood from my body. The sensation was horrible yet fascinating, I was attracted yet repelled. It was a life struggle when caught in an inextricable morass, a course for rats and lice to run over. "My skin bleeds; my body becomes a course for rats to run over."

My mind would slip; a period of forty eight hours would have gone by. I thought: "I'll die and the rats and lice will eat on me and the pass-erby will use me to defecate on, I am not human, I am below an animal". It's better to let the soul go before it too is reduced to this craven thing, and then reason would come to me and I would say: "No, I'll beat this and them and I'll go back and tell the world of the rot and filth that is under the guise of Communism".

Mine is nothing, some of the men have spent a week or two in this place. Hank Petticone and Bill Funchess, both Army officers, have been in here. They both have been quiet and have a haunted look on their faces when they were finally released and allowed to come back into camp. A week of kindness from the other POW's, a bath and a shave did wonders for them. I, too, will come out of here.

About the 50th hour the log was again rolled back and I was made to come out. The guards were shouting 'Amerika Amerika, come here'. I crawled out stinking rotten through the filth that had piled up around me and on the ledge where the passerby would relieve themselves. One horrible old crone, who looked like the witch from Hansel and Gretel, stayed in a loft directly above me. I can still hear her hollow cough like drawing up parts of her lungs to spit them into the hole where I stayed. I crawled out there stood the company commander and an interpreter. They made me walk to a little building and stand in the door way. I was asked if I had reflected over my past misdeeds which they enumerated: causing disruption in class, cursing them for being commies, my belligerent attitude. I stood there like a fool and said: "I am innocent of the charges that you are giving out and I have nothing to say". To which they replied: "You lie, you lie, you cursed capitalists' friend of the money bags in America, you tool of the Wall Street aggressors, you have not had enough reflection in the quiet place to change your mind". I knew that I didn't want to go into the hole again, but there was no way to avoid it. I tried to pretend that I had a bad case of dysentery and that I wanted a smoke. They laughed: "You do not need to smoke, it is injurious to your lungs, and besides, the dysentery is what you brought into this country from America. You are pigs there, look how many men in camp have died". I thought 'yes, look because they have been in the holes, have not been fed and have had no medicine. That's why they have died, you Murderers'.

That last I said to them and it did me no good. I was hustled back into the hole and given a brutal shove with the butt of the rifle of one of the guards. I landed in that filth and the squeals of the rats, felt the fleas take over. I wondered just how smart am I, to go through with this, how much longer, how much longer. Perhaps I should confess to the things that I have actually done. But I knew that wasn't what they wanted, they wanted a confession that I had raped and pillaged and was an aggressor, a tool of the capitalists in America. That I wanted destruction and war as long as it served me or my country's purpose. These were all lies but that is what they wanted me to do – follow their own pattern of lies and more lies.

About 70 hours had gone by and I was getting weaker and sicker. The rats had started into boldly eat on my hands and neck and ears. When I reclined, the nights were nightmares of hell itself. I could hear the fellows across the way sing out 'Keep you chin up, keep your chin up' and I wondered if it is worth it. Can man be reduced to this state and ever go back to sanity and decency again or will he be forever marked with the brand of filth and degradation. Then sanity would come back and I'[d realize that I had been through the same treatment on the 'Hell Ship' going to Japan and in the coal mines. It was all the same. I'd come back.

I was fed again and taken to the toilet and then they came back. They were softer with me then and asked me to sign a confession. I said I would if they would let me write it and not add anything to it. They promised and I wrote that I had been causing friction that I hated communism, and I had called them sons of bitches because they were commies. They took the confession and left, I was put back in the hole for another night of hell. In the morning an interpreter stuck his head in the hole and said: "come out, come out" as though I should have been out and waiting for him. They always acted that way as though they were surprised at the fact that you were suffering or were not completely free. They knew full well that you were not.

I came out of the hole and the guards made me sit on the porch of a house that was across the street from the jail. I could see the fellows in there and envied them. I had not rated the jail. They were giving me the V sign and thumbs up. The interrogator gave me a cigarette and lit it for me. I was a pretty sorry sight, shaking and filthy dirty. The Koreans even turned up their noses at me. I took the first drag of the cigarette and it floored me. My head spun and I got sick to my stomach. A horrible depression took over and I threw the cigarette down. Even now when I smoke a cigarette I get that same feeling of depression. The interrogator then said: "You have had time to think over your past misdeeds in this quiet place, so I want you to change your confession. You will say that you came here to rape and rob the Koreans and that you curse the Chinese comrades. You will also say that you are an aggressor and should be shot if you ever do anything again. Then you will make a daily report of the activities of your friends activities in camp to us so we can protect them and keep them out of the reflection rooms like the one you have been in for 80 hours". I thought 'yes, or rather put them in the hole like I was if someone informs on them to the Chinese for their activities and escape plots'. I answered: "I will sign a confession and say what you want because part of it is true. I do hate you and I have called you sons of bitches. I don't want to be crapped on again and I don't want the rats and lice to eat on me. I want to breathe air again without feces in it and I want to cleanup in the river. Yes I'll sign".

The interrogator said again: "But comrade you were only in a quiet place. You must mention that as we wouldn't want anyone to think that you had been mistreated when you read your confession to the men." I thought 'brother, how crude can you be, but I'd better sign the damn thing or I'm not going back to the camp – period end of report and end of McCool'. I agreed to sign and make out a new report of my bad conduct and bad attitude, but I said: "I'll do what you say about writing but I'm going to balk on informing on my fellow officers. My opinion of an informer is that he too fits the category of a son of a bitch. Now, comrade, do you want to call me a SOB"? He looked at me and said: "No". So I said: "Well, if I inform I'll be one, so the fact that you don't want to call me a name that I have chosen for you and the fact that I don't want to inform means I won't. I will make the confession".

All the time I was looking with horror at the hole and watching across the street. I saw a momentary glimpse of Colonel Guy Thrash, USMC, who was in solitary at that time, but he didn't see me. I made the confession and was put back in the hole. The squealing rats sounded like it was with delight as their portable meat house came back. I sat down and thought, remembering a picture called 'The Informer' that Victor McLaughlin played in years ago. There was a craven way that he portrayed the character with shame on his conscience and I vowed to myself that it would never happen to me. Anything but that. It was sacred to me like repudiating my God and I couldn't and wouldn't do that.

I think I cried a little. I was getting soft in the head and thought of suicide. I would put my head in a crack at night and draw my body up, knees to chin, and hand myself. It never had to happen as they came for me about dusk. I crawled out of the hole, rotten and stinking, and was taken back to camp. Some of the fellows were walking in the yard and said: "Hi Mac, welcome back. Did they break you?" "No, not exactly but I did confess to cursing them and to being a rapist and murderer and I wouldn't be an informant", was my reply. To which they replied: "Good boy, Mac".

I went into my old sleeping place and saw Doctor Anderson. I told him I needed to be cleaned up so he gave me some clean clothes and a bar of soap. Chet Osborne, Hector Cordero and Ding Bell came down to the river and poured water for me, Allan Lloyd gave me a smoke and I began to feel like a human again. I left the filthy clothes outside and talked about half the night to Doc Anderson and Jerry Fink. Jerry was the senior Marine Officer present as Major McLaughlin was in the jug again for some infraction. I was plenty proud of them. Andy talked to me for a long time, I thought he might be worried about my mind as I kept saying 'I wouldn't inform, I wouldn't inform'. God how I hated those people, hate them and always will. I don't have that feeling about the Japanese. They were my captors and were brutal but they had character. The god damned communists have no character. Wherever they are I feel like I could pound the keys off this typewriter in the saying of it. I should have brick bats to pound on to relieve this aggression I have. I say God pity one of the sob's if I ever run across one or one crosses me – it will be suicide for him or her.

The next day I washed out my clothes and boiled them so I wouldn't contaminate the rest of the men.

Well, that was the hole!   It wasn't nice but I lived and still do!

CHAPTER SEVEN
FUTILE ESCAPE

Back when the first of us were captured or, rather after about six months of capture, I was approached about an escape plot. There were four plots going on while we were at Pyockdong, just about as far from any of our troops as we could get.

The mountains were awesome; the weather was cold in winter, and rainy in summer. There were little trails winding throughout the mountains as well as small camps of Chinese guards and the civilian defense with spears (Korean men, women, and children).

We had a modicum of food, and were dressed in tennis shoes; a small residual of the clothes we were captured in was fast wearing out.

The first of three attempts were by Hector Cordero, Deakon, and two others. Frank Noel and Zack Dean, and Major McDonald, were another. Major McAbee and three others including myself were in the one that ended tragically.

We were set up by a Korean from the south and a young Japanese boy who had been a dog robber for someone in the army and was captured.

We had it planned that we'd all take off together and use the knowledge of the terrain by the Korean. He was also to use his native language to convince anyone we met, that they were our guards and we were being taken to another camp.

The plan depended on our leaving the camp as a work party. We had knives, food, a compass and courage. Two days before we were supposed to take off, the Korean disappeared, and then Major McAbee disappeared for two days. We heard pitiful moans and cries coming from a little compound about 100 yards from camp. We had a suspicion who was being tortured and why, because the interrogators had questioned all of us about escape plans.

The Major was returned to camp, and he was in pitiful shape. His arms had been bound behind his back for 24 hours and he was raised from the floor by the method of a pull up rope that held him suspended from the floor, arms behind him.

A rope passed around his neck and tied to his feet had been drawn up, so when he tried to let his feet down it pulled the rope around his neck choking him. By the same token he was enduring the entire weight of his body on his upraised arms which were pulled up behind his back. They then kicked him and beat his face. This type of treatment lasted all day. It is a wonder he survived but he did. We were captured before we started and after seeing the condition of the Major, which lasted for months, it kept us in line.

One Marine escaped and was gone for nearly a month but was finally captured. I never heard of a successful escape from the place where we were held. We tried to contact the guerrillas but we were too far north. Capt. Gillette, the Marine Officer who escaped ran into a giant bear so the story goes, and he didn't speak bear.

CHAPTER EIGHT

GUARDS AND LIES
OUR INDOCTRINATIONS

We were surrounded by guards most of the time, either in their function of duty or off duty.

When off duty they would be training in mortar, small arms and field problems. They trained constantly and when not in training, they would study.

We prisoners called their studies 'Hate America Week' because they would always be particularly mean when coming from one of their schools.

They would soften up a bit between times but would immediately return to meanness when coming from one of their classes. They were taught that we were an aggressive race, and that under our domination they had nothing but poverty, but under their leader Mao Tze Tung they had everything.

That seemed to me to be incongruous as hell. They were receiving only a meal or two a day of rice and had some pork occasionally.

I remember back when I was a kid in Pawhuska, Okla. and was told to gather up tinfoil to turn in at Church. That was how we were able to save. I used to have a little bank of pennies, saved for the Chinese babies. I gave it to our Church, for the Missionaries to spend in order to save the lives of Chinese babies.

Our pennies and time were for China to aid them.

Their lessons were lies. They didn't make any sense to us. We felt that our captors had been bought off by their overlords with a bowl of rice and a promise of being a ruler of the world.

They were duped into thinking that as soon as we were indoctrinated, we would go back to America and preach the gospel of Communism.

They must have really thought that the lectures and teachings they were giving us would influence us as it has swayed those other dupes here in America who embrace communism.

I feel genuinely sorry for the communists or those who profess the communist belief here in America; if they only knew as I and the rest of us who have suffered under communism, just what communism really is, they wouldn't be so hasty to want to sell Uncle Sam down the river believe me.

The communists, in my opinion, are divided into a few groups. Initially there are only a few 'dyed in the wool' communists, by that I mean; true believers, fanatics would be the better word for it. These are the opportunists, who go along in hopes that they will be leaders and can run things the way they want when they take over, in other words, dictators at heart.

Then, there are the rice bowl converts who never having much under their government, plan through cussedness on their part or just plain laziness, become the anarchist who wants to change things, only his way. He wants a revolution, and doesn't care who gets hurt in the process.

Finally, there is the 'phony as a three-dollar bill', super intellectuals, who have never channeled their thoughts into productive work and want things easy. For them, as long as they go along with the party, become commissars, and then can order the poor dopes that do all the work around.

At the bottom end are the peasant laborers who can be changed from one job to another at the commissars' beck and call.

This is what I mean when I say I'm sorry for the poor fool who thinks that communism is going to aid him. He is a dupe now and will be a dupe until the day he dies.

Imagine your home built on sand at the beach with only a mud retaining wall holding the sea back. That's what communism is built on! Lies, deceit, murder, lies, anarchy, revolution, lies, the loss of the family value, lies, denial of God, integrity lost, trivial pursuit of material goods, lies' inferior products, lies, more lies, and damn lies! That is what Communism represents. When I compare it to my home, I am thankful for my blessing.

They attempted the same types of schooling on us, to try to convince us theirs was the way of the future.

They were conducted in so many different ways and in so many different places.

We could have the comparative comfort of seats in a movie house in the town of Pyockdong, or it could be on the cold ground, in a Pagoda, for about six to eight hours. We would sit there for hours, in the rain and listen to them. Sometimes it would be in a small room with only a few present, and then we would be forced to have a discussion about all the merits of communism. What a wasted effort.

We'd be called out, into the yard for a roll call. We would be held there and told to sit right there where we could be seen. There wasn't any place else to go. We couldn't hide as they would search the rooms. So we would sit in the cold or the heat and listen to the ranting of Communism.

We might be told to go into a room; about fifteen of us would be put into a room that only three or four people could occupy comfortably. It was about 8ft by 10ft. There we were, fifteen of us and three instructors.

We could be sent into Pagodas. These were located all over Korea. They are little shrines that had been built by the Japanese during their occupation in WW II. They are found on hilltops and were wind swept and cold.

Other times we were directed by them into a theater. It is a pity to call the things theaters but there is no equivalent name unless you said an outhouse, and they are used for that purpose too. They do not observe any sanitation just go on the floor.

The place is small and cramped, with rows of planks from the wall to the center of the place. Those are the seats, and that's your theater.

Our lessons would begin with a harangue of how we had been duped by our leaders and that we were tools of the Wall Street Money Bags. We had only to sign their papers and they would make number one communists out of us. We'd listen for a while and then someone would let out a curse, or stand up and yawn or do anything that would annoy the instructor.

He had his henchmen mingle amongst us and in the crowd you couldn't make them out. Well, we'd end up standing at attention in the snow or the hot sun for hours for not paying attention to the gospel according to 'Tse Tung'.

It had its effect. The Officers and men would finally listen in self-defense. It would go on for a couple of hours before they would let us have a short break for five minutes then it was back to the grind of listening to them maligning of our country.

After four or five more hours, they would start what they called discussions, and if we didn't discuss, or ask a question, they would take our name and we'd end up in either the hole or standing at attention somewhere, or being taken away from the camp to God knew where! I heard that some of our guys were taken to Siberia.

We would knock off for what they called supper, what I called slop, and then they'd come into our quarters with little questions written on paper and we had to discuss what had been said that day again and to then write down our comments.

We'd draw straws as to who would write the report, that way not everyone would have to write every night. We gave them a report, with plenty of ambiguities in it. If we didn't comply then there would be trouble for all of us.

One day when we were being forced to go to class, they had brought in a lot of their goons to hurry us along.

We were going down a long corridor, and it was winter.

The Chinese were dressed in tan padded trousers and jackets, and the padding was highly flammable cotton. One of them was directly in front of me, so I took a lit cigarette that I rolled out of newspaper and Korean leaf tobacco and I applied it to the seat of his trousers, it ignited, in a few seconds I saw smoke, so I drifted back in the crowd.

About a minute later I heard a yelp, and one of the Chinese goons was on his way out of the school room holding the seat of his trousers, while trying to tear it off. He had already dropped his coat.

That got rid of him for a while, as he couldn't sit down.

That trick worked so well, that all winter, I kept a small piece of smoldering wood nearby, igniting any Chinaman who walked by me. They never caught me. All the training in the world doesn't make up for guts!

A bunch of our barbers and carpenters managed to procure a couple of buckets and were boiling their water and then cooling it in a stream. They would take the water up to their shop for drinking in the summer time. Some of the more aggressive slope interrogators learned about it and took most of the water.

One of our men decided to put a stop to that, so they took another bucket and filled it with the ditch water that ran freely through town.

The community stream was where the children washed their feet and often urinated, and the women washed out the slop jars.

The stream ran right in front of the houses and the water wasn't fit for human consumption.

The number two bucket was filled with the stream water. The number one bucket, which had the good water, was kept hidden.

After about a week of drinking the stolen water the commies got sick, one of them was sent back to China and the others were taking dysentery medicine. They soon started boiling their own water.

We had many a good laugh over that. Despite our miserable state, all wasn't lost; we kept a sense of humor, to help us fight back.

There was a bell that the chinks would ring to bring us to class. Well they rang that bell once too often, and it disappeared. About half of the camps were accused of stealing the bell, but they never did catch the right man, even after he confessed. They were using the bell incident as a lever to get confessions out of us.

They put up pictures of all the great communist leaders of the last 40 years, including William Z. Foster, they were plastered all over the walls of the compound. Someone or a group stole all of those pictures and put them in the toilet, we used Moa Tze Tung's face for our aiming point, when we used the head. Many of the boys would look over and say "over to the left, or over to the right, or fire at will, you are on target."

We had no use and little regard for anything they had to offer. Even when they brought in their soft music and the dancing girls from "Liberated Tibet" with their snake like necks that darted to and fro.

We remembered the beautiful women in America, our homes, our friends and family. Nothing the commies had held any interest for us.

There was one little character who claimed to have been in America once and said he knew all about us. How we let the little guy starve and go homeless and so forth. This old commie line of accusing someone else of what they in reality are doing to themselves.

We were on a hillside one sunny day listening to him vituperate America and Americans. He said, "You men come from America, I have been in America, I was in Detroit for two hours, in New York for four hours, and in Los Angeles for a day.

I know all about America, all that I saw were slums and bums, it's all slums. The only people who have homes or automobiles are the big shots in the government. The other people who drive cars there are carrying out a big propaganda scheme to fool you poor people. You have nothing."

I'd think of the corner store, the family car, the movies, the popcorn stand, See's, or McFarlane's Chocolates, public schools, free buses, dancing on the beach, and thought what in hell is this maniac trying to sell us. He would go on, "I got shoes, you have no shoes in America but I got my shoes, they come from Chila" (meaning China, he couldn't pronounce the 'N'), then he would go into a tirade of, "it's the truth, you don't know black from white but we'll teach you and we'll change the world, and we'll conquer nature, there is NO GOD. HA NO GOD NO GOD!"

This fool, I thought, is a fanatic; no doubt he was a dangerous one.

Just to show him up, we took a risk, stood up, and started to sing "All God's Chillan got shoes."

"He's got shoes
Chinese shoes
Chilla shoes
When it rains there'll be no shoes
Paste board, only paste board
But all us God's Chillan got shoes
With leather** leather Chillan shoes"
This got him and he left talking to himself.

I remember now his name was Loung we called him Leon. He never came back to The Officers compound, but later on we heard he was assigned to the enlisted men's compound.

I remember Frances the FANG.

I met him the first time at capture. He was a self-effacing young man, with a cultured manner. His use of English was very good. He tried the soft method in putting over communism. He was of a slight build, very yellow, a slight slant to eyes, said his father was well connected with the Peking government in some important way.

I called another one Gin.

He was a half way decent Chinese. Had a swarthy complexion, and smiled a lot. Some of the guys called him "smiley." He disappeared right after I wrote a paper on the differences between Chinese and Japanese treatment of paws'.

Sigh (tsie) was short, brown, very slanted eyes, but had a large nose, somewhat European in appearance.

"Who say, Tsie say?!" was our favorite expression whenever he came around us. This half way amused him and but also made him fearful. This explained a lot to me. I knew FEAR was the motivating power of communism, and of any dictatorship. A decent compassionate thought wasn't permitted to live if it wasn't party line.

The Snake:

Ding was Commander of The Camp. He was tall and snaky.

His tongue would dart a lot out of his mouth and curl around his lips whenever he became agitated, and was often when he was around us.

He had a wife, pretty and cute, and we men would whistle and make funny sounds at her, which she seemed to enjoy, whenever she came into the compound.

She came in every day for water. One day I was holding a cup of water near the well. An inspection was called by the commander, so I had to remain where I was and not move. The Chinese lady came forward to get her water and I, holding a bowl, had to keep it from falling upon her head. She paid me no mind and was bent over in front of me looking at some lice on the floor. It became an uncomfortable situation fast. I couldn't let the bowl fall upon her head and I couldn't push any further forward than I was, in order to keep hold of the bowl. She didn't seem to mind, so who was I to complain.

I stood in this position and it was tense. All the boys let out a howl when she finally left. They said, "Come here Mac, old boy and tell us about it, just how did you feel after so many years, etc., etc. ... I lived it down but my dreams were disturbed that night!"

Wong: shoestrings under the neck:

He was an ash. .! He started in as a glorified house boy to the political honcho and then wormed his way in by ingratiating himself to the Chinese commander. He did this by spying on us, getting men into trouble and used the excuse, that he was watchful for the commanders' interests.

He would create incidents then take the upper hand. He became an interrogator but needed an interpreter since he couldn't speak a word of English. He was tall, very serious, and couldn't take a ribbing. We took advantage of that, by kidding him constantly.

The name 'shoestrings under the neck' came from the fact that he tied his winter cap to his head with shoestrings, giving him a very ridiculous look. He had a particular dislike for me and was the cause of me being locked up in a hole in the ground for 80 hours.

It was a small hole, wet and full of rats—I was ready to confess that Mao Tze Tung was my hidden relative before they let me out of the hole.

I did confess that I was a warmonger and had done many things which were wrong, namely to call the communists sons of bitches!

Lily, The dragon lady

Very pretty for a Chinese, oval face, a creamy complexion petite in appearances, walked gracefully, had a lovely smile. I used to call her 'Kuniang', a name I had picked up in Shanghai in the old days, an endearing term. She didn't take too well to it.

She walked holding hands with another girl we called him Goy, as it was a tossup whether or not it was a boy or a girl.

Their behavior did not please us. We couldn't stomach the familiarity between the two. The Chinese men would also walk around holding hands. Their conduct lent an atmosphere which was slightly on-the eerie side, sort of a masculine, feminine stickiness which didn't fit the standard of our culture.

Their deviation was unlike anything I had seen. None of their feminine charm or snakelike fascination rubbed off on any of us, thanks God,

When I would see 'Lily' walking down the path, I'd say, "Good Morning, Kuniang, Wei!" She would answer: "Good morning Comrade, I hope that you are studying diligently." I would think, yes, I'll study your figure but not your literature.

Sometimes I would openly admit that to her, but it was like talking to a tree. She wouldn't respond!

When I would be called in for interrogation by her

I would enter the hut, having previously removed my shoes. She would be in a padded pair of trousers, her shirt removed, no bra, her loose coat unbuttoned. There would be a pile of papers on the table, some of my dossier, some of the type of interrogation put out by the Chinese for that particular month, no originality.

I would sit down. Sometimes there would be cigarettes on the table, or tea and sometimes both.

"Comrade what are you thinking lately?" She would ask.

"What are the rest of the men in camp saying about Communism?

Are you studying hard to learn the truth so that you may go back to America and fight The Wall Street money bags? You must know by now that they started the war in Korea so that Taiwan should be allowed into the UN."

I would reply with either defiance or timidity, how I happened to feel at the time.

My defiance would manifest itself according to the amount of times I had been interrogated in the past. If there had been many, then I wasn't very defiant. Their WEAR DOWN process had been used effectively. Tired, hungry, despondent I wouldn't act defiant, unless out of desperation. I showed that at times, but mostly tried to play it smooth, get out alive was the motto geste.

"Comrade you are reported not paying attention in my classes, why is that?" Well I would sometimes say, "My interest in the lessons drags especially when you low rate my country, as I know it isn't true." This was a mild defiance.

"Stand UP! Stand at attention" she said and called out to the guard in Chinese. The guard would come in and poke at me with a bayonet if I slouched; this might go on for two or three hours. My time limit was four hours, then I had to rest as the blood would fill my legs and my feet would swell.

Some men could stand all day, 12 hours or more. I couldn't stand too long, because I had Beri Beri in the Jap POW camp. That was the reason. I don't doubt it.

"Comrade are you willing to talk reasonably now?"

"Yes, comrade, you dirty son of a bitch, I am ready"

"Comrade what are you saying in your mouth"

"Nothing, I was just moaning because my feet hurt"

The interrogation might go on for an hour or it might go on for twenty-four hours, a relief would come and take over when one of them was tired. The time would drag, but the cigarettes tasted good and I'd butt them and bring them back into camp.

One day when I had dysentery quite bad, I was called out by one of their smooth-off men, a nice looking and friendly young Chinese but a 'dyed in the wool' communist who later became the chief of the interrogators.

He said, "McCool, how are you, you don't look so well?" I answered, "No, I am not well, I have dysentery and Doctor Anderson tells me that I need some Emetine or Sulfa drugs, do you know where some are?" He answered "There are Sulfa pills, the comrade who wants to interrogate you has just returned from China and has brought some with him."

We entered the mud hut, first removing our shoes, a common custom in the Orient, one of the few which seems to make sense.

The comrade, who I was to spend the next three grueling hours with, sat in a large woven bamboo chair, perfectly at ease leaning back with a leer of Satan on his face. He threw a pack of butts on the table, his orderly brought in some tea which I eagerly took as I was nearly dehydrated from the dysentery.

My interpreter then said something to this demon, which immediately opened up a drawer in the desk which was in front of him, pulling out a vial, opened it and out rolled some sulfa pills. I immediately grabbed two and swallowed them, making out that I thought he was giving them to me, he wasn't, it was just bait.

He then spoke in Chinese to my interpreter who turned to me and said: "Comrade, why are so many men in camp dying, and why are they so weak and fearful?" "Why do they not want to study communism, it would go easier for them if they did?!!

I answered: "we are starving to death, and those who are not starving are weakened by wounds and malnutrition, this allows illness to fall on them."

He was told what I said and I could see the pills fading into the dim past. I was pissed because I knew that they were starving our men and then blaming illness on our 'weakness' our way of life in America.

It made me 'G.D. sore'.

He answered "Buduey" or some such word which I think means "it won't do." Then gave the oriental shrug. I then knew my chance for the pills was a thing of the past.

I didn't care, I felt that I would die along with the rest so I told him this, "there is no weakness in any of the American boys other than what you inflict on them—even an animal will weaken if you feed him straw. We need food, and medicine too. As for your communist doctrine, you can jam it! There is no truth in it, and anyone who has eaten it has been eating "horse shit."

We always said, after one of the commie lectures, "don't eat that pal, that's horse shit."

I went on to say, "our American youth is of pioneer stock, they are strong and restless, but they are not weak. Think of our history, our revolution, the progress that we have achieved in the past 150 years. You can't tell me anything about our boys, just feed them, and they will live!"

He threw down his pen, picked up the pills and I was hustled back into camp. I fully expected to be put in the hole.

By some dumb luck I was returned to my hut. I found out later that he had come down with Typhus fever. I think that is what saved my life; the hole would have finished me.

I went over to Major McLaughlin and told him the story, he gave me a hug, didn't say much, he and I had a brotherly understanding.

I also spoke to Dr. Anderson, who told me to get some burnt charcoal and eat it. So with a faith in his ability and a determination to live, I ate the charcoal, and finally overcame the worst part of dysentery.

The Chinese who had been our interrogator stayed with us POWS' for more than two years, but was never one of the primary interrogators again, he was in the background.

The Chinese had a doctor, he was a small man with a swarthy complexion looked as if he might have been a field hand, a coolie type, with dirty habits. He spit on the floor had a terrific cough. He provided very little medicine to us.

He would grunt when told of our distress. He always wanted us to sign testimonials as to the good treatment and fine medicine that we had received. Sometimes we did sign because one never knew when the medicine would be needed. To fight off dysentery or pneumonia we might survive if given just a little sulfa drug. So we POWS' went for survival.

Another Chinese doctor came into camp. This man seemed to want to help us but he was spied upon and written reports were given to headquarters daily on him. Slightly build, long tapering fingers, an olive complexion, no slant to the eyes, I accused him of being a Eurasian mixbreed, he neither affirmed nor denied.

One day when I was flat on my back with a back injury from carrying too heavy a load of rocks off the mountain, I asked him why they wouldn't give me the right kind of care and why they wouldn't allow me to go home. He said that I was getting good care. I then said, "Doctor Wong, you know that 1 am sick, why do you lie to me and say that you are giving me good care?" He looked at me, and then peered out the slit of the door for anyone listening, then drawing very close to me said: "I tell

71

you what I am told to tell you, no more, no less, we Communists are not allowed to think for ourselves."

I knew that this man could be on our side if he could only break away, but he was motivated by fear, yellow cringing fear. We talked again while I was still on my back. He asked me if I had heard from my family lately. I said no but that I had some pictures. He turned to me and said: "Let me look at them please." The please surprised me as they aren't very polite. I said: "Why do you want to see my family or friends you don't like Americans?" He just hung his head and asked again. I gave him the pictures. Two were of my sons and the others were of my sister standing by her car in Glendale.

He looked at them all and then said, "The government furnished your family with this car for propaganda so that you would be able to tell us that you have automobiles, and freedom."

I was stunned for a moment and remembered everything we have in America; homes, cars, the corner malt shop, Bob's, movies, the newspapers that tell the truth not the party line. I realized just how much this poor and misguided fool was missing, and how absurd their claims were.

He later admitted to me that he had been told what to say to me just a few days ago, at one of their "HATE AMERICA MEETINGS."

CHAPTER NINE
CAMP ACTIVITIES

At first there wasn't much to do, our activity was taken up in head runs, some of us had the nasty squirts, helped along our diet of poor cracked corn, the kind that is feed for hogs, a lot of contaminated water, and no salt. Our bowels were in bad shape. The camp overlords used this opportunity to feed us more of their commie drivel.

Later on, we were given a little better diet which consisted of rice and a modicum of cooking oil, a turn for the better was not much better but we had hope.

The Officers and Non-Commissioned Officers and some senior enlisted men realized that we should think of other things than a false promise of going home, which was nebulous at the best. They suggested that we try to keep our body active by exercising. Which would tire the body and mind and give us some spiritual hope? We organized physical activities, and mental activities.

I remember that we would try twenty questions and the name of the states, and their capitals. We played a game called "ghosts." We did anything to keep the mind active and resilient. It would work, but with starvation dragging us down, we slowly lost interested in games. Some of our efforts did have a positive effect for instance:

Some fellows would sing. Lt. Robert Saksa, would sing many old songs to us. Lt. Petticone would sing the song called, "Heart of my Heart" and we would sing it together by the hours; it was real and inspirational to us.

One day I asked Walt Mayo, from Boston, "say old man, is there a Catholic priest here in camp?" I hadn't been to Confession for a long time and it began to look like I might never have the chance.

Mayo said, "look over there in that burned out building, you'll see a man rummaging around in the debris, that will be Father Kapaun. He is the Chaplain from the outfit I captured with."

I looked over there and spotted him, he had a patch over one eye and a stocking cap over his head and ears. The weather had become bitter cold. I approached him and said, "Father!"

He looked up at me, smiled and replied, "say fellow, help me scavenge this cellar. I saw a water crock that we can use to store water. If we boil the water maybe can have a sanitary water supply for the men. It might help knock out the dysentery."

I inspected the hole above the cellar, and saw the crock.

It had a dead rat in it, not that it would make any difference to us. I said, "Wait a minute, Father, I'll drop down into the hole and pull it out."

Easier said than done. The hole was too small for the crock to pass out of. 'Father' looked down at me with a woe be gone expression. Quickly I assessed the situation and said to him, "it isn't so bad, if you can pull up some of these loose boards, I can maneuver the crock over to another hole."

He started in, but the dirt and other debris covering the boards were too much. Dirt started cascading into the tiny space I was in. A large rock loosened by the dirt began to fall toward me. Father Kapaun tried to stop it by putting his foot in its path. The rock was diverted away, but left its mark on his foot and leg. A nasty bruise formed and may have been the cause of a blood clot that later formed in his leg.

The rock came crashing into the pit, hit the rim of the crock, cracking it, then rolled away. The crock wasn't too damaged, so we called out to Hank Petticone to come over and give a hand. We worked through the rest of the day and finally were able to get the crock to the surface, where we would make good use of it.

Father Kapaun was the custodian of this precious water supply. He would boil the water; place it in the crock, so that the sick men could get a drink of clean water. The rest of us, well we had to fend for ourselves. Sometimes I could mooch a small drink by bringing in some sticks I has gathered to burn in his campfire.

Once I saw his helmet liner laying in the yard and I asked him about it. It had the Cross marked on the front in white lettering. A representation that the wearer was a Chaplain. He said, "Mac, if I wear it that would only antagonize the Chinese, so I won't. But by the fact it is laying on this garbage heap causes every man to see it and remind them of their God." "You know Mac, I often wonder just how many silent prayers are said by this old heap of trash." "God moves in mysterious ways" he said.

Father Kapaun would hold evening devotions for all of us, and would always preface it with: "Gentlemen, Evening prayers!" An immediate hush would fall and everyone would listen to the Lord's Prayer: 'Our Father who art in heaven, give us this day our daily bread (here everyone would remember bread) as we had known it, I remembered what my mother used to say, "sonny, don't waste your bread for someday you may be in need." The prayer would continue to the catholic ending and then to the protestant ending. He was for all of us and showed his devotion in all of his actions.

I remember one day he went to the death house and gave the last rites to all of the dying men, men who might have lived with proper food. Father Kapaun would care for the extremely sick too, and then come back with sticks that he had picked up along the way out of the debris to feed the fire for heating water.

The dysentery could only be whipped in this manner. Hot clean water and rest, a lot of the runs were caused by some psychological reactions to our degrading treatment in camp. The men just couldn't accept the fact that they were prisoners and subject to these deplorable conditions. As a consequence they gave up and died.

The Chinese would sit back and say, "0 so solly that you Americans are such weaklings you should be made of sterner stuff" —Well, we were and we continued to confront them at every opportunity and they found out we weren't so weak after all.

We didn't go along with the programs, as their poor ignorant peasants would. We knew the truth and only waited for the time when we could express it.

Some of their lectures would go like this: "You liberated Officers are receiving extreme lenient treatment, but some are not, the reason that some of you are not is, that you are belligerent, now you should learn from Major Hume that belligerence doesn't pay. Major Hume tells us our policy is pleasing!" Hume, a man who had been subjected to about one week solid in a hole in the ground without care retorted, "Yes, you men should be good and do what our captors tell you to, I was a bad man, but I have learned the truth, listen to them, it will be better for you than if you don't!"

We knew what he meant, as we would be subjected to the same treatment, if we didn't swallow their line. I hope that Comrade Sun gets to read this, he was always worried that I would write the wrong thing, and often threatened me by using my confessions, if I did write something against the communists. Goddamn his filthy little guts! I get carried away when I think of those bastards.

There would be days of total inactivity, we'd think up things to do, I talked with Hector Cordero about setting up a camp school, as I knew that a school would solve many problems. It worked and soon we had a big program to set up, Lt. Deakon, Paul Docker, British, Dr. Anderson on Psychology, with Major McLaughlin on Public Speaking, and many others, too numerous to mention. This school would drive the commies crazy.

We were allowed to set up a water carrying program for the men. I volunteered as one of the initial members. We made about 40-50 trips a day, carrying two and a half gallon buckets of water from the river, so that the men could bathe, and wash clothes. We built a little bath house, many of the men set up little cliques of bowl washing, and clothes washing, using cigarettes to credit for pay. It was fantastic set up but it worked.

Our glory was of aiding to keep the sanity of a group of men who had begun to feel that we "would never get out!"

The mental stress at times was terrific, thinking of home, worrying about the fact that some of the wives were beginning to show strain and lonesomeness which could be easily fulfilled in our home towns, but we could do nothing about it.

I remember one man received a letter from his wife and she said, "You should know John, he is such a nice man, he plays with the children and sings to them, even helps me to put them to bed at night, don't you think he is a nice man to do all those things for me dear, and when the children are tucked into bed, he grinds my kitchen knives for me, he is such a nice man dear, you don't have anything to worry about as John is such a gentleman!"

Well after this husband read his letter he was foaming at the mouth thinking just what in hell was "John the Grinder" doing at his home this night, this very hour! It was a hell of a thing to have doubt and mistrust, and the commie bastards would take it up telling us that our families had forgotten us and were remarrying. Some of the letters were pretty heart breaking.

I remember one man received a letter that his ex-wife, one who had just remarried and had custody of the children, two sons, wrote him the new father didn't want them to know their own daddy, and she didn't want them to either. If he hadn't had a faith in his God he'd have given up hope, but fortunately he placed his trust in God, and he couldn't be shaken. He also had good memories of the decent people whom he had known in the past and knew his future was in the good old United States.

He would confide in me quite a bit and I with him, helping each other through the damnable days.

Fights among us were reduced to a minimum as we soon realized that we weren't fighting for pride in petty disputes, but we had a common enemy and when we fought amongst ourselves we were fighting for the enemy not against him.

We'd sit around and talk about everything under the son in the evenings. A makeshift carpenter shop run by Lt. Bill Watson was frequent topic and of course we discussed our favorite foods. We would plan what we'd do when we got out, how we would always appreciate everything we received as long as it was American. How we should continue our education, and to improve our knowledge to our own Government. In order to defeat these bastards who knew so much about communism.

Sometimes our talks would drift to women, that were usually when we had a full belly, and only then would we talk freely. I wish Lana Turner, and some of the others whom we had gossiped about could have heard us.

My secret passion was Maureen O'Hara, who incidentally was the only woman whom I have ever written a fan letter to (that is in the movies). It was in Shanghai, China during the years 1940-41 when I wrote the letter, I had just seen a picture of her at the Uptown Theater on Bubbling Well Road, and with a "Scotch" thimble in my hand, sat down at my typewriter and told her all about what I had seen her in. I also placed many Chinese stamps on the envelope, so she would know that the letter had come from China.

I was captured by the Japanese on Corregidor soon after so never found out if she had ever answered it or not—I'm still wondering!?

Mike Lorenzo, an American Officer had been captured with the Turkish advisory group. An intelligent man of high principles, he was a staunch fighter of communism. He spent many days on solitary! or in the hole. One night, he stripped himself of clothing and walked out into the snow. That convinced the commies that he was out of his head so they let him come back into camp.

Rotor Head John Thornton, a Navy Lieutenant helicopter pilot, he used to harass the guards in any way that he could. His classic was the dead rat on the small handkerchief which was supposed to represent a parachute holding a diseased animal dropped on the enemy, a representation of germ warfare. He would also ride an imaginary motorcycle around the compound much to the chagrin of the guards, and the interrogators, and instructors. They thought him nuts.

Lt. Bob Howell, USA was a great one to kid the instructors and ridicule the interpreters, who spoke the English language very poorly. He had a deep voice and wonderful sense of humor and was absolutely foolhardy.

Colonel Guy Thrash, USMC, strong, fearless, god fearing and entirely unafraid of the communists, he gave them many a sad hour.

They wanted him to salute one of their privates during roll call. He wasn't having any of it; this plus his uncooperative attitude in general, put him in solitary.

Major John McLaughlin, USMC, courageous and resourceful, would always try to do the greatest amount of good for the greatest amount of people. He is responsible for the fact that the Kanggye bunch came through with such flying colors. He saved many lives by using an intelligent attitude. Those men whom he aided will remember him the rest of their lives, I know because I am one of them. He talked me out of many foolish moves. His escape plot was disclosed by one of the informers and he and all of those in it were subjected to intense punishment in the hole and in solitary.

Pop McDonald, Major McDonald, USA he was our chief cook and bottle washer, he could steal a garlic clove out of the hands of a Chinese and did often, this helped to flavor the slop they were giving us. He and I lived in an abandoned kitchen which was nothing but a dug out. We blocked all the rat holes, lined the walls, and bricked up a couple of fairly comfortable beds, in fact it became a haven for the Chinese, so they moved us out and took over the comfort that we had made. Pop hated the Chinese with a passion but went along with it so that he could continue to steal food from them, and feed us.

Zach Dean, USAF, Capt., provided a bit of 'chef de cuisine' for us. He had a severe lung condition and was released on operation "Little Switch." When he got home, he sent letters to all of our families and told them about the real conditions in camp and also told them to stuff our letters with some kind of gift hoping something would get through.

I noticed Father Kapaun's helmet liner was still rolling around through winter and spring. Father Kapaun died there in the camp among the men he loved and cared for. I picked up the liner, broke off the cross emblem and hid it. I kept until I was repatriated, then sent it off to the Father Kapaun* memorial.

*-The following comments regarding Father Kapaun were contained in other writings by Felix. As a side note, Father Kapaun was awarded the Medal of Honor in April 2013.

Then I met a man, a man of god, a Catholic priest. He was in one of the camps where we were held. His name was Emil Kapaun. A chaplain in the U. S. Army, he ministered to all: Catholics, Protestants, Mohammedans and Jews. As I said, He was a Man of God. He would hold evening prayers, wash the clothes of the sick and hear confessions. Doing all this while he was slowly being eaten by disease, caused by lack of proper food, sanitation and clothing. He died in agony, the agony of Christ on the Cross. Before he died he called me to him and said, "When I die, say the last rites over my grave!" They never let me do this. He was spirited away before he died. We never had the privilege of knowing where he was buried in that cold ground, not even the comforting thought of a coffin. He heard my confession and told me to dedicate my life to the Blessed Virgin Mary and that she would intercede for me to Jesus, her son. He told all of us the story of the seven McAbees. A mother with seven children, all of whom would not repudiate God to their Emin, the King. One by one they were killed. She cried not tears of pain and privation but tears of joy. Her children were with God. Father Kapaun said, "I, as you see, am crying too, not tears of pain but tears of joy, because I'll be with my God in a short time. And he is! After his death we grew into a solid group, fighting the Communist: Catholics, Protestants, Jews, Mohammadans, all fighting races. He was our "Beau Ideal".

Lt. Ray M Dowe, Jr of Arlington, Va was the officer whom Father Kapaun spoke to just as they carried him out of the yard. He said, "Mike, I'll come back and kick the so and so out of you" just kidding. Mike remembers him so much that if you mention Kapaun he shows tears in his eyes.

At Freedom Village, Korea, the crucifix carved by Major Gerald Fink is examined by Father (Capt.) Leonard J. Paznonskas, Capt. Joseph L. O'Connor, Capt. Ralph Nardella, Warrant Officer Felix McCool and 1st Lt. Paul O'Dowd.

(See page 15.)

Official U. S. Navy
Photograph

DEDICATION

Who might have no tomorrow?

Had men like these not lived today?

CHAPTER TEN

HUMOR AND INCIDENTS

This particular thing happened to me one day when one of the interrogators decided to call me out. I was taken to a hut outside of my compound. It had a small room, a mud floor and a small bed set up in the corner. The guard told me to drop my gear, I did on the floor. He then closed the door and posted a guard around the house.

About two hours later I heard a call outside my door "American, American," so I slid the door back there was a Chinese coolie from the Honcho's kitchen. He had a five gallons pot of some sickly looking broth and a small wooden container of rice. He indicated for me to get my bowl and chop sticks, which I did with rapidity, I hadn't eaten since morning: He slapped the bowl full of rice, and covered it with the soup, made of sea weed, greens and pork flavoring, highly seasoned - that smell stimulated my appetite as we were never given enough seasoning.

I took everything I could get, and he left, the door was slowly closed, as the guard was watching me eat with his big bug eyes, and I was slurping it up with gusto.

Sometime later the door was opened and a slimy looking young Chinese man came in. He looked like a caricature of all the Orientals you have ever seen, big glasses, buck teeth gold rimmed, slick back hair and slant eyes and yellow skin, about 5 ft. and 4 inches high, small boned, tiny hands and feet. He said, "Sit down," I asked "why am I here?" He replied, "Never mind, you will soon learn; now I have some things to ask you."

He threw a cigarette to me which I threw back, I told him the polite way to give a cigarette was to offer it to a man, and that I was not a dog. He took the cigarette back, I knew this was a bad start but I didn't like his approach.

He then said, "My name is Liang! Do you know what that means?" I thought for a while and the only thing that came to my mind that sounded like his name was, cool water, which in Chinese is Ling Swee. I said, "Well comrade, it sounds like cool to me. Or is it what Liang means to me, which is quite similar to my name, McCool." He threw the pen he had in his hand down and said, "Do not make a joke without permission."

I thought what a prize prick they've picked to interrogate me, no sense of humor. Well old boy you asked for it and I'm not going to be nice in any instance.

He then said, "No comrade, it is not 'cool', it means dragon." He sort of rolled out the name dragon and his eyes lit up with a glitter of malice. I thought brother he's a nut too! "Do you know what a Dragon is?" I said, "Why yes, comrade, a Dragon is a SNAKE on two legs!" He said, "Are you calling me ·a SNAKE?" I said, "No, I believe a dragon is the beast, anyway it's either a beast or a snake. Do you think it will get any colder tonight? I only have one blanket, and there is no fire. Do I have to sleep on the floor?" "The supper was very good because it had flavor of pork in it." I then took a breath.

He just stared, and said, "Go to sleep." I lay my pad down on the floor, and listened to the rats gnaw on the cloth, where the grease of my head would contact the cloth.

It didn't matter to me then as I was mentally exhausted and worried about what tomorrow would bring. I slept fitfully, he tossed and turned also, and I could hear him gurgle noisily in his sleep. I awakened about dawn, inched the door open and slid outside looking for a toilet, the guard let me go and I grabbed some snow to rub in my face to wash the sleep out of my eyes. I got back in the room, and he was awake - the snake beast, I wasn't sure which.

He lay on the cot watching me. He said, "Where you go?" I answered, "I went to the toilet, and washed, I couldn't do it here in the room." He said, "You westerners are weak aren't you, you are afraid of me." I said, "listen I'm not afraid of you, but I'm afraid of what your report will be, I'll frankly admit that, because its cold and I know how you work on a man when it's cold." He said, "You accuse us of cruelty?" "No, I don't accuse you I let the facts speak for themselves, look through the crack in the door, there is a man tied to a post, it must be about 40 degrees below zero, how do you think that you could fare tied out there?"

He answered, "That man is an enemy of the people, he refuses to confess his crimes, he has dropped insects and germ infested bugs on our poor innocent people, and we will make him confess, or he will freeze to death!"

With that logic I had nothing to say, I knew they could get anything that they wanted, they only had to find the breaking point in the individual, the breaking point that all men have, because life is more precious than death, unless you are crazy.

I told him that it would be easier for me to talk if I couldn't hear the cries of that unfortunate man. This was at Pingchong Nee, the Officers camp, about 150 yards out of the POW compound, close to a mule barn. I know because I could hear them bray.

If I were a donkey, I would bray as an Ass, or as a wolf howls to the Moon but being a knowledgeable human I can only sit here and ponder.

The interrogation started that morning, the Dragon man threw a group of papers in front of me and let me glance through them. In them I saw the name of Subic Bay, where I had been on duty in 1949, and the name of my birthplace Pawhuska, Okla. They had quite a few other pertinent things that made me realize that they had a fairly complete dossier. I remarked on that fact, and he said "yes and we have one on every prisoner, and everyone who has ever written to a prisoner". It was food for thought. He could have gotten it from no other source than the Communists in America, and it made my blood boil to think about those bastards safe in my America.

I still had to fight with the scum who had us here as prisoners. I wondered just where justice begins!

I was burned, and told him if I ever ran into one of their dirty bastards in America, I would try to throttle them with my bare hands. I still feel that way, I see Red when I hear the name Communist and it isn't the color of their flag but BLOOD!

I stayed in this place for three days. He wanted me to tell him about our naval districts. I pretended ignorance of what he was talking. He then said to me, "I know more than you know about your country."

I came to the conclusion that I was an experiment for him. He failed miserably in extracting anything out of me, I stayed either dumb or belligerent, which is how he reported my conduct. So he hurried me over to the Chief.

At that time they had just brought back Major McLaughlin from solitary confinement for organizing resistance in the camp. Colonel Guy Thrash, USMC, was in solitary at that time for the same thing, resistance to the Communist doctrine. And I had been warned by Major Fink, USMC, before leaving to say nothing of importance, as he had received the word from Colonel Thrash and Major McLaughlin, to fight them for all we were worth.

Major Fink was taken out, so Major Jack Perry, USMC (aviation) got the word to me to continue the fight.

The word was passed in this way: A working party would go out of camp, they would start singing as they passed by the hovels where prisoners were confined.

They would sing out any current news, sing patriotic songs and in a general way try to bolster the morale of the unfortunate persons who were confined at that particular time. It was one thing to be strong when you were around your fellow prisoners, and quite another to act the same way when you were alone.

The chinks also had Lt. Allen Lloyd, Capt. Robert Messman, Capt. Ernest R. Reid, of Dallas Texas, and all of the USMC or USMCR prisoners on their list to harass.

I later found out that Chinese were being attacked by the 1st Marine Division out on the front lines, and so, they would try to get something on us for propaganda.

The Turkish Officers were putting up the same kind of resistance as were the British Officers. I believe that Colonel Carne, a British commander was held in solitary for nearly two years. He was a fine strong man, and I hope that he wasn't ruined by them.

Chaplin Davis of the High Anglican Church of England was carrying on his own campaign to thwart them, and doing a fine job - in my estimation they lived up to the oft repeated phrase of "stout fellow."

Capt. Arthur Wagner had already been through his ordeal and was in camp lending us his moral support together with Capt. Smith and the other Marine Officers.

The US Army had their resistance set up, as well as the British, the Turks, the Filipinos, and the Puerto Rican Officers.

We were united, all doing anything that we could to block the inroads of Communism. We knew that we all had a common enemy; any petty differences were quick to fade. Many spent miserable days in the hole and in solitary confinement. Capt. Bruce Shaw, USAF was one of the strongest.

Many times after 'one of their particular intense days of schooling we would come back to the room and discuss the happenings of the day, some would say, "Mac, we're never going to get out of here, they have us lock stock and barrel."

I would make the reply that our names were out there, they couldn't hide the truth. The fact that the Chinese wanted into the UN was one of the major reasons that we would be allowed to return home, and in fair shape.

In the spring one of the Army Officers started gathering up all of the woven or knitted things he could get his hands on. He also got hold of some of our old boots which were worn out. He made them into some softballs. His name was Ralph Nardella.

He did more for the camp morale that spring, than the sudden increase to our food supply. More food was a harbinger of the peace talks.

I'll never forget their 'Bug Warfare campaigns'.

They had a room rigged up with some pictures out of science magazine enlargements of bugs that we were supposedly to have dropped on them. I remember one picture of a dead fox or dog in the last stages of decay, chin on his forepaw, hair falling out of the skin, a picture of skin and bones. The caption on the picture went this way: "This infected animal was dropped out of a plane, in order to contaminate the country of North Korea; the contemptible UN Forces continue their germ warfare."

Now if this animal had been dropped five feet he would have completely fallen apart, I know this, because I've hunted in Colorado, in Oklahoma, in California. Any man who has ever run across an animal carcass in that stage of decay knows that all you have to do is to push it with the butt of your gun and it falls apart.

We pointed out to them the ridiculousness of their entire program to discredit us, they would counter with the fact that probably the animal had been wrapped in heavy paper which had since disintegrated due to the rain or cold, and thus left the animal intact.

I give you this for an understanding of what we had to listen to, stupidities, and absurdities, until we'd wonder if they knew enough to button their own pants, much less run a country.

Pictures of some of our leaders of industry as rats carrying rifles, and they the mighty and invincible CPV Chinese People's Army, with guns, and can you imagine the feeling we had.

They were crazy and we knew it, but we had to put on a front at times in order to eat. Sometimes when the study program was in full swing, about half the camp would act sick, and go to a sick call. Be given some burnt chalk or a placebo that the Chinese doctor would hand out and the next day the other half would do the same. This was planned, but when they got wise to our trick, the really sick men would suffer, because the Chinese would cut out all of the medication. It was a tough grind any way you looked at it, but it had its sense of humor, and we never lost our sense of humor, because if we did things looked quite bleak.

They would play excellent records over the loud speaker but then when we were enjoying it, a communistic broadcast would start, the volume would be so loud that we couldn't escape the noise. Sometimes it would start at 4:00 A.M. and last till ten or 11 at night. It did nothing to aid in keeping sanity; fortunately they became tired of it too, just as we did so it would finally stop. Another attempt of Brain Wash.

The beast or Snake left soon after I was allowed to go back to camp. I don't think he made many points with his bosses.

We had another little snake or rat. His name was Sun, Comrade Sun. He tried everything in the world to break into our consciousness, from bribes of candy, food, strong drink, to threats. His particular threat to me knowing the strong feeling that I had for my sons, especially after receiving my 'Dear John letter', was to say, "it would be too bad if something happened to them."

They never knew where my sons lived nor who had them until I received my Dear John letter from home, then of course they knew everything. This was a devastating personal attack. To have in their dirty hands, to hold against me, is an episode that might have broken me had it not been for my faith in God and Holy Spirit.

I had been in that black place before, when captured on Corregidor, in May 1942. Three years and five months as POW of the Japanese where I was a ditch digger, shithouse tender, gravedigger, animal herder, then sent to Japan on a hell ship, and forced to work the coal mines for the last year of the Pacific War II.

Now I suffered the loss of my sons by divorce, and had the letter to tell of my loss to the Chinese. A fact they tried many times to use on me, to break down my resistance.

CHAPTER ELEVEN
LETTERS HOME

We were forced to write home, having to say that we were well treated; we used to wonder if our correspondents really believed it.

Many attempts were made to get a point across, to the persons whom we wrote, to let them know that what we said in the letter wasn't really as decent as we were describing. We also wanted our Government to know that we were still loyal citizens even though we were being pounded with communism rhetoric.

This was how I did it.

I wrote to my sister Mary, "Dearest sister, my birthday is coming soon, so I want you to display my birthday banner outside, it is a great old banner, a reminder to me and to my friends here and I know it is to you."

The banner in question is the American Flag, which is displayed nationally on Flag Day, 14 June, a day that happens to be my birthday too.

Mary answered me: "Dear Felix, I received your letter and have hung out your birthday banner, when we see it we are also reminded of the song which accompanies it and appreciate it more now that you are gone."

The song in question is "the Star-Spangled Banner."

With these kinds of messages going out and in I knew that anything that I had to say in the way of describing the Chinese was being rescinded by our word play.

Like our saying in camp. "Don't eat that its horseshit." Another was when I told her of the study programs. I mentioned that our captors were teaching us, but we older persons were slow to learn, so the commies were patient with us, and would repeat and repeat, just like our dear departed Father used to do with us children. I knew full well that my sister would remember that Dad was one of the most impatient persons in the world with us kids when it came to our way of study, and many times gave me a kick in the pants if I was too slow.

In the same letter I told my sister to tell the rest of the family and especially to tell cousins Frank, Beatrice and Inez. (I have no relatives by that name) I also told my sister that firsts always come first, meaning to take the first letter out of each name, leaving FBI.

I wanted them informed, hoping that, by this method I could negate anything that might be done by the Commies there in the US.

The Chinese berated us many times about their agents contacting our families. One time I mentioned to my sister to buy me some stamps for my collection. I told her to buy a Swift Premium Stamp. I believe a Swifts Premium Stamp states "US Government Inspected and passed Grade "A." I wanted them to know that's the way I really felt, but I couldn't say it, because our mail was heavily censored.

I told my sister that we were being fed well. I told her that we were receiving eggs and warm food, and then followed it up, remarking "I wish that I could eat with Pete as that old Red Heart was good!"

Pete was our dog. My sister got the message. And the story went out to the right people.

When they finally gave us the beds after two years on the floor, I told my sister that finally we were being allowed to sleep on a plank and not on the floor. This backhanded compliment was allowed to go through by their censors, as they didn't realize the fact that I had said I was made to sleep on a floor for two years.

They were blinded by the compliment that I gave them by saying they had given us beds. They were blind then and are more blinded by their own propaganda.

Many of the men kept up this style of letter writing, by misleading and absurd comments about our treatment. It was effective, as long as we knew that the people of America were with us. We couldn't lose faith even though it looked grim many times.

I remember the two thousand who died at Pyockdong ni, and were buried along the banks of the reservoir. When the water rose in the spring floods, the bodies were washed away, and became fish bait. That is another edition from the communist book of lies.

When decency enters, communism propaganda flies out the Window.

CHAPTER TWELVE

STOLEN CHOW

Pop McDonald and I were living in the old abandoned kitchen in this Korea house and we had made it habitable, which the Chinese seemed to resent as they moved us out.

Before we moved out and having an inkling of the main reason that we were being moved, we pried a nail out of a small sliding pantry type of door. This aperture led into another room in the house. We pried the nail out and left it loose, and then we could pull it out from the adjacent room.

The Chinese stocked this room with small stores from their supplies. There were tobacco, oil, sugar, sea weed, dried fish and garlic, salt, and red peppers.

We left it alone for the first day but hunger for sweets and a smoke drove us to raid the storehouse. We waited till night and pulled the nail through, slid into the room, breathlessly watching for the guard.

An Officer who was in the small kitchen was making a lot of noise, and they were so used to hearing large rats scurry about, they didn't pay too much attention to any noises we made. Well, we had smokes, sugar, and fish, garlic with salt and pepper in our soup for quite a few days.

This alone gave us quite a bit of renewed energy and the fact that we were fooling the commies was enough to bolster our morale. It ended in a near tragedy, the guard and kitchen honcho came down one night when we were raiding it, and we got out just in time. They had been suspicious about the use of so many of their stores. They didn't catch anyone, but they discovered the loose nail, and held a search of our room. No one was caught, but all of our names were put down in the little black book they kept for future reference. They kept the book handy when they wanted to punish any of us.

Food was constantly on my mind we would lay around and daydream about it. I said "My mother used to make the best pineapple upside down cake. She used three pineapple slices on the top and she put chopped walnuts on the top, when she baked it." Someone said, "you are almost right, but use two pineapples instead of three." Another guy said, "I don't know if that is right or not, we don't use walnuts, we use pecans with syrup over the top. The next guy says, "I don't give a 'diddle doo damn squat' how you think pineapple upside down cake is made. I happen to know, and by God I can prove it." Someone says, "Put your money where your mouth is." "Ok I will," he answered "I'll bet $50.00 dollars that I'm right."

Some choruses of voices say, "fifty dollars? , What in hell would that do here? Make a reasonable bet." First man responded, "Ok, I'll make a sporting bet, I'll wash bowls and I'll roll two Korean tobacco cigarettes each day for a week, if I'm wrong."

With the bet agreed on, it was decided to consult the master of all information, Harry Wignau. "Might as well be Harry," we said, "he lies better than anyone and some actually believe him?" We in the group go over to Harry. He is engaged in a polite conversation of telling some Major or Captain that he doesn't know what he's talking about. We interrupt and ask Harry to tell us the ingredients of a pineapple upside down cake. His answer is, "in a pineapple upside down cake, there is one slice of pineapple and is topped by peanuts, because they are cheaper."

Harry always the politician was a proponent of doing things reasonably.

We go away angrily, while Harry stands there scratching his head and says, "I wonder if they know that I can feed 35 people with six hot dogs?" -

The night goes on with similar arguments, while some groups of intellectuals debate Einstein's theory of relativity, or whether Pythagoras ever applied the Pythagorean theory, or if he used the Sine of trigonometric function to calculate the right angles' in a triangle.

This buzz of conversation would go on till the Chinese would scream out, "stop, you mellican alIa time walla walla talk, you no stop this talka talka. Why you no stop, all mellican is crazy."

We would then begin a discussion of 'marsh' gas. Did it really burn? Someone was always ready to produce a sample. So we would light it and get some color. Green, blue, red. A large flame would travel up a man's backside. There were many noble attempts to produce the most spectacular flames. This would send the Chinese into frenzy. They would have men standing in snow up to their necks if caught demonstrating 'marsh' gas.

We hadn't had a bath for about four months, summer was coming along and we were miserable, so we put up a serious protest that our poor sanitation conditions were one of the causes for so many deaths.

Comrade Sun gave us a classic speech, "You say that you are dirty, we know you are dirty, why don't you clean up?" "Sun, we can't clean up if there is no water. Is there any water in camp except the water which we use to cook with?

"You won't let us go bathe in the river!" Sun said to us "never mind, you must keep clean, why don't you keep clean!"

We ended up mumbling to ourselves, "What the hell does the silly son of a bitch think we are cats, we're going to lick ourselves clean!" "Try the bastard again!"

"Sun, you know there is no soap in camp, and there is no water, why can't we go to the river and use sand on our bodies, it is warm enough now and then we could boil the clothes and kill the lice." He said: "Silence! You try the patience of the great CPV, we are kind to you, we do not kill you, why you not patient, your planes bombed the barge which was bringing the soap to this camp, just like they bombed the tobacco barge."

Someone in the crowd said, "Did they bomb the meat boat, and the salt boat, and the mail boat." Sun said, "Comrade, come to my Quarters when this discussion is over!" (He went and came back a week later, beaten up and fatigued.)

We knew that we weren't going to get anyplace.

Sun ended up, "Go back to your quarters and reflect on how you can keep clean, you do not try, you are lazy pigs of Americans and do not try, I know that we do not have soap to give you but you can keep clean anyway." Some of the men started to drift muttering to themselves "the dirty S. O. B.'s, they are the pigs and expect everyone else to follow suit.

They tell us of their five thousand years of culture, those filthy dogs haven't any idea of what culture is

They are best described by the grease on their necks, their spittle on the floor, and smell of them, as garlic mixed uncleanliness wafts off their bodies, noticeable within five feet or downwind from them.

We were battered by our circumstances. How we faced and dealt with our conditions would determine our future. Our fate was not by chance. We must learn to channel our mind to believe that 'I am a creative power and capable of change within myself, to accept that which is, and begin to grow from inside.'

We each and every one of us did just that, some more latently than others, but we inexorably followed a similar pattern striving for excellence in our mind.

This belief was impossible to capture with the body, but soon it became more noticeable, some were more distressed than others, injured minds physiologically unsound and needing time to recuperate.

If condition and environment allowed there would be no permanent injury to the body or mind.

What if the political decisions of a foreign government choose to tamper with the mind of one who went through these hellish experiences, by disguising the truth? The result would show up later. The thought that there is no truth-when he cannot find it in the people who wasted him for two years in the purgatory of camp.

"A man only begins to be a man when he ceases to whine and revile, and commences to search for the hidden justice which regulates his life. And as he adapts his mind to that regulating factor, he ceases to accuse others as the cause of condition, and builds himself up in strong and noble thoughts; ceases to kick against circumstances, but begins to use them as aids to his more personal progress, and as a means of discovering the hidden powers and possibilities within himself." James Allen

This thought served as sustenance, as many of the men in camp did just that by study, and concentration upon the grace of God, and with the inculcated spirit of mankind.

CHAPTER THIRTEEN

IN THE CAN

The can was a six holer, with no seats but a slit in the floor which you would squat over. In the summer the flies would drive you mad by crawling over your balls and ass and up and down your spine.

Conversation was held to a minimum due to the fact that a man wanted to do his business and scram. In the winter the cold was so bad that our fingers would cramp into a locked position and we couldn't use them unless you put them under your arms or between your legs to get some of the body heat.

Then and only then could you have the flexibility to button your fly, therefore there wasn't much conversation going on.

But at times though, the rumors would fly thick and heavy this way: Man on the first hole is just out of hearing distance of the man on the last hole. Man on the first hole says, "Boy, it will be great when we get out of here!" Man on the next hole mumbles, "Yeah, it sure will, could be any time now couldn't it?" "Yeah", says the man on the last hole. "What was that you said, WE'RE GETTING out of here?" New man just entering the can, "What's that, WE ARE GETTING OUT OF HERE?"

Man on the grounds outside passes by hears the conversation and goes to the courtyard where a group of men are talking. "Boy, did you hear the news, we're getting out of here, I just heard it and from a reliable source, of course I'm not permitted to tell who said so, as he might get in trouble with the commies, but its straight dope,"

"WE'RE GOING HOME SOON." Man in the school house hears the last part and runs into next room, "Men I just heard from a reliable source, whom I can't mention that we're going home any day, he got it from a reliable chairman, one who has never lied to us." Chorus: "Wow, were going home soon, the armistice is SIGNED!" Men on the hill who have been carrying dirt all afternoon hear this and scream to the men in the toilet, "did you hear we're going home soon the armistice is signed and trucks are on their way here to pick us up, there is also a chance that we'll get Red Cross packages. I just overheard a Chink tell the top dog 'Ding', and 'Ding' smiled."

"I'll bet the bastards give us pork and rice now to fatten us up, just like they have done in the past."

Men in the yard: "Brother did you hear that they're going to give us pork, rice, and flour, and sugar to celebrate going home, it's about time the bastards did something." Voice in the corner: "We ain't ever gonna get out, I tell you Mac, they're lying, and won't stop lying. The dirty commie bastards G.D. the S. O. B.'s!"

Men coming out of the can buttoning their pants: "Boy it's just like a dream isn't it, here just a few minutes ago we were hoping that we were going to get out and now here it is finally."

After talking about the rumor at night some of the more cool heads try to pin the rumor down, and everybody denies starting it but they heard someone else say it was a fact! A delegation goes to the Chinese to find out; if the story started there.

"We have heard that we are going to be released soon, and that the armistice is signed, and that there will be an increase in food." "Is it true?"

A Chinese with sickly grin on his face said, "Your side is insincere comrades, you will have much time to study and learn the truth before you are allowed to go home. Your side has violated the previously arranged agreements and is very stubborn, just like you. You here are all the same way, you will not go home until you have learned the truth."

The group goes away mad at the chinks, and mad at themselves because they believed the rumor, never realizing that they all contributed by their own wishful thinking.

If this happened once in camp it happened 10,000 times, and that is the short side of the estimate.

We lived on hoping, and kept on with wishful thinking, but realized if the UN had to go through the same crap as we, that hope was dim.

CHAPTER FOURTEEN
THE MARCH TO NOWHERE

To leave was a wonderful thing. We were like fractious horses ready to break the ribbon and go. Our frantic desire to leave and with the plum of possible freedom dangling before our eye, we played a little hard in that crowded room of fifteen people, breaking the flimsy paper windows out of the doors. Those paper shells were all that kept the cold out.

When we left, the straw mats, heavy with lice, fat from our blood, were torn up. Well, we left and when we neared Kanggye they turned us around again and we marched back into camp.

The Korean women were overjoyed. The old lady just stood there holding a cloth to her eyes and smiled through tears, but we had to go back into that room discouraged, tired, and with a hopeless feeling of nothingness. This was part of their breakdown program.

We took some rice and papers to the windows, closing out the chill, ate a rice ball a piece and were undecided between unpacking our pitiful rags and just flopping on the now hard dirt floor. The march had determined that for us, so we just lay down on the dirt.

During the night I heard a door slide softly back and the young girl slipped into the room. She had brought us a pot of hot soup. It was like nectar from the Gods. Her presence brought about that longing for home and life. But this was life then, and a new chapter was being written for many of us. That we live for now, not yesterday, nor tomorrow, but now.

The next morning we started our march again. At night we got into the Kanggye Rail Road station. They handed each of us a fish head and some kind of a sweet fruit and cigarettes. We were sure now we were going to be freed.

We boarded the train with high hopes.

Each night they opened up the doors and let us stretch. We arrived some place in Korea in a marshaling yard. They pulled us out of the train and we marched about 15 miles. By that time the spring rains had started.

It was a mile by mile of soppy, sloshing, slop to walk through, loaded down with Chinese gear.

We stayed out there about three days and they stopped and separated 18 men from us. We didn't know where they went. Later found out they were freed. Why? We never knew.

They marched us again for a couple odd days and threw us back on the train and then were taken off the train again to bury the dead.

Their burial custom is quite degrading. The deceased is taken to a hill near a town. There usually isn't much grass on the hill but I could see large rounded mounds that were covered with grass. These were the graves. I have been told that the dead people are planted setting up. They made us turn our back when the burial was going on.

We marched through two more villages, were isolated into groups and moved about. They would go into the huts and tell the Korean women and children to go into one room and then they would pack twenty five to thirty of us into one small room.

There was nothing to keep us warm except the warmth of our bodies.

For a while we did have little bowls but most of the time we used our hands to eat. We were under guard all the time.

Guards were well dressed. A typical commie soldier had rubber soled shoes, layered with thick horse hair.

The sergeants and above had better clothing. They wore thickly padded trousers, with coats. They carried Russian rifles about 27 caliber with bolt action. Later on they got some modern rifles. The first class troops had Russian automatic weapons.

They changed guards often, but we still kept on going. There was no possible way of telling how many men dropped off. They kept us so well spread apart that we couldn't tell. They never kept any groups together. If men dropped off ahead of us, we never saw them.

They must have done something with their bodies. We were marched in small groups. This was all done in a confusing way so that we couldn't keep track of the other men.

They were doing this for a purpose, so that we wouldn't know who fell.

When we marched we never saw any POW's on the road. They must have buried the bodies because we saw fires up in the hills in the night time. We wondered what the fires were for a long time, but finally we found out that they used the fires for softening the ground to bury the dead.

Major Mac and I were talking about it one time. Frank Noel and Curly Reed were in an open shelter one night and were just sitting there wondering what all the fires were for. Some Koreans had told one of them that they did this so that they could bury people. "Who is it that they are burying?" They are burying our people.

Imagine yourself in a vast space of white emptiness, nothing else. All we can see is white and feel its icy grip. All we hear is a constant 'whoo-whoo' of terrifying wind. The frigid snow is all around us and we march mile after mile. We look around and there are miles and miles of nothingness. The faint sound of water flowing is heard from miles below.

During the falling of the snow it is very windy and after the fall of the snow it is quiet and the snows brightness is blinding because it is so white. We would take a piece of cloth and make a slit in it for our eyes.

The entire march was in the winter and spring. We were starting to cross a river. We called it the "Unnamed River" at that time. The guards ordered us to stop, saving, "The weather is changing and the ice is breaking up. " The march stopped.

Many times, if we were on the march and were not heavily guarded by the Commies, the Korean families would bring a bowl of rice to us, if they were not endangering themselves of being caught. This often took place in a hut where they would be positive of not being caught. But when the Commies came by they would act very cruel to us. This of course, was all an act.

There weren't many young men. Generally if a young man was not accounted for the family would suffer for his not being there.

The Commies had a government set up in each town. If the villagers had something of value it would be collected for distribution, but it was obvious that these things were sent to China.

The Commissar was generally a Korean. Sometimes he was a long time Commie. There was one that I can't remember.

She was not about to accept Communism and we would see her fade away by a lack of food and in ill health.

By now, I had seen two Russians. That is, they had Russian type of clothing and were dressed well. They were white men, Caucasians. I heard them speak in a guttural language.

We used to see those Caucasians occasionally, driving in foreign made sedans' a limousine type. I saw this Burchett fellow one time. I never noticed him spoken to-directly by any of these Caucasian fellows.

We arrived in the valley close to Pyockdong Ni. A long valley heading down toward the Yalu River. A reservoir on our left and an estuary on our right, and Manchuria to the north. We approached the town from the mountains by a well-traveled road reminiscent of a winding staircase.

We spotted a group of dark, dirty, bearded prisoners behind barbed wire fence. We yelled greetings to them but they hollered back in a foreign tongue.

Hector Cordero, the linguist in our group, tried out his languages. We learned that they were French speaking Turks.

A Korean guard who spoke English took us into camp and the Chinese guard who took us in disappeared.

The place was guarded by a perimeter guard and had a roving patrol inside the camp. At vantage high spots there would be a machine gun or automatic weapons, with a guard where we couldn't get at him.

I turned to a group of the first ones in and I remember looking at Bob Messman. I said, "Bob, this is a prison camp. This is the end of nowhere," and with a hopeless gesture, Bob turned and gestured toward a hut where a group of dead, frozen Americans lay. There was an undershirt hanging on a stick that they had just taken off of one of the four bodies. The undershirt was worn and gray and seemed to be moving.

Major Mac and Allen Lloyd took the stick and started banging it against the rail on the outside of the building. It was moving and upon closer inspection it was woven with lice. Barro Turner, he was the tanker guy I had been captured with, said, "This is a new weave. I don't think it will catch on in America."

We had reached the end of our march to nowhere.

CONCLUSION

Peaceful! How often we have heard that term used by a nation whose "Bill of Rights" is their almighty "Fist". Who fostered such efforts as the "Stockholm Peace Appeal" and tried to divert the people of a free world from necessary measures of defense and create through the free world a popular demand for peace at any price.

Low, cunning Communist leaders, knowing that if pacifism becomes a prevalent mood among the free people, the communist can easily conquer the world. Then they can confront the free people with successive choices between peace and surrender; and if peace is the absolute goal, then surrender becomes inevitable. In this connection while modern developments have made war more terrible, they have also made the consequences of retreat and capture more terrible. Modern war could now destroy much of life on this planet. Peace, under certain conditions could lead to a degradation of the human race and to subjecting human beings to a form of mental decay which obliterates the capacity for moral and intellectual judgment. We cannot but shrink from buying peace at the price of extending over human beings the rule of those who believe that men are in fact nothing more than animated bits of matter and that to insure harmony and conformity, they should be deprived of the capacity to form moral and intellectual judgment. Man, we read in Holy Scriptures, was made a little lower than the angels. Should man now be made little, if any, higher than domesticated animals which serve the purposes of their human masters?

The great deeds of history were wrought primarily by men with a deep conviction and dynamic faith. They were sure they were right.

Our nation was founded as an experiment in human liberty and rights.

Our institutions reflect the belief of our founders that all men were endowed by their creator with inalienable rights and had duties prescribed by moral laws. They believe that human institutions ought primarily to help men develop their GOD GIVEN possibilities and that our nation, by its conduct and example could help men everywhere to find the way to a better and more abundant life!

AND IT DOES!

FJM

date unknown

"Felix repatriation photo"

PRAYER

Christmas was near by the calendar, this time a year ago, but it seemed terrible for the Communist POW Camp in North Korea.

Still, there were prisoners whom no Reds could keep from having Christmas in their hearts.

One of them, W.O. F. J. McCool, USMC. of Glendale, Calif., composed a Christmas prayer, that a fellow prisoner preserved. It's a prayer for others, including the Communists, as well as for you.

When the prisoners were released this year, Capt. Joseph O'Connor of Spring City, PA., brought back his "POW Anthology" in which he had written favorite poems and the prayer of Felix J. McCool, Marine Officer.

Dated 16 December 1952, it runs,
To You, Sweet Infant Mild
by W.O. F.J. McCool, POW

Born of a woman in purity for mankind, dear Infant Savior, come to us this day. Drive from us, by our faith in you, thoughts of personal selfishness, that we may be one with your teachings.

To have Hope eternal in our hearts for our soul and our loved ones.

For us to understand our natural enemies and by virtue, to overcome the evil that may be existing in their hearts.

By the forgiveness that you gave to those who persecuted your ideals, personified in the ultimate crucifixion of Your Sacred Body, give us charity for all mankind. To love them, to give examples to them by our actions of love and charity even to that our nature despises.

Let us open our eyes to limitless horizons, never again to descend into the valley of ignorance or deceit in man's nature. Let us stay aloft with our "Lady of the Mountain," eyes descending with compassion, hearts lifted with pure love, all for you, "OUR JESUS!"

Mini Bio

The time that elapsed between Japan and Korea was Sept 45 till November 50 about 5 years. I got a job after arriving home with Base personnel at Marine Corps Base San Diego, Calif. Nine months later I was headed for Pearl Harbor. Stanley Bronc, an old buddy of mine in San Francisco delayed my transfer to the Pacific area so soon. I was there at Treasure Island about two years then I was off to Subic Bay, Philippines. I was billeted near the old place where General Bull Ridgley, USMC had been put aboard the Jap Hell Ships.

The Bull is now commanding General of the 2nd Marine Division. I stayed in the Philippines for two years, saw Corregidor again, then back to Pearl Harbor for a few months then back to the states.

Mother died then, and I was sent to Camp Pendleton near Oceanside Ca. for duty with Service Battalion of the 1st Marine Division. When General Craig started up his Brigade, the 1st Marine Brigade, I volunteered to go with them to Korea. There wasn't any billet but Laundry Officer, (Mobile Units). I took it and embarked in July for Korea, landed at Pusan 3 August and was committed with my outfit at Changwon, Chingdong, Nee, Myrang, then made the Inchon Seoul landing, went over to Hamhung then out to the mountains to Koto Ri and Haggeru Ri. I was on my third trip to Haggeru Ri when I ran into the road block which was my down fall. Frank Noel, Capt. Curly Reid, Major McLaughlin, Allan Lloyd and Capt. Barrow Turner were there. So with whomever we could find set up a defense of the place till daylight, many men ahead and behind us got out but we were stuck and ended up prisoners. If we had crawled away during the night, it might have been easy to do, there was much confusion, but a Marine is trained to fight where the fight is so we stayed and were stuck.

First Korean camp prison at 14 day place, next Kanggye, then Camp #5 Pyockdong Nee and then Camp #2 Pingchong Nee our final spot. The reason we were switched around was that we weren't very good students, and they were trying to "reeducate us."

116

It didn't take as I've been studying more about my country since I came back then I ever did before. We have the greatest and it will continue. I let a little of it interject in my instructions at Freight Transportation school. I had taken a lot of history courses at San Francisco Golden Gate College. The Marine Corps sponsored me and paid part of my tuition. I've also been taking Psychology from Eastern Carolina at Greenville North Carolina, and will be enrolled in University of Tennessee extension the next semester, working for my Bachelors' degree. I hope to teach Transportation History and/or Geography when I get my Master's Degree, probably about four more years. I will continue to write, and belong to a Poetry group in Camp LeJeune

ANNEX – 1
POW LETTERS HOME

These are letters Felix wrote from his Prisoner of War camp to the family. This is a small sample of letters. These are hand written notes from the early 1950s on thin parchment paper with very small script to increase the contents. Some of the handwriting is not legible. I've tried to do my best to transcribe accurately. There are some hand written notes in red which Felix wrote upon these letters after his return illuminating his hidden messages.

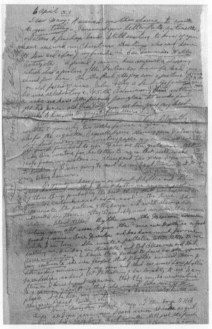

Actual letters home from POW camp

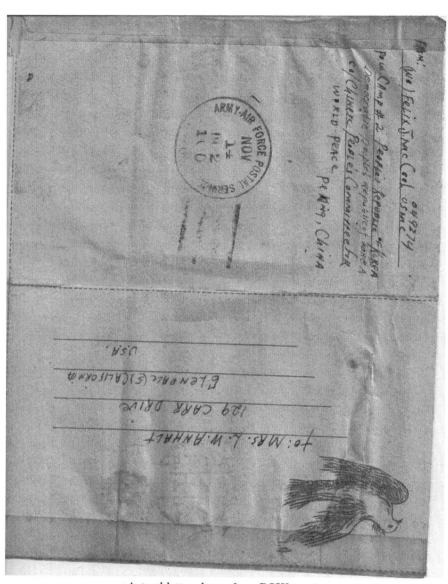

Actual letters home from POW camp

15 April 1953

Dear Mary: Just received your Jan 13, 53 letter
thanks for all the kind words - Honey I do write
to you and often twice _____ each month
I'm so sorry you do not receive them. Thank Pete only
for his consideration of me however I'm still jealous
of them - I saw something today which for the first
time gives me definite encouragement of getting home.
The sick and seriously wounded men went by in
trucks supposedly heading for home the trucks
_____ carrying a red flag in the rear and had
a red panel on the hood We were told that
they are to be released on the 20 th of this month.
This coupled with other news we received is
highly indicative (to my way of reasoning) that
our time is drawing to a close. I pray for that
day - and the one which lands me in the
U.S.A. any part of it!
We still have a touch of winter in the air
has been cold in the mornings had a slight snow
this morning.
I'm so happy that Carl has decided upon a profession
and quite a lucrative and helpful one - he should
make quite a fine dentist. Also happy about Tom
nearing his C.P.A. You two Mothers should be
proud indeed!
It's Lois now - still have the "Old Crow" it
is an old crow now isn't it?
I hope darlin that you are over your
heart ailment by now - Please take care as I want
you to be at the landing field with all of my rest-
_____ _____ me.
Have to go to roll call now last one
for the day and afterward can relax Will finish

Seoul Korea

26 Sept 50

Dear Pat, Dick & Frances,

Here I sit on the banks of the Osan River. I've been over but have 60 men and 13 units to move up now so came back. This place is a mess believe me, had to bury 40 NKs right where I'm sitting now in order to be able to work, War is Hell!

Did received your pictures and they are fine, Frances is lovely!

I picked up a poor woman who had been held by NK's. She had a broken arm; her brown eyed baby boy had an arm nearly shot off. I carried them to a safe place and got the town (illegible) to take care of them. The mute appeal in her eyes was a tragic thing Pat and the little fellow actually smiled at me-I hurt inside but know that God has a special place for those who suffer so very much. Perhaps she's safe now. I got a little panicky and wanted to run but couldn't. We received some mortar fire for breakfast but no harm done. I made the landing at Inchon and hope to make them all.

You keep mentioning Phyllis to me-that was a mistake. I leave her to heaven and do not care to hear about her again. The boys are a different thing but a just country of law gave them to her- I have no recourse- Smallness of nature(illegible) hell out of me so I

couldn't reconcile with her- I'm not sore at her Pat
she just "never happened."

I have to take a Reconnaissance into other side of
Seoul now so think of me and pray.

My love to all,

Felix J

To: Mrs. L.W. Anhalt

129 Carr Drive

Glendale(S), California

From: WO Felix J. McCool USMC 049274

Dear Mary:

I have again been offered an opportunity to write to you. I am in good shape. The Chinese Volunteer Army in North Korea treat all of us very good we have good food warm quarters-warm clothes and fine treatment. It is the exactly opposite my treatment the Japanese who captured me in 1942.

I wish to extend my love to you to all of my sisters to my wife and to my boys Mike and Tim. I love all of you very much. I hope this foolish aggression we have subjected the Koreans to will soon close and that we can come home to peace and happiness.

Please inform my outfit and Dr. Berry of that we can someday resume our political interests and discussions of Oriental Arts.

A history of who I am alive though I had said I would never be a Prisoner of War again. I was on my way to a new position in convoy we were surrounded and fought for 14 hours close battle with many exchange of shots people all around me were killed and wounded too. Bullets went through my coat but I only had a small scratch. I was saved why (?). I don't know-I stood up in the midst of battle but could not be hit! My captors told us to close firing and surrender before we were all killed, only a handful were left so our leader (illegible) surrender to Chinese, gone as good food and (illegible) our needless fears. They are fighting for peace a good peace. I will have much to talk about when I come home. I would like to see my family all of them very much love to all.

Felix J. McCool

28 January 1951 Sunday

To: Mrs. L.W. Anhalt

129 Carr Drive

Glendale (S) California

From: Felix J. McCool

Dear Mary;

I have again an opportunity to write home. I am in good health and receiving good treatment, we are in a warm room receive adequate food, and we are allowed an opportunity to keep clean. All of these things are contributory to good health which everyone has. We can thank our liberators for all of this kind treatment. The Chinese have shown a definite friendly attitude throughout.

Mary I would appreciate if you would tell Phil Jones that my final "will and testament" should remain the same as it is my wish. I do not want any change to be made in my financial status there in California or in Florida any changes will be made by me upon my return which God willing I hope will be soon. Please inform my ex-wife my two sons Mike and Tim my sisters Patricia and family, Cecilia and family, Aileen and family, Antoinette and family, your family especially Louis of my good health, good treatment and hopes for a hasty renewal of our family ties. Also inform my dear Aunt Mary and Kathy also Dr. Berry of all these good things, and include Mary Lou and Phil and family. I have tried to reason why I was saved again — it must have been for a good reason — my mind is clean and I have no bad feelings. Will you write to the following names people and tell them that their respective husbands are being treated fine and they are in good health:

(Editor's note- the next paragraph is a list of names and addresses of fellow POW family members. I decided not to include due to privacy concerns)

Thank you for them and for me, my love to all until we meet again.

Your brother Felix J

[Editor's note-this is a hand written note from the early 1950s on thin parchment paper with very small script to increase the contents. Some of the hand-writing is not legible. I've tried to do my best to transcribe accurately There are some hand written notes in red which we believe were Felix illuminating his hidden messages, after the fact.]

6 February 1951

From: Felix J. McCool

To: Mrs R.L. Swift 1752 W. Flager St Miami Florida

Dear Sister Patricia,

I have been offered an opportunity to write again, I have written to Sister Mary Anhalt before. I wish to let you, Dick, Ernest Lynn, Patsy, and Francis know that I am in good health and being treated excellently. We have been given a warm room clothes from the extreme cold and good tasty food by the Chinese Volunteer Army who are our captors. They are friendly and feel justified in their actions. Before I digress I am with fifteen (15) other men from various units who were captured at about the same time as I. I will include (10) ten of their names and addresses for you to forward word of their good health and treatment to their (illegible). The names will be on the back of this page, please do this for them and receive their extreme gratitude.

I had no intention of ever being a Prisoner of War again after my last episode with the Japanese-I was in a convoy on a mission in heavy mountains roads snow covered and icy. We ran into a road block which extended for miles we fought all night when our trucks were hit and dead and wounded were all around us at dawn the remnants were offered a kind opportunity to surrender, the alternative was obvious so the surrender was carried out-from that minute on we were treated with upmost generosity and friendship. This was exactly opposite from what I had been led to believe. God willing I will be able to come back soon and visit all of my sisters. I have not mentioned my ex-wife Phyllis or my sons Mike and Tim. I have their pictures which I received Christmas 1950 they are nearly worn through with handling. Please give Phyllis my kindest regards and hug and squeeze the boys for me. I wish I could also say the same about Phyllis but I know she doesn't care for me and I do not want to distress her more than I have but I do love all of them. Tell Mary to ask Phil Jones to see that no changes are made in any financial arrangements I have made and that any accrued monies I have be left for my disposal.

Love Felix

PS- My best to all of my sisters to Aunt Mary Katie (?) and all of the family; I promise I won't do it again. Be captured I mean. Love Felix

[Editor's note-Names are included but addresses not for privacy concerns]

Hector Corderro

Lt. Messman

J.N. McLaughlin

Frank Noel

A.L. Lloyd

Ernest Reid

G.P Shedd

Geo. Snyan

Chas. Peckham

Fred Soriano

R.E. Alley

28 February 1951

To: Mrs. L.W. Anhalt (sister)

129 Carr Drive

Glendale (S) California

From: (WO) F.J. McCool USMC

049274 P.O.W. Camp Number 2

C/O Chinese Peoples Committee for World Peace

Peking, China

Dear Mary:

I received your letter of 18 January 52 today — It
is a wonderful letter! The little snap shot of Mike
and Tim included gave me great joy- I live a little
world of my own about them with my 4 pictures of them
sometimes they eat with me and often at nights I take
them out for a good night talk, life deals some unfortunate circumstances at times but it's a good old
world.

It's strange that Nadine sent the picture to you
(why?) and so far I have not received her letter or
letters perhaps soon. I hope I'm there in spirit at
times when you and Louis are talking in the warmth of
your room. I know I project myself to you too often
we have a wonderful closeness I wouldn't trade for a

million dollars. My family are all fine. I'm proud of Tom tell him so for me! Heard about the rain there — remember New Years' 23 (?) you and Louis went to the (G) I was going to say the Glendale but it was the theater on (I think) Glendale Blvd close to your home now- well the gist of the story is that you were nearly flooded out and the "wash" was overflowed "ridin around in the rain" Sentimental one!

I'll bet Mike and Aileen Ann are fine looking children they should be look at their parents. Do Joe and Aileen still live at the same place? Yes, I surely did want to hear of Louis and I'm glad the old alarm still goes off. Is it still set 15 minutes early I used to like the comfort of that extra 15 minutes and if you don't laugh now I don't know Mary and Louis. I've many things to tell you my dear I've grown much mentally since being a P.O.W. believe that! Sort of like the way you told me of the "pipe and tobacco" as Antoinette would say "I'm honored!"

The word of Jack and Donna is good and I like the "for keeps" way it sounds my best to them. Tell Carl to move over and I want the 2 top drawers "dub-bies?" I'm holding the Stations of the Cross on my worn out prayer book this Sunday you sent the pamphlet to me "Way of the Cross for Servicemen" —my Rosary was blessed by a Saint and it can be used for Stations with all (illegible). I surely do know how Paul drives on Saturday night had a few of those wild rides up (illegible) sign boards with him unfortunate he doesn't go easy isn't it? He surely must hate life to hit the old bottle like he does its no cure. I know and only intensify pain.

I have met a particularly good American doctor here who is thinking of going into private practice out of the service we have had many talks, his wife is now in Long Beach, Mrs. Clarence L. Anderson (street address) — his name is Captain Clarence L. Anderson, A.S.N. USA perhaps you could call her sometime. Andy has had many "pow wows" with me and I've told him about you Louis, Jimmy practically all of the family, incidentally he has one hellova good Basso voice. We always have a few songs before going to sleep at nights — then my Rosary.

Incidentally I thought Ernestine a charming person, the old "Green Eye" is a very poor medicine I know because I suffered it with Phyllis.

Tell all the girls hello for me. My love to you and Louis

Love Felix

P.S. Do you ever hear from Dr and Mrs. Berry if so send my regards to them.

[Editor's note-this is a hand written note from the early 1950s on thin parchment paper with very small script to increase the contents. Some of the hand-writing is not legible. I've tried to do my best to transcribe accurately. There are some handwritten notes in red which we believe were Felix illuminating his hidden messages, after the fact.]

16 September 1951

From" Prisoner of War WO Felix J McCool USMC 049274 Democratic Peoples Republic of Korea

Committee of Chinese Congress of the Defenders of World Peace Peking China

To: Mrs. L.W. Anhalt 129 Carr Drive Glendale California

Dear Mary and all of my family:

Although I haven't heard from you in over a month I am still given this opportunity to write again.

I want you to call all of the girls and tell them to write me; Mary, use the address given above. If Phyllis can release pictures of my sons Michael and Timothy I would love to have them, one of all of you would be pleasant.

We have been given an opportunity to read quite a bit by that I mean outside of class reading there helps to pass the time pleasantly and aid in the instruc-tions we are given so by that you can see it isn't unpleasant here. Our instructors are quite patient in there manner of instruction and have to be some do not respond to study as well as we did when younger but as our own dear departed Father use to be infinitely patient while trying to teach a lesson to one of us children, so do our instructors and day when I return I will tell you all about it.

Now for some personal things will you drop a line to (illegible) for me as the last time I saw him he was quite sick Eddie knows him well so if you haven't his address ask Eddie

3 September 1951

To: Mrs. L.W. Anhalt

129 Carr Dr

Glendale, 5, California U.S.A.

From: (WO) Felix J. McCool, USMC 049274

Dear Mary,

I again am given an opportunity to write to you and now I can say I have received three letters from you and dated May 9, 1951 and June 9, 51, and July 15, 1951 you must know how happy they made me.

Give all of my family my warmest love and tell them I look forward to the day we will be reunited. Possibly soon?

I hear quite a bit of negotiations going on for a peaceful settlement of this conflict for which we are all hopeful.

I would dearly enjoy having pictures of my sons Mike and Tim and I hope that you are successful in receiving them from Phyllis. Perhaps if not through that avenue, Pat might be able to get some and then you could send them on — I still have ones taken

Christmas before last but they have been put to heavy use- They and my Rosary.

Happy you were able to say hello to Dr. Berry for me and yes I do know that I have good friends- and especially a special family of lovely sisters it is a nice thing to look forward to seeing them all again. Also, Louis and his "old crow" it should be mellow now. I know I am! Jack and Donna are fortunate in having a son, congratulate them for me- presents forthcoming/ later. Glad that Jack will get to see Dorothy I hope he passes my regards to her. Give May Lou and Phil my love and kiss the new baby for me, a nice name James Vincent isn't it! Did Pat come out also Antoinette and Gordon (?). I'll bet you had a fine holiday and didn't worry too much about the "bird lover." If you see Eddie O'Brian on the streets say hello to him for me — I was very close to him at one time but unfortunately took the wrong road. Tell Nadine hello also Betty Pargl thank them for their interest- I enjoyed Nadine's and Val's company so much while I was in O/ City perhaps again?

If you do see Eddie O'Brien tell him to tell Mr. Stone that I am O.K. and didn't lose a pound. Did you enjoy the 4th of July with Billy and Clara, I'm sure you did perhaps we should plan for the next all together. I'm happy your recovered from your operation and have no more occurrence-there is so much to say to you and my family I love all of you — and I do miss the little family I had started, especially tell Louis I'll try to get some Manila Cigars when I come home so that we may resume our splendid male after dinner conversations. Give (illegible) and Ernestine my love- and I'm happy Paul Anhalt is (illegible). Like to see Midge and Paul for a (illegible).

My love to all,

Felix J

Address: (WO) Felix J McCool

USMC 049274

Prisoner of War Camp

Democratic People's Republic of Korea

c/o Committee of Chinese Congress of the Defenders of World Peace

Peking, China

24 December 1951 Christmas Eve

To: Mrs. L.W. Anhalt

129 Carr Drive

Glendale (S) California

From: Felix J. McCool WO U.S. Marine Corps 049274

Prisoner of War

C/O Chinese Peoples Committee for World Peace

Peking, China

Dear Mary and all,

I once again am given an opportunity to write on this Christmas Eve. I have written before, but lately have not heard from you. I wrote to my sons Michael and Timothy last time, I do hope they receive the letter.

It's a sentimental time of year so I wax sentimental — I'll be there the next Xmas for sure, I hope!

Writing has never been my specialty (penmanship) being poor. But my thoughts are there as usual with all the best for now. I hope the boys will be home for Christmas. Suppose that Mary Lou and you have been preparing for her tribe give them all my love. Tell Cidy, Aileen, Pat and Antoinette hello and to write if they are able at this time and a world of love to them. We are having a "white Xmas".

Best to all give my love to Mike and Tim someday I'll be able to give them a good Christmas — I hope.

Love Felix

[Editor's note-this is a hand written note from the early 1950s on thin parchment paper with very small script to increase the contents. Some of the hand-writing is not ledge able. I've tried to do my best to transcribe accurately There are some hand written notes in red which we believe were Felix illuminating his hidden messages, after the fact.]

From: W.O. Felix J McCool

049274 USMC

POW Camp #2

C/O Chinese Peoples Committee for World Peace

Peking, China

To: Sister Mrs. L.W. Anhalt

129 Carr Drive

Glendale (S) Cal

18 January 1952

Dear Mary:

Honey, I was very pleased today, quite a few of the P.O.W.s received mail and I was included. I received your 30 December 52 (Editor's note-dates don't match) letter and it was newsy. I received your Christmas card a few days before, it too made me feel great.

141

All the very nice things you say and mean to me aid my morale 100% believe me. I understand why I have received no letters from the rest and it's OK. Just keep giving my love to all of them and my hopes we'll see each other soon. Louis attitude toward me is appreciated and reciprocated also he's always been tops in my estimation, would have to be seeing the girl he has for a wife! All of you see "fine as silk" and believe me have carried me through many hardships in that knowledge.

Now to the meat of the letter that picture of Mike and Tim is wonderful I have looked at it laughed and cried in the same breath. They are growing aren't they? Thank Patricia profusely for getting (?) the picture for me, never could understand why I haven't received one before but I guess it takes all kind of people to make a world doesn't it? I was very happy to hear that Aunt Mary is well tell her I'll be seeing her soon. She reminds me so much of our dear little Momma that I'll have to give her one big (?-illegible)

The BAWL that Phil proposed sounds good, did I spell it right or is it with and (R) give the "tribe" my best and new babies? Glad for E.L. and Betty give my love to them the time before Baptism I do remember! Would love to see all the Anhalts and am happy for Paul that he is OK.

Had my picture taken the other day with all the Marines and Navy Officers by Frank Noel no doubt you have seen it by now don't we look massive it's the heavy padded clothes that does it! (Red note to that sentence-"no meat")

Anxious to see and hear the Record player. Does Carl like his new job keeps him "hopping" (red note in margin-"USAF") I'll bet Peggy is a "doll" you do have some beautiful daughters but don't you tell them-huh?

I have a rosary which has been broken and patched —re broken and patched-but it has a blessing on it that was made by a saint (underlined in red with "Fr. Kapuan" in the margin. Referring to the Catholic Priest Father Kapaun) who is always with all of us believe me!

Is Aileen's eye all right I think of it often and hope well for her.

For all that I have not said and missed ("missed" is underlined in red with "could not" written in red in the margin) please know each and every one of you that we'll make it up. Keep the back screen open I like to come home that way so that I know my way to the Palm tree in the yard. Brother those days look good to me. Did Phyllis re-marry? You haven't said.

Love, Felix

Post Script

I've shown the picture of the boys to everyone and they comment as handsome, (illegible), and strong. Some Scrappen's Ding Bell said.

I've been studying Spanish in the evenings under the tutorship of Hector Cordero, AUS, (address deleted for privacy) San Juan Puerto Rico.

"Ding" Bell Lt Richard Bell USMC aviation, E Church Santa Maria California, myself Captain Jack Perry USMC aviation of Laguna Beach California, Lt Larry Taft USMC (aviation) and some others we have all learned quite a bit under Hector's guide he's a great American. Well dear ones, All my love, Felix

[Editor's note-this is a hand written note from the early 1950s on thin parchment paper with very small script to increase the contents. Some of the hand-writing is not ledge able. I've tried to do my best to transcribe accurately There are some hand written notes in red which we believe were Felix illuminating his hidden messages, after the fact.]

WO F.J. McCool USMC 049274 POW CAMP 2 c/o Chinese People's Committee for World Peace Peking China

TO: Sister Mrs. L.W. Anhalt 129 Carr Drive Glendale (S) California

21 Jan 1952

Dear Mary;

We are being given the opportunity to write; almost at will-so I'm taking full advantage of it. Firstly the letter you wrote on 30 December 52 was registered to me and I signed for it this is an insurance of getting the letters and works pretty well! I'm going to take time out to re-request certain things which you haven't answered me on or perhaps the letter was misplaced that contained an answer.

Please answer these things if you are able to carry them out! First let the Bank in Oceanside know that I'm still OK and wish to maintain my status quo. I also told you (illegible) to tell Phil Jones that I wanted the Will and Testament to remain the same plus my dependents care no changes!

Will you ask Louis to enquire the cost of a new Plymouth Sedan or Dodge with accessories I intend buy a new car when I come home and want to get the best buy that I can. See if Peggy Jean would like to pick up some extra change by attaching all of my old scrap items in my scrape book plus any news during the time I have left up to now. Imperatives (illegible sentence).

How is Jack now is he with Carl or Dorothy and how is his wife and new baby. [editor's note-red notes indicating Dorothy is US Army and Carl is a Captain Childers USAF]

Is Mary Lou still playing the piano(?) the Xavier Cugat records "Pendan" in Spanish I understand has a nice piano score also "negra and yours".

Sometime read in the bible Matthew VI I find it one of the most enjoyable of the testaments.

Well my dear I have to attend a class now so I will close I'm thinking of you constantly

All of you

My love Felix

Felix J McCool

PS-Hector Cordero says that "Martha" in Spanish is a beautiful song for your collection.

28 February 1951 (Editor's note-Probably 1952)

To: Mrs. L.W. Anhalt (sister)

129 Carr Drive

Glendale (S) California

From: (WO) F.J. McCool USMC

049274 P.O.W. Camp number 2

C/O Chinese Peoples Committee for World Peace

Peking, China

Dear Mary:

I received your letter of 18 January 52 today — It is a wonderful letter! The little snap shot of Mike and Tim included gave me great joy- I live a little world of my own about them with my 4 pictures of them sometimes they eat with me and often at nights I take them out for a good night talk, life deals some unfortunate circumstances at times but it's a good old world.

It's strange that Nadine sent the picture to you (why?) and so far I have not received her letter or letters perhaps soon. I hope I'm there in spirit at times when you and Louis are talking in the warmth of your room. I know I project myself to you two often we have a wonderful closeness I wouldn't trade for a million dollars. My family are all fine. I'm proud of Tom tell him so for me! Heard about the rain there — remember New Years' 23 (?) you and Louis went to the (G) I was going to say the Glendale but it was the theater on (I think) Glendale Blvd close to your home now- well the gist of the story is that you were nearly flooded out and the "wash" was overflowed "ridin around in the rain" Sentimental one!

I'll bet Mike and Aileen Ann are fine looking children they should be look at their parents. Do Joe and Aileen still live at the same place? Yes, I surely did want to hear of Louis and I'm glad the old alarm still goes off. Is it still set 15 minutes early I used to like the comfort of that extra 15 minutes and if you don't laugh now I don't know Mary and Louis. I've many things to tell you my dear I've grown much mentally since being a P.O.W. believe that! Sort of like the way you told me of the "pipe and tobacco" as Antoinette would say "I'm honored!"

The word of Jack and Donna is good and I like the "for keeps" way it sounds my best to them. Tell Carl to move over and I want the 2 top drawers "dubbies?" I'm holding the Stations of the Cross on my worn out prayer book this Sunday you sent the pamphlet to me "Way of the Cross for Servicemen" —my Rosary was blessed by a Saint and it can be used for Stations with all (illegible). I surely do know how Paul drives on Saturday night had a few of those wild rides up (illegible) sign boards with him unfortunate he doesn't go easy isn't it? He surely must hate life to hit the old battle like he does its no cure. I know and only intensify pain.

I have met a particularly good American doctor here who is thinking of going into private practice out of the service we have had many talks, his wife is now in Long Beach, Mrs. Clarence L. Anderson (street address) — his name is Captain Clarence L. Anderson, A.S.N. USA perhaps you could call her sometime. Andy has had many "pow wows" with me and I've told him about you Louis, Jimmy practically all of the family, incidentally he has one hellova good Basso voice. We always have a few songs before going to sleep at nights — then my Rosary.

Incidentally I thought Ernestine a charming person, the old "Green Eye" is a very poor medicine I know because I suffered it1 with Phyllis.

Tell all the girls hello for me. My love to you and Louis

Love Felix

P.S. Do you ever hear from Dr and Mrs. Berry if so send my regards to them.

[Editor's note-this is a hand written note from the early 1950s on thin parchment paper with very small script to increase the contents. Some of the hand-writing is not ledge able. I've tried to do my best to transcribe accurately There are some hand written notes in red which we believe were Felix illuminating his hidden messages, after the fact.]

26 March 1952

From: (WO) Felix J. McCool 049274 #2 C/O Chinese Peoples Committee for World Peace Peking China

To: (sister) Mrs. L.W. Anhalt 129 Carr Drive Glendale (s) California

Dear Mary,

Received your dear letter a few days past and do hope you receive all of my letters as I know they re-assure you that I am being well cared for and that is important to both of us.

Frank Noel whom I was captured with the 29th of November 1950 was in this camp last week and took pictures of us in small groups I hope you see them in the papers at home he took one of the group that was captured together (another man took the picture as Frank was in the picture with us) that one particularly I would like for you to see and if O'Brien still visits be sure he see it too as he is such a good friend.

Your cheery words never fail to make me happy and pick up my morale-I have never given up hope that someday I will return home.

We have been conducting "Stations of the Cross" during the Lenten season using "My way of the Cross" for service men and Easter is fast approaching it should be rather enjoyable we P.O.W's as the Chinese have promised us some eggs as a special chow for that day and possible some wine you can see what a joyous and festive an occasion it will be!

Heard from Bette Penny a very nice letter and I answered it!

I have been in a Bridge tournament in the room (24) men and made the "top of the Ladder" once, am now in the middle but have improved my game considerable-Antoinette and Patricia will probably be interested in that.

We have a freak snow three days ago snowed all day and night, looked like Christmas time again, it is mostly melted now excepting that sunless side of the mountains.

Glad Jackie is closer to home seems as if that is the same distance as I am from Japan now, about; what a big difference a few miles make. I'll bet he's very proud of the new baby isn't he?

Many of the men have canned chess sets and some tables were furnished for us to play on so we have much of that type of recreation when we aren't busy.

At the present time we are on a big cleanup of the camp inside and out getting rid of "Old Man Winter."

I am completely well now except my eyes and you know how bad they were anyway and have a very good appetite which is undoubtedly fortunate as Momma used to say: "Good appetite is the key to good health."

All of my friends who are familiar with my family due to my talking so much of you send their regards.

Give my love to all

Your devoted brother

Felix

27 March 1952

P.S. - I had a very good dream last night seemed that I was home again had visited everyone and then went to my sons I found a changed Phyllis soft and sweet who really loved me and I her naturally. Mike and Tim were happy about this. We had a small cottage, etc. I awoke about 3AM lay awake for some time in the darkness trying to analyze my true feelings about the

whole thing and I realized that the dream was the
real answer I have been looking for —who knows (?)
Life is frustrating at times isn't it?

Well any way it was nice

All my love Mary

Brother Felix

[Editor's note-this is a hand written note from the early 1950s on thin parchment paper with very small script to increase the contents. Some of the hand-writing is not ledge able. I've tried to do my best to transcribe accurately There are some hand written notes in red which we believe were Felix illuminating his hidden messages, after the fact.]

From: F.J. McCool   049274 C/O Chinese Peoples Committee-free for world Peace, Peking China

To: Sister Mrs. L.W. Anhalt 129 Carr Drive Glendale (S) California, USA

8 July 1952

Dear Mary: Haven't heard from you since your 18 April 52 letter, but I have stationary so I'll write any-way letting you know I'm still OK. Have completely recovered from Amebic Dysentery as far as I know. Received good treatment in getting rid of. The rainy season has started and when it rains it pours. We go to bed about 9 or 10 in the evening and it stays light till about nine so we aren't bothered by darkness (red note-"no lights") too much! How is Louis' back and leg now I hope ok I've had pulled muscles myself and know they are painful. How's everyone, tell them all to write personally in your letter to me just a note and also try for some more pictures of Mike and Tim-I'll pay $200.00 two hundred dollars apiece to Phyllis for two (2) pictures, that appeal might touch her tender heart, that quote you can use any way you see fit! Have written something for you and Louis in

154

retrospect and thanks for all the past years tell me if it is to your liking. (Editor's note-this is an embedded poem) "Yesterday" to Mary & Louis (FJMC July 52) "The years have passed and blended into times immutable law; A misty veil from here to there, thoughts go back to retrospect! A baby is born, the first: 'It looks like mom, no like dad well perhaps like both'-another and now one of four and thru those times-the banging of the kitchen door-warm spring-cold winter-quiet afternoons, the incessant bass and treble of the scales-hard struggles-how a youth and now a miss; coming out introductions "this is so and so' aside 'He's so nice mom and I think he loves me' Another voice youthful, masculine-deep yet fine with springs eternal surge says, 'yes dad, the prof tells us what you have always said in a different way; but seriously dad isn't she a lovely thing'-'not the engine but the girl.' A baby is born-a new life and we sit back and say "why it was only yesterday!" FM: this is to your little family Mary hope I put my thoughts clearly enough. Until I hear from you again-by the way one of the Filipinos is teaching me the phil language tag-along and another friend is giving me speaking German should keep my mind well occupied-please write often.

Love Felix J McCool

[Editor's note-this is a hand written note from the early 1950s on thin parchment paper with very small script to increase the contents. Some of the handwriting is not ledge able. I've tried to do my best to transcribe accurately There are some hand written notes in red which we believe were Felix illuminating his hidden messages, after the fact.]

From (WO) Felix McCool

To Sister Mrs. L.W. Anhalt

19 August 1952

Dear Mary: Just received your letter of June 19, 1952 and was certainly happy to again hear from you. Yes March is a long way off and I hope by now you have received my numerous letters to you since then with all of my messages of good cheer. I'm very anxious to buy that "Dodge" car that Louis recommended and I'll go to his shop to see it and visit. Yes the picture did make me look fine didn't it (?) I'm happy that it impressed you as much! Haven't see Frank Noel in some time but when I did he looked good and could still deal a good hand in bridge, rather miss his fine company, but have many Officers of all the services to keep me company. Would have to act as 'teacher" as you suggested would probably teach many interesting things with the knowledge I have gained while here. I do remember Mrs. Slaussen (chemist) of (?) and feel honored that he and Mr. Bell are interested, give he and all of the old last Frank Meham especially still owe him @20.00 (joke). I think! Do remember Tony Beck of

Subic and will appreciate hearing from him. Bet Peggy is happy visiting Jack and Donna in Monterey; Dorthy used to take me to a big estate there is that where Jack lives (?) What College is Peggy going to perhaps "God willing" I may be able to see her off! Mary Lou is beautiful enough to vie with any of Petty or Yarga models so that should be "no strain." Hope Louis and you enjoyed the vacation tell him I'll expect a "day off" for us to go hunting together in my new Dodge. Is it a deal? Carl enjoy his new work-he seems to be having a good time of it and "pant-pant" what happened to that lovely person whom he used squire-Carolyn? Give my beautiful sisters Cecilia, Antoinette, Patricia, Aileen and Mary my best love I want a date individually and collectively when I come home! Hope Betty A and Midge are doing fine and I'm glad Paul A is well and traveling. Tell Betty A and Midge I'd like to go to the Palladium with them some evening, but watch out as I'm not such a good Uncle at least I find it wearing. Did the Century Plant reach its peak yet and go into the dying shudder? Use all of your pages for writing please. Honey, I get so D—lonesome it get the "so and so" but can't help things now-but someday will be home I know! Tell Uncle Frank, Billy and Beatrice also cousins Inez and Patsy I still love them and all that they mean would like to drop in on them when I come back. Yes also Aunt Mary she's a sweet old thing. Perhaps I can teach their children when I come back. I'll try anyway. You know that banner that Dad used to put up on my Birthday? I've grown to love it very much guess because I can't be there on my birthday to see it but you remember that! By the way if you see Dr Berry tell him hello from me especially. Honey I've rambled on but first is first and I come first with you. How's your radio now still coming in well if so let me know.

My love-Felix J

3 September 1951 (editor's note-probably 1952)

To: Mrs. L.W. Anhalt

129 Carr Dr

Glendale, (5, California U.S.A.

From: (WO) Felix J. McCool, USMC 049274

Dear Mary,

I again am given an opportunity to write to you and now I can say I have received three letters from you and dated May 9, 1951 and June 9, 51, and July 15, 1951 you must know how happy they made me.

Give all of my family my warmest love and tell them I look forward to the day we will be reunited. Possibly soon?

I hear quite a bit of negotiations going on for a peaceful settlement of this conflict for which we are all hopeful.

I would dearly enjoy having pictures of my sons Mike and Tim and I hope that you are successful in receiving them from Phyllis. Perhaps if not through that avenue, Pat might be able to get some and then you could send them on — I still have ones taken Christmas before last but they have been put to heavy use- They and my Rosary.

Happy you were able to say hello to Dr. Berry for me and yes I do know that I have good friends- and especially a special family of lovely sisters it is a nice thing to look forward to seeing them all again. Also, Louis and his "old crow" it should be mellow now. I know I am! Jack and Donna are fortunate in having a son, congratulate them for me- presents forthcoming/ later. Glad that Jack will get to see Dorothy I hope he passes my regards to her. Give May Lou and Phil my love and kiss the new baby for me, a nice name James Vincent isn't it! Did Pat come out also Antoinette and Gordon(?). I'll bet you had a fine holiday and didn't worry too much about the "bird lover." If you see Eddie O'Brian on the streets say hello to him for me — I was very close to him at one time but unfortunately took the wrong road. Tell Nadine hello also Betty Pargl thank them for their interest- I enjoyed Nadine's and Val's company so much while I was in O/ City perhaps again?

If you do see Eddie O'Brien tell him to tell Mr. Stone that I am O.K. and didn't lose a pound. Did you enjoy the 4th of July with Billy and Clara, I'm sure you did perhaps we should plan for the next all together. I'm happy your recovered from your operation and have no more occurrence-there is so much to say to you and my family I love all of you — and I do miss the little family I had started, especially tell Louis I'll try to get some Manila Cigars when I come home so that we may resume our splendid male after dinner conversations. Give (illegible) and Ernestine my love- and I'm happy Paul Anhalt is (illegible). Like to see Midge and Paul for a (illegible).

My love to all,

Felix J

Address: (WO) Felix J McCool

USMC 049274

Prisoner of War Camp

Democratic People's Republic of Korea

c/o Committee of Chinese Congress of the Defenders of World Peace

Peking, China

21 September 1952

To: Mrs. L.W. Anhalt

129 Carr Drive

Glendale (S) California

From: WO Felix J. McCool USMC

POW Camp

Democratic People's Republic of Korea

C/O Chinese Peoples Committee for World Peace Peking
China

Dear Mary:

Haven't heard from you since last week the letter
which I answered was your 23 Jun 52 letter which
I received 7 Sept 52 and answered 10 Sept 52 but I
thought I'd write anyway as I have an envelope to
send. It's fast approaching winter again and it seems
to be expected that it will be a cold one as we have
already felt "old man frost" the weather this Sunday
morning is particularly nice as the sun is shining
as it briefly does in these thick mountains. Give my
love to all Mary especially and Antoinette, Cidy,
Aileen, Patricia and their own also Aunt Mary. I'll
not mention more but any that you think of let them
know I'm OK and anxiously waiting for my return home.
One of the officers here (allied) has been giving me

a course on Inorganic Chemistry so I've just about completed my college education with the exception of Math which I shall start in October all up to Calculus the Officers of the (MC) Air Force, & Army plus the British Officers have been splendid in helping me to further my education, a fortunate thing in these slow times.

I hope you receive my little (illegible) to you regarding you family Louis etc. and one I sent to Antoinette and Aileen & Cidy to please write and send pictures, so for I have received numerous letters from you -2 from Patricia, 1 from Antoinette and a could from outside the family. My dear for all that I have space to say I'll say there. I have not changed only more settled and am the same person whom you have known so whenever the Refrigerator door opens remember me and Pete. We are both anxious to be eating together again in your home — give Pete my special regards and a wee! Bit of my jealousy as I am! HOW MUCH WILL IT COST ME TO BUY A NEW (BRAND NEW) DODGE? (2) Plymouth (3) Pontiac (4) Chevrolet (5) Ford — two door type with appliances radio, heater etc listed extra please. Answer

All my love,

Brother Felix

21 November 1952

Dearest Sister Patricia,

I was the recipient of two letters quite recently, one from you and one from younger sister Mary Anhalt. Due to the fact that your letter had news of much interest and directly connected with me I will consolidate the two answers into one for obvious reasons. To say I was surprised that Phyllis had re-married would be a fabrication of the truth; however, I had hoped though these long months that it would be true and that we could someday patch up our troubles and give our sons their heritage a father and mother endowed by their maker not a Court of Law. I had detected the weakness in Phyllis' faith many months before our divorce so that this too does not come as a surprise. I do not condone a weakness of this nature, and although you say the new man is giving them a home and normalcy, I say it's impossible as "Blood is thicker than water." The brief span of years that Phil was to have worked and formed the children out was nothing to the eternity that I have known in their loss, and will know-however I accept and wait. I do not believe that anyone can escape their fate who deliberately pull the shade of darkness for another and expect to remain in the light undimmed (illegible) by darkness, as I have said I wait! I had written to Dorothy just about a week before receiving your letter asking for pictures and news of Phyllis and my sons. It will not be necessary for her to answer now. I have complete control of my faculties and good friends here so the patient will be a recovery. Do not worry either you or Mary or any other of my sisters. I jot down thoughts occasionally and find it as much a relief of expression as I need. I quote in part, "I find in the part truth myself search the one important note was in myself a thing I'd failed to do through life — to find the truth within myself and once found I knew the key to the entire panorama was in my grasp before I find the truth in others, I must first find it within myself." If I sound rather philosophical it is the truth I am today. To quote something from Goethe, "Nature has left us tears, the coy of pain when man can hear no more and most of all to me, she has left me melody and speech. To make the full depth of my anguish known; and when man in his agony is dumb. I have God's gift to utter what I suffer."

I have God's gift to utter what I suffer! I like that picked it up out of a book. I read here in our library. To you my dear sisters I shall quote something (a poet!) or a Sonnet from Shakespeare, "(Illegible)."

I also found this in a book here so the patient can recover. Many say your eyes. Tell Antoinette to play "Sertless in Spring" my graying hairs would love to feel the sound again. My dears you kept something from me for a long time not knowing my temperament now do you know? I'll be back some happy day and we'll visit though all the Country. Have thought if possible to visit the farm remember so well the din-ner from (illegible) so very capable hands the last time while there. However it is — I intend to visit each and every one of you. Thank you Patsy and Bill for giving my name to one of your sons. I hope he always finds the meaning of his life. Come on Aileen and Cidy write to me through Mary if there is no other avenue than I will have received a letter from all of my whole sisters. Give my love also to your families also our half sisters and brothers. Christmas is approaching and we are all anticipating. Place a wreath at Momma's grave as her wishes are fast becoming fulfilled is it not so? Things bigger than we are fast becoming a reality she always wanted us to overcome our natures. I shall try on the two halves of this paper to put down on paper a thought or thoughts I've had this was written after receiving your letter Patricia. My love to each and every one of you.

21 Nov 52-p.s.-the pictures of Michael and Timothy the two I speak of is a wonderful picture and timely. Some have given me the joy of hearing "they look so much like you."

Two lives in one November 11, 1952 — Felix J. McCool

"Twice I was born and twice I've died, someone gives and some takes some one has to be the striking bag to keep the world rotating round its infamy and pleasure — again it strikes and this time low and hard. There was an island night of terror — a crescendo of sounds, meteorite like objects hurting through the sky falling —falling! One blow before had limed my soul, two dear ones gone —this was my time! And again it struck with strong staccato in my soul — the drums echoed in my brain and the ball of fire kept increasing and there was I death all around — I still alone

standing and again another blow, the drums reechoed
in my brain, harder, my captors, applied methods old
yet new and all in all, a life gone — a good life
gone a bad begun # a different man came through the
crucible of fire. The elements melt into a new compound -. A new man — he doesn't know who he is now,
no! the prior life still floating in the outer orbit
of consciousness —tormented with the new — sorrow-
ful combination of man in man, brain within a brain
— wonder of man, who does not know what makes him
sad —thoughts poignant reminiscing, pulse beats — go
back to the old, old drums — sound. Pin point lights
in this reaction —the whole world falling but why?
Forthcoming loss foreshadowed culmination and to —
wait, wait! The blow came hitting hard and low three
dear ones gone-the drums echoed again and a world
fell night covered all! Three dear ones gone a cyni-
cal twist of fate or was it this: the man who lived
had died and gone; a man of clay, soulless wraith
like. Left instead, knowing all knows that the man
who died was or in his wake this time the second used
new ways of making known that the man who died was
dead in spirit — a new man unknown to himself had
been born by using he burden of time terrible pressing time and reiteration — the final blow fell: total
severance from reality and hopes the drums of death
resound, must he rebear himself, NO! a new man must
emerge but does he know that the man who was no longer
comes and does he think that he'll come back again-it
cannot be, the new man comes, the old one is gone.
The man stands alone, the island night with pinpoint
lights and hated sound envelope his brain —the world
opens, blood flows then a radiance is throw upon him,

he knows that he's alive in two, then a cry, an an-
guished cry-it is joy, a gasp for air, ok, is it not
a cry of pain, it is a cry for life, new and clean,
behold the man, he has been born!" FJM

(Editor's note-there are a few more sentences that
appear to wrap up the letter but it is too faded to
read but only a few words)

[Editor's note-this is a hand written note from the early 1950s on thin parchment paper with very small script to increase the contents. Some of the hand-writing is not ledge able. I've tried to do my best to transcribe accurately There are some hand written notes in red which we believe were Felix illuminating his hidden messages, after the fact.]

13 February 1953 Friday

Dear Mary,

Have not heard from you in a very long time but still hoping. We had a mail call a few days back but I was not lucky! Also have never received the letters you said that Nadine Lechter (?) and Mary Lou and Phil had written perhaps soon?

We had a very cold winter, sometimes I witnessed -35 below © but the "back is broken" on "old man winter" as it is becoming warmer.

We took a couple of trips into the mountains for wood; it was very enjoyable as you know I enjoy hik-ing (written in red-"I don't")

Our camp is quite clean now, we have a daily river trip to the little branch river for water and keep hot water for washing etc daily. It also keeps down the insect pest which seems to thrive on a dirty body, as I say we are quite clean.

I still pursue the Spanish I have been taught and have quite worn out my source material a Spanish speaking P.O.W. I need new material if I intend to progress in that language. At present a fellow P.O.W. is teaching me Mathematics, we have stocked our minds with all the available material that from other P.O.W.s it is really amazing the amount of material that is retained in the human brain and is forthcoming upon stimulation; applied stimulation can practically drain the brain of knowledge held. I find that the Algebra and other facts of higher Mathematics come to me quite a bit easier-whether it is my application or the complete lack of outside stimulus I do not know but it does come easier now. Intend going into trig, surveying, map reading, analytics, plane solid and spherical geometry and calculus this program I have mapped out will last me until late spring. I hope you received my list of completed studies and my request for the Junior College to recognize them?

I want you to give every one of my sisters and their husbands and families my half brothers and sister and my Aunt Mary and Kathy my love-Hello dear Patrica, Cecila, Mary, Antoinette and Aileen my cousins Charles, Cole, Paul, Inez, Uncle Frank and my little niece Beatrice-I love them all and will always remain myself in their gratitude and to give all of them my regards. (Editor's note-written in red in the margin is F.B.I. and the names Frank, Beatrice and Inez are underlines. Felix was sending a message to the FBI and family about his loyalty and love of country despite brainwashing alluded to in a previous paragraph). Naturally my two sons Michael and Timothy even though I have lost them in their extreme youth I hope to spend many pleasant times with them when they are able to choose for themselves. I can wait. My birthday will be in June so be sure to put my banner out on that day as my family and I are proud of my birthday banner. Honey, this probably sounds like sentimental dither-but it's my heart speaking. No matter what happens or how long it takes I'll always remain the same toward you, all of you. My loved ones-write in hopes that the gods of fortune may deliver the mail to me.

Your loving brother

Felix J. McCool

P.S.-If you see Reg and Ruth give my best regards

16 March 1953

Dear Mary,

Your loving letters were received yesterday (Dec 5th & 15(52) was the home date on them. There are a most welcome part of spring and to see you Louis and those two lovely young women and know that I am so closely related makes me doubly proud and not to say the least envied. I share all my mail with my friends and the praise of all of you is never ending. I hope now that you will send pictures of all my family Aileen, Tony, Cidy, Pat. Your (illegible) looked enjoyable and the beach pic of M.L. caused a stir tell Phil I had to warn a few that M.L. was taken and by a Marine too. I did receive the pics of Mike & Tim and Rosita Patsy Jerry and their family the boys surpass my wildest dreams of young men-I am proud of them. No I don't remember what I said about the dance except I'd love to with all perhaps I had lapsed into a crude expression at times. I do. So much for denial I guess. I'm glad the banner is still ready for my birthday and no matter how long I take coming —cherish it and (illegible) the family to cherish it a proud thing in our family never been dishonored nor will it be. I hope Aileen & Joe are doing OK hope (illegible) thought now that I'm denied of my own boys and wife that I could be an Uncle John to the kids would like to take them on a trip with me Is it possible-Would Peggy like? New York City. Make to keep my accounts and a (illegible few words). I'm open to suggestions I want to travel alone again. Perhaps Havana after Miami? I was thinking some time later of doing duty in Honolulu if possible and all of you could visit one at time well dreams are made of the same material as reality. Happy you received the little poem-my meager talents are used by some of the boys here to express an idea- I like doing it. Did Pat and Tony receive theirs too? Please have Cidy & Aileen write with pictures to include with yours or however you want.

Sorry you are having trouble with your reception on the radio is it local interference and I do hope it doesn't bother your television too? Mary I can't say how anxious I was when finish hearing of your ill health please please take care I need you too! You work sounds exciting the knitting some beautiful work is done how about some of the MODEL's pictures both Louis and Mary Lou & the gremlins never seen #4 yet.

If one could be seduced by music while here we would be yesterday Sunday a medley of all type came in over the Loud speaker very beautiful music Chopin's Nocture in "D" Flat Major Opus 27 #2 Andante Contable Tchaskski opus #11 Remsky Korokoffe Schezade also a beautiful Piano Concerto by Kornsakoff in "L" Minor also Chopins treatises Opus #10 and two (illegible) called "So indefinitely Lonely" and "Two Tickle Eyes" by Gezza Dusik. The afternoon was spent well (illegible) in good mentally.

My love to you-Felix J

20 March 1953

Dear Mary,

I'm answering your third letter of the new stationary dated 15 December 1952. I'll ask my questions first. How are you now I hope completely recovered from the heart attack and please take care! I answered the other two letters also but in case you didn't receive them —I am sorry that Aunt Mary has pass away please extend my condolences to Katharine. I also had wished to visit Aunt Mary because she was so much like Momma. How are Patricia, Cecilia, Antoinette, and Aileen now? Give them my love and ask them drop a line and some picture late ones, properly identified.

Have you seen Al Leman and Frances lately they are very close friends of mine Mary and tried to help when I was in trouble before when the family dispute came up. Tell Al I've gone over my 6 years and may I expect any changes in status when I come home? I'm vitally interested. Did Phil get to take care of my claim was it for damages etc., or being my money or both. I would like to know. Did you have a fine Xmas give me the details I'm so much interested in all of our intimate family news. The pictures of Mary Louis, Peggy yourself and Louis were very good, Peggy has changes so. M.L. as lovely as ever. You and Louis just like you have always been to me! I'm happy you have received the "M&L" poem. I've sent many others. I hope you and the family receive them have tried other and seem to be pleasing the eyes and taste of other POWs slightly lazy though and as many distractions. We were given a list of good books lately "Black Beauty" "Grimms Fairy tales" Andersons Fairy Tales, "Treasure Island" and a host of equally good books to read. We also have been finally given bunks to sleep in off the floor and it is very good. 33 inches wide and 6 ft long all our (illegible) to use for sleeping. I've certainly improved my disposition since receiving this treatment. Easter is fast approaching and Lent has been the same we few Catholics say Rosary and "The Way of the Cross" from the book you sent to me in 1950. Tell Mike Galvin about that I know he studies things of that nature-Antoinette told me in a letter I received a long time ago that the ladies on Lake Street were thinking of me. I appreciate that too! (Editor's note-red note and line pointing to "Ladies" written "nuns city")

Sorry if Aileen &Joe have sold the store. I hope it was not a loss to them. I still would like to give Mike Hiss a trip w/me like Uncle John did when I was Mike's age 14 years old. I will take advantage of Louis' offer if it will not (illegible) him in any way regarding the purchase of a Dodge or DeSoto the price seems terrific. Is a standard or Special the least or the best type with all accessories? Your radio &

television must be a source of pleasure to you. It should extend to all my kind. Perhaps a little technical advice on upkeep and repairs would be instrumental in your better reception. There are technicians there in whom I place the utmost of trust in Repair Maintenance and better reception. I've heard of the song, "Wish you were here" it's nice I understand one of the boys here wrote one call "Wish I were there" we have enjoyed it mucho!

I hope Francis Swift is not suffering her attacks. She needs a good dose of Love from Momma, Daddy and the Half Sister &Brother plus more recognition from all of us a sensitive nature like hers and the hears she was deprived of genuine love in opposition to smoothing spasmodic affection have been the contributing factor in her condition today in my opinion. A little food and affection and less "I now Will" does wonders in human nature. I know! Hope Jack & Donna have their home and perhaps the new grandnephew or niece is on its way for sure. Congrats to both of them. Tell Tom "stout fello" I'm glad he had continued school — A young man need that very much in this day and age-I'm going for a BA when I come home for sure and I'm not exactly young. HA!

Honey my love to all of you

Your Brother Felix J

Felix J McCool

175

[Editor's note-this is a hand written note from the early 1950s on thin parchment paper with very small script to increase the contents. Some of the hand-writing is not ledge able. I've tried to do my best to transcribe accurately There are some hand written notes in red which we believe were Felix illuminating his hidden messages, after the fact.]

Easter Sunday 1953

Dear Patricia,

Received your so very kind letter the first of April. It was your 26 December 52 letter in which you men-tioned hearing from me however you failed to tell me which letter by date, it was that you answered this information would be more than welcome of all times. I'm happy Frances is well again she is a darling girl. Thank Patsy for the pictures she managed of Captiva. I appreciate them much. Also the pictures which you say Phyllis had sent to you for forwarding to me. I shall take this opportunity to say Happy Birthday to my love Michael and Timothy in May and June-please extend that to them. If I were there I would send gifts with all my love-they exceed any of the dreams I've had of them believe me I'm very proud of them. I appreciate the core which has caused them to be so fine. This master play a subterfuge which has been go-ing on for so long has finally reached the ridiculous hasn't it? Are you on friendly terms with Phyllis, medium terms, with Phyllis or outs with Phyllis? By her demand the first (one) and last letter to me in-forming me of her marriage stated she did not see you wrote to you, nor did she intend to, nor to let the boys see any of my relatives-a rather childish & immature attitude which I hope she has overcome. The laws of nature are stronger than the laws of man-Blood will tell —a fact not fiction. Outside of that she's ok I guess- I hold no grudge nor revenge. Have you the courage to answer this in the same vein in which it was written or do we go into the Roundley (?) again? I'm anxious for the trip to Miami to see all of you as I love each of you very much. Thank Patsy and Bill for the baby's name "Felix" they certainly have a family and they all love fine. I enjoyed the slightly perplexed look on Lynn's face when she was looking at her second cousins Mike & Tim. You look fine Pat quite calling yourself big say comfortable, I intend to be also. Is Dick gaining yet hope so. About the car whenever I can buy it most reasonable and convenient is the place for me. I can always fly there and drive back. I certainly do remember old "Woody" we had fine times together in Miami, give him my best and I want to know does he still carry a pen knife in his watch pocket. He Dick, Bill and I will have to go stay some place for a cold one or two? Tell Norma W to invite to me with all the "Hot" news about cars? Himself and family.

Honey I do think our mutual friends the Landers. How's Earl now I hope ok Marion, Ruby still beautiful girls? I dreamed of Billy Blockwell the other night we were together on a long trip funny thing about dreams as I woke up with a very clean and fine feeling about the day-How's her children. They must be quite grown by now-Is she married-How's Murtha (?) they are both very charming people. So sorry Harvey (?) isn't there now. [editor's note-Illegible sentence]. Ever see the McGanns'-hello from me?

If you see or hear from Dorothy or Jerry extend my regards. I'd like a fishing trip with 4 cases of good cold beer to put out the fire with. Give Grey, Pat my temples and mustache. Listening to some music this beautiful day the classics and they always stimulate me. A list of the Notre Dame line up" Village Polka's by Karel Vacek- "A crowd riding in a carriage" by Soloyel Syedor — Violin Concerto Miaskovskky Bethovens' symphonies #%-Flower Gargen in Autum by Moktowhn. Concerto in (D) Major Brahms. This is a violin concerto done my Szigeti-last but not least (Italian Cappiccio by Tchaikovsy. One of my favorites

Love Felix J

ANNEX – 2
KOREA

This annex is a collection of speeches, reports on his capture and time spent in Korea and two letters written by fellow prisoners about Felix's conduct.

"Felix with Ralph Edwards."

"Felix on the Ralph Edwards show with Marion, Lieutenant Commander John Thorton, Major (Dr.) Clarence Anderson, Captain Allan Lloyd, Major Ernest Reed, and Lieutenant Colonel John McLaughlin.">

"Felix with fellow Korean War POWs Captain Allan Lloyd, Lieutenant Commander John Thorton, Major (Dr.) Clarence Anderson, Major Ernest Reed, and Lieutenant Colonel John McLaughlin."

TO WHOM IT MAY CONCERN:

On the morning of 28 November 1950, I was called to
Battalion Headquarters by Major J. Stone, at that
time Executive Officer of First Service Battalion, who
informed me that his regular dispatcher and liaison
officer was ill, and that due to the fact that I had
one quarter of my unit at Hageru-ri, Korea, he was
sending me on a mission to deliver the critique and
company commander's reports of the Inchon Seoul landing, 15 September 1953, to Commanding Officer First
Service Battalion for his OK (yourself). He instruct-
ed me that there were numerous (I believe he had
three) road blocks held by the opposing forces and
that I would incur difficulties and danger in reaching my objective, and gave me the direct question
of whether or not I wanted to go. I accepted gladly
and left at about 0900. My driver was Corporal Leon
Roebuck, USMC, and one other whom I cannot identify
at this time.

We left Hamhung in the Battalion Headquarters jeep
with trailer. The army military police stopped me
at the traffic circle, telling me that no unescort-
ed vehicle was to be allowed through. I then, realizing that the purpose of the mission would be
lost, told the military police that I was going up
the road to the Fifth Regiment (Rear) First Marine
Division. He allowed me to go through, and at about
1200 28 November 1953) I arrived at our First Service
Battalion Dump where I left the mail and picked up
the outgoing mail. I then proceeded to Koto-ri, where
First Regiment, First Marine Division were in biv-
ouac. Heavy traffic had held me up until about 1600

183

the same date. I met the commanding officer of the regiment, who at that time was Colonel Puller. I was allowed to attempt a call to you at the Lumber Mill and also to First Service Battalion Rear at Hamhung. The lines were jammed and I could not get through. The conditions at Koto Ri were, enemy troops close in three directions. Regiment would not allow traffic through that day stating that there were heavy road blocks and the enemy along the road in length between Koto-ri and Hageru-ri. I was forced to remain at First Regiment Headquarters at Koto-ri First Marine Division, 28-29 November 1950.

I left about 1400, 29 November 50, to proceed forward through to the position of First Service Battalion at the Command Post. We were under constant attack from about 100 yards from First Regiment Headquarters. We drove in spurts, stopped and battled when forced, then proceeded. This happened innumerable times. I mixed with a convoy which was en route to Hageru-ri and which was commanded by a British officer. There were some United States Army and elements of Military Police Company Headquarters First Marine Division. Major John McLaughlin, USMC, Frank Noel, Associated Press photographer, Lt Allen Lloyd, USMC, Lt. E. Reid, USMC, Lt. B. Turner, USMC (Tank Commanding Officer were also in the convoy. We were heavily hit and could proceed no further. We set up a last ditch stand, and after fighting all night long, were surrounded completely, depleted of ammunition and with a group of dead and wounded around us (both United Nations Forces and enemy Chinese). I could have run away during the night, but felt that the Marine Corps requires a Marine to stand fast, so I remained. This choice was difficult to make. I was a free agent, but placed myself in Major McLaughlin's hands. We were captured at early dawn. I jumped upon a burning truck and emptied the contents of my pockets. The reports were completely destroyed by fire.

The enemy did not extract any part of the information nor know what my position was at capture. By devious methods they diabolically extracted information regarding strength, type, and size of the First Service Battalion from me. Primarily, I gave the contents of a (50 in 1) Px ration box and mechanical parts of laundry machines.

This report is in my opinion, completely true, and dates are authentic.

Submitted,

F. J. McCool (049274)

Warrant Officer

U. S. Marine Corps

STATEMENT OF COMMISSIONED WARRANT OFFICER FELIX MC COOL USMC

ESSENTIAL ELEMENTS OF INFORMATION OF INTERROGATION OF RETURNING PRISONERS OF WAR

Marches from place of capture to collection point of camp.

Place of capture was at a road block in the mountains close to the Chosen Reservoir between Koto-Ri and Haggeru-Ri, Korea.

I was captured by the Chinese Communists forces about 5 a.m. 30 November 1950. We left about 2 days later, I believe, on the second of December 1950, marching through the mountains for about 4 or 5 days, I believe the march was about 100 miles. We arrived at a place we called the "14 day place", so named by we, prisoners who had been captured at the Koto-Ri-Haggeru-Ri road block. This was a sort of a collecting point.

There were numerous South Korean, wounded, American Army Forces and a few Marines also wounded. Enlisted and officers were put into a room about 10 feet by 10 feet square. There were 15 to 20 men in this one room, no wounded. In the other room, which was slightly larger and contained about 30 men of which numerous were badly wounded. The ones becoming infected were subjected to total lack of sanitation facilities. They crawled from the room to the door to relieve themselves. At this place we were interrogated to a small degree. About 2 days prior to leaving, some of the wounded men were taken away and we never saw them again.

All who could walk left this place. We had stayed there about 14 days, which makes it about the 16th or 17th of December 1950. We left for Kanggye Korea, marching through the mountains. It was bitterly cold, at one place between the "14-day place" and Kanggye, we met a group of South Korean prisoners. This was about 9 o'clock at night, it was snowing.

We were made to stand against the side of a mountain while the Chinese scattered around, we were finally put in a cow shed, which was made of slate about 6" apart, no protection against the elements whatever and no covers of any type. The South Koreans whom we had met, also prisoners, were clad in summer clothes and most of them were seriously frost bitten, either on the feet, hands or face. One particular I noticed was standing next to me and both of his ears were frozen black and nearly dropping off. His nose was black and also his hands. He was standing on feet bound in white cloth and he appeared to be in great agony. No one gave him aid. This was one of the things that I considered an atrocity-in allowing a person to suffer in this manner when there was shelter available. He was one of about, I would say, 200 men.

We separated from them the next morning and marched on to Kanggye, Korea, arriving about the 27th of December 1950. I estimated the entire trip was around 200 or 350 miles. It was very difficult to ascertain the distance because there were times that we were taken off the roads and marched through the mountains, up and over, breaking trail which led to confusion.

When we were on the march, we went North mostly and ended up at Kanggye, Korea which was about 20 miles from the Yalu River. While at Kanggye we were separated and placed into various small huts.

It was impossible to actually ascertain the amount of neglectful death. I remember one place that the officers were finally put into a room about 8 by 10 feet. There were 15 of us in this room and in an adjoining shed; there were numerous American GI clothes, which were covered with blood spots. They appeared to have been taken from the bodies of American GI's who had been wounded and died; they were marched to this place without aid. I'm quite sure that this room we were in had been one of the chambers where they kept the sick men until they died. They were buried on the side of a hill we noticed the ground being burned off at a certain point which was the only indication that might be as to what was going on. I would ascertain that about 40 men had died through neglect of wounds and improper feeding and housing. The names of the men, it was impossible to ascertain as they were from various units of the Army, Marine Corps and South Korean Army.

At this place in Kanggye, the food was 2 very small bowls of Kooleang, which is a rice type of food and an ounce or two of a protein substance twice a day. A small Chinese boy used to come around occasionally with a RED CROSS bandage on his arm and snip off the putrefied flesh of the men who feet had been frozen. It could not be classified as adequate medical treatment.

I would say that at Kanggye, we were guarded by approximately a Company (identifying a company as the regular company in our own army) of Chinese personnel. In the mountains around us were numerous guerrilla forced and/or local police forces. At the onset of capture there were 2 Marine Officers by the name of Lt. Colonel Chidister and Major Eagan, USMC. These two officers had been wounded on the road and were left all night lying under a bridge by the Chinese at which time their feet were badly frozen. They were carried to a hut about 8 miles away where they were supposed to be receiving medical treatment. It is my opinion that these officers were not wounded enough to cause death. Knowing that their deaths are now being presumed, it is justifiable to say that if they died, they died through total neglect by the enemy, the Communist forces.

The men who had been on the road prior to capture who were wounded badly or lightly had been informed by Chinese Communists and also the senior officer in our group, Major McLaughlin, that they would be released immediately and sent back to their own lines.

I saw at least 25 or 30 men who had frozen to death overnight who could have quite easily been either housed by the Communist forces, or taken back to a spot close to the lines and released, or at least allowed to be picked up by our own forces. In my estimation there was a total lack of humanitarian attitude, although the Chinese manifested that they worked under a policy called the "Lenient Policy".

My first talk with any Chinese was a young man by the name of Feng from Peking, China. He told me that the Chinese had no desire to take any of our personal belongings; however I saw looting going on — of prisoners both wounded and well.

The main thing throughout the initial part of the capture was the fact that the communists tried to instill in our minds, that we were the victims of what they classified as "wall-street aggressors", and that we had been tools of them and we should by all rights turn toward communism and try to fight the American way of life as we knew it, and by doing so, we would have better treatment and be released sooner. This some people believed but they soon began to realize the fallacy of their belief, as anything that they did in cooperative spirit was immediately followed by more stringent requests (a sort of "Fuller Brushman" sequence).

We left Kanggye, North Korea for the center part of Korea at about the 15th or 20th of March 1951. We were placed in cattle cars and taken to an unidentified spot at which place, they separated one officer and about 18 enlisted and took them to another point. They told us they were going to be released.

We stayed at this place about 2 days and were put on a train and the Communists told us we were going to return North because we had showed a belligerent attitude and should be given more education. I gathered from this the fact that we had refused to sign leaflets to be dropped to our troops was the cause, also that we had refused to take any such literature back with us.

We listened to their indoctrination until such times as we became thoroughly disgusted and then we offered an argumentation and rebuttal. For this our food supply would immediately be cut and as inadequate as it was at that time it became worse. The cutting of it had serious consequences, in health of the men, many died. We rode the train for possibly a day, were taken off and marched or about 50 or 100 miles to a place called PYOCKDONG-RI in North Korea which was called camp 5. We arrived there in the latter part of March. Upon arriving, it was quite obvious that this was a death camp; there were living skeletons starved emaciated (UN) personnel walking and dead lying in two houses.

I estimated between 20 to 30 persons died daily in this camp, from nothing but lack of food, proper medication and sanitation, for the first 6 months. We were told by the Chinese that it was our own American bombers fault that food and clothing was not forth coming and as soon as we learned the truth and would write back home and tell the American people the truth, to stop this bombing that we would be fed better.

We realized the trickery of this because by the same token, possibly two or three days later they would

come in with some eggs and extra rice and try to make
a gala affair of it, proving that supplies were available. This would immediately be followed by a request for us to sign some kind of pamphlet or leaflet
or something that would tell our families back home
to intervene in this war or stop the war and make the
people realize what they (the Communists) classified
as the truth, that we had gone into North Korea and
we were the belligerents in this Korean War. This,
the majority of us, generally laughed at. Any time
that one ridiculed anything they said, the food supply was cut down, medications would cease and also
sanitation.

The majority of the older hands, officers more mature
in nature, began to realize that suicide of the entire group was being performed by us. As a result,
they tried to temper the feelings against the communists, at least to curb feelings and to curb us, so
that we would not continue this suicide. In other
words, to soften our attitude toward the Chinese so
that, at least on the surface, it would appear that
we were beginning to accept to a degree or at least
to be peaceable in the camp.

This attitude was reflected in an increase of food but
still inadequate. We realized that there was a limi-
tation and took a code, a much different code than can
be supplied in normal living ethics.

The primary purpose of the ethics was: (1) to stay
alive so that you might fight them again and also to
tell the American Government the actual truth of what

went on. (2)To do nothing against your country, say nothing against your country and to avoid saying anything against anyone in camp that would cause them difficulty with the communists.

We classified persons who talk of fellow UN forces as informers or rats, in the main the personnel whom I associated with followed a pattern of a more or less, not a passive resistance but a degree of passivity rather than constant belligerence. However, each one of us would reach a point at times when we felt that we didn't want to take any more that which was given out and on the advice of a senior officer we would sound off to the Communists and suffer, as a consequence.

At Pyockdong I knew a Major by the name of Major Hume of the United States Army; I believe he was artillery Major. He was a very slight man and quite sensitive. We were given some papers to read one day, something about our country of a derogatory nature. Major Hume grabbed up the paper and said something to the effect that "this crap isn't worth the paper it's written on". There happened to be a chinaman close by the name of Low Quo who came in, took the major out and called the guards. The next time the majority saw the major he was in a hole in the ground about 30 feet away from camp.

He was kept in this hole for about 8 to 10 days. Prior to his being put in the hole he was made to stand at attention until he fainted. After he fainted he was kicked about the head and shoulders and stomped in the kidneys, a thing I personally witnessed.

When he came out of the hole, he had lost about 40 to 50 pounds. He was terribly emaciated and his mind was completely gone. When he spoke to us as he was forced to do his appearance was as a plucked sparrow. He spoke in a very weak voice and told us we were all foolish and that we should accept communism. The situation was obvious to us, he was driven out of his mind. He died about 2 days later.

While at Pyockdong, I was approached by Captain (or) Major McAbee US Army. Most everyone called him Major McAbee , of the Army. He was quite aggressive and he seems to be a well-adjusted officer. He knew I had a knife which I had hidden on my person and asked me if I would give it to him. I told him no, that I felt I might need it later on in an attempt to escape. He told me then that he had also intended to escape and that he had about 3 or 4 other men and he said that "You seem to have your bearings and I think you should try to escape with us". He told me he had a compass and that he had a North Korean who was friendly and could speak Japanese. Most of the men he had chosen were quite hardy and tough characters and if I would come with them I should start gathering little bits of rice and food to sustain myself and walking softly to practice for sneaking through the mountains.

At that time we had no realization as to the distance to friendly lines, nor did we have any realization of the total coverage of the mountains in this area by guerrilla forces or North Korean volunteers.

About a week prior to our attempted escape, a group of four officers left the camp. One was an officer by the name of Amandq Aries, another Hector Cordero, and another one by the name of Deacon. They were all Army Officers and one other officer whom I do not know, left the camp but were captured by morning.

That afternoon the Chinese came for Major McAbbe, the Army officer who had approached me to come into the escape plot. He was taken out of camp. The next morning about noon I heard my name being broadcast over a loud-speaker system. It sounded as though it were the voice of this Major McAbbe, who told me to give up my attempt of escape that the Chinese knew all about it. He also mentioned an officer by the name of McDonald and another one by the name of Harold Kouck and told them to give up their attempt to escape. We were totally confused and didn't know which way to turn.

I took an attitude of belligerence and when I was approached I told the Chinese that it was a bunch of "poppy kock", that I had not intended to escape and that I wasn't doing anything about it. And in the same voice I turned right around and told them everyone was going to escape. I also told them any man that belonged in the services of his country should try to escape any time that he saw fit. This infuriated the Chinese but they obviously had their sadistic impulses taken out on Major McAbee. Even though I had felt a great resentment for what he had done informing on me, I was told by Captain McDonald of the U.S. Army that McAbee had been hung by his wrists for 6 ½ hours. His arms being twisted behind his back and hung up, a wire band put around his neck extending down to his feet, so that when he relaxed his body and let his feet down so that he could touch the ground, he would choke himself. When he pulled his feet up he had the full weight of his body on his arms. This lasted for 6 ½ hours plus beatings about the face and shoulders.

I realized that he had chosen to live rather than to die in this instance. I do not feel any personal animosity or blame connected with this man. He continued his actions throughout the balance of our captivity and seemed to be totally afraid and ashamed of his actions.

He was afraid of the Chinese and ashamed to face us. Nevertheless, I considered this an atrocity against an American Officer by the Chinese communists. When he arrived back in camp, he practically got on his knees to me and apologized as to what he had done. He told me that the pain was too great that he couldn't take any more pain.

He had been very seriously wounded during the war about the head and shoulders. He had a deep scar running from his temple all the way to the back of his head, and also into his ear. One bullet in his shoulders, this coupled with the torture he went through, I believe was the cause for his breaking down and telling about our escape plot, which naturally was thwarted at that time.

There seemed to be a definite group of persons in camp who would always get the information of what we had intended or were intending to do. The carrying out of an act of aggression or getting out of camp or trying to escape, were nipped in the bud. This created quite a furor in our minds, because we never knew whom we could trust.

At this place I would say we were guarded by about battalion of Chinese volunteers. Also in the hills surrounding the camp, there were possibly a company of guerrilla volunteers, and the local security police of the North Korean Army. As I said before it was very difficult to know whom we could trust. However, we officers in the Marines knew each other pretty well and began to form a Marine clique. The senior man at that time was a Major John N. McLaughlin. His instructions were that we should not accept or do anything which would jeopardize our country in anyway, nor any of the U.N. Forces. We knew what we signed was a blank sheet of paper and that they had our signatures before and could apply them to anything which they wished, and which they did.

One reason for putting your name down on anything was the fact that your name got out and it was a proof to the people and your government that you were actually alive. We had no doubts, and had often been told by the Chinese that if we did not do as they said, and accept their policies, we would not go back home and that we would be buried right there. They even showed us a hole in the ground at one time that we were going to be buried in.

Most of the men having had previous knowledge of the Russians in Russia and how they act, under the Communists knew very well that this was not an idle threat. And, that they would carry out just exactly what they said, especially if you name wasn't out. The thing that became important to all of us was to get our "name out" someway.

There were many times that we would write home hoping that something would get out and in a letter that would say we were being well treated, or we have a warm room. We would also say something in essence such as we wish we were eating with Pete (a pet dog's name at home) "or had a little can of red heart (this is a dog food". In other words to show a little humorous attempt to let the people know back home that they should not believe everything they read. I have letters in my possession at the present time which were sent home of this nature, such as personnel aboard, type, Army, Navy or Marine Corps, name place and location, also locations by direction.

Upon going on work details I noticed throughout the camp, there would be quite a few enlisted personnel scattered from the upper part of the valley at Pyockdong down to the estuary or lake which led into the Yalu River. Pyockdong was adjacent to the Yalu River. These men would be sitting around, emaciated, starving. This was the first year, after that the conditions began to improve.

We left this place in the latter part of October and went to a place called camp 2 at Ping Chong Nee, Korea. This camp was located about 10 miles away from Pyockdong, southwest. Numerous men tried to escape at various times. As a general rule they would be brought back into camp and their arms tied with wire and I saw many instances of men who had "dropped wrists" from this tying and cutting off of circulation and lack of use of the muscle caused the wrist to drop. They would then be put into places of isolation or holes in the ground and given half-food. There were some instances when actually it was better to be in isolation because you were fed better and it was more of an isolated spot and they just couldn't cut your food down that small. In other words, when you're feeding 200 men with a bag of rice, you have to make it go for 200 men. Being in a hole of solitary you would probably be fed out of the Chinese galley and they were pretty well fed themselves. As a result anyone who ate out of the Chinese kitchen would probably receive a more sufficient quantity. They are a frugal race and they do not throw away food.

I would approximate that at Pyockdong there must have been over 1600 to 2000 personnel who died from starvation and lack of proper care of their wounds. Upon the move from Pyockdong to Pingchongne food improved to a certain degree. An increase of grain was given and our sanitation was increased greatly. We were still sleeping on the floors, but we were allowed to go to the river for our bath and given quite a bit more of some type of grain and floor. In some instances one pig, sometimes it was once every 2 weeks and sometimes it was once a week. That was our protein for 200 to 300 men.

No men died in this camp, however that does not say that any man who came to this camp and through the camp did not: because they were never heard of or seen again. Numerous young aviators who were shot down after January 1952 were not seen or heard of again although they came through the camp for interrogation.

There was one small road leading into Pyockdong about 8 miles up the road. There was a junction at this road junction, there was a road that went on one side of the lake and went on the other side of the lake and went on the other side, and one that lead back into Pingchong-Ni. It was quite mountains in that area.

At Pingchong-Ni they had various small quarters and isolation quarters and room which they called "reflection rooms", where a man could think over his past misdeeds, so they said. There were 3 holes in the ground, one covered by an iron lid, 1 under a bow grain shed which had been a toilet and which was considered the "quick break down hole". A hole that would make you change your mind in a hurry. I don't believe it had been made originally for that purpose as it was a portion as it was a portion of a building which might have been used as a disposal, toilet or storage room. It was about 3 foot long by 3 foot wide and 3 ½ feet high. Generally articles of wood or something of that nature would displace a certain amount of room and putting a man or two men in this hole was extremely and discouraging.

Twenty-four to forty, fifty or eighty hours of this type of treatment coupled with the fact that the place was infested with rats caused a great deal of mental and physical torture. It caused many men to do and say things that they normally would not have done or said.

Each man seemed to have a different point of break. At this point, I believe it would be and should be interesting to note this fact that this was considered more or less a passive punishment. They would put you in and let you sit and sit, and wait with the constant threat of death at hand. It caused quite a bit of mental anguish coupled with total lack of food and sanitation.

One had to urinate and defecate in the hole where he was with all the rats all coupled to make the place extremely distressing. To a person who after two years of capture was already quite mentally distressed in mind. The way that the mail was mishandled caused a lack of real knowledge of home. Letters were used as another wedge to get inside of our minds to see how were reacting. A "Dear John" letter from my past wife telling me of losing my sons was used as a wedge on me and a promise of better news which wasn't existent.

Everything seemed to be based on a psychological approach. There was, as I stated previously, quite a bit of physical torture, but that did not seem to be their initial policy. It seemed to be used as a last resort on persons upon whom they actually had an animosity toward.

The policy seemed to be, by a slow process of mental and physical starvation and psychologically threatening, depriving one of personal comfort and to allow complete freedom of thought of mind in steady work or play, and then completely depriving you of that effect in a day or two. A man could be brought to complete disorientation and unless you were very stable you would find that you had said or done something which would give them an "in" into your psychological nature. They had definite information coming from America regarding we and our families, and used these methods again to threaten or to frighten us.

Now in the same token, in the last year they furnished addition food, they let us play sports and they even went so far as to have a sports meet. This I did not attend nor did I condone it, but I heard about it.

At this time, in the early part of 1953, I was still considered to be belligerent after cursing them as Communist SOB's, they decided they would definitely punish me for this. I was taken out in the middle of the night stood at attention for quite a few hours. I was put in this quick break down hole, the small 3 by 3 by 3 ½. I was kept in there for 80 hours and was made to confess that I had cursed and was an aggressor against them and also that I was a tool of the wall-street aggressors. I was requested to inform, the thing which I did not do, nor did I ever intend to do. As a result, within a few days I was made to carry a terrific load of rocks from the mountains.

The carrying of this load placed a strain on my back and being already weakened from the hole and various starvations that I had had there and previously, I feel that they realized that I was in a weakened condition and that my back was injured and deliberately made me carry this load so that they could continue the process of humiliation and pain. The result was an injury to my back from falling I was paralyzed for 2 months.

On the main, it was quite obvious and apparent that these people used any means in order to get their information and/or psychological breakdown. There estimation of a human being is that unless he is a member of the communist party he is not a human being, but he is an animal and as a result may be treated as an animal, providing he is not of a friendly nature and does not go with the party.

The first year the food was not enough to sustain life, the second year the food improved and continues to improve up until the time of repatriation. Initially, we had no clothing. Later clothing was furnished, a cotton padded uniform and tennis shoes. For shelter we were put in a wooden mud hut, the first two years or first year and a half rather, the last year we were in a large a one panel school room. During this time, we slept on the floor.

We were allowed a fire in the corridors about 3 hours per day. Those corridors were open and drafty and the rooms were icy. So icy that on the inside of the room you could cut ice off the wall on any part. We kept warm by huddling together. Then the last year, blankets, a comforter and small blankets were furnished, prior to that one blanket for two men.

Regarding medical care, I was called in at Pyockdong and asked why so many men were dying. I told them I felt that they were being starved to death and that if they would improve the food that the men wouldn't die. At that time I had a bad case of dysentery. The interrogator had 6 to 8 sulfa pills on the table which I knew would be of a great aid in curing me. He also asked me why American men were such weaklings, why so many men die. I told him that I disagreed and that they were not weaklings, but that the different diet was the reason for the numerous deaths also coupled with the fact that we weren't receiving enough to eat.

He knew I had been a Japanese prisoner of war and he said: "what do you suggest we do about it?" I told him increase the protein diet, give oils, salt and bulk to fill the stomach and he said he would agree to do such, if I would show by my attitude that I realized the aid that they were giving. He also promised the 6 to 8 sulfa dyazine pills.

I asked him what was it he wanted me to say. He told me, he wanted me to write home and tell the people, as he called them, that the men were weak and the condition they were in was due to the fact of their way of life in America. And if they would accept Communism and follow the rigid routine of communism they would not be that way.

At the same time he was promising the pills. I told this, that I did not believe this to be a fact and I believed that American youth and men are pioneers still and that if there is any reason for the numerous deaths, one of them was the two discussed previously, the treatment and the association they had with the Chinese. I was denied the pills.

I received a black mark in my book that they kept on my actions, but I noticed about 2 weeks later that the bulk did increase in the camp. I recovered fortunately for the effects of the dysentery.

The next year I had another attack which was at Pingchong-ni. While there, I was put into the hospital and met what I would consider a complete reverse treatment. There was a Sunyen, a Chinese nurse, who was very kindly disposed and she got additional food stuffs and sulfa pills and some other form of medicine which completely cured me of this disease I was having at that time.

I found soon after that, the reason for same was that the Doctor expected me to write a big treatise, on the treatment, so that it could be published in the Shanghai News. I wrote the facts. That I had dysentery, that the dysentery was caused through improper sanitation and had it not been such, I would not have been in there. I also mentioned the fact that an American doctor, G. L. Anderson, U.S. Army, who was in camp, had given much more to me and that if it hadn't been for his interceding to gain entrance into the hospital for me, I would possibly have died in the camps. This was not accepted as good propaganda for them, I don't think it was ever published.

I was told by Lt. John Fox, U.S. Army, that he had been captured by North Koreans and that he was in a column of 200 or 300 men and that every few miles someone was taken out and deliberately murdered in order to speed up the balance of the march. This was June 1950. I did not witness this, but I gave further credibility to the officer who spoke of it to me. Lt. Fox was in the U.S. Army.

I believe that in the same column was a Lt. Colonel Dunn of the U.S. Army. He also told me there were numerous women and children; one woman was carrying a small baby. These people did not make it through on the long march up north. There were Nuns, Priests, and Ministers, all on this march.

Kanggye I would say there was about, possibly 300 men captured prisoners rather. At Pyockdong it appeared to be 5,000 or so. At Pingchong-ni I believe, there were at one time around 350 officers and senior Air Corps enlisted men. The Chinese explained that they were taking the Air Corps men and isolating them with the officers. They felt that the Air Corps had a high-er caliber of enlisted men and that they would also be capable of influencing the lower ranking enlisted men away from the break down that the Communists were working on in trying to indoctrinate these enlisted men into communism. Something they attempted to with us for about a year and a half, but finally gave up. Many men initially flatly rejected their communist doctrine and would never listen to anything they said, but they soon began to realize that unless they knew what they were fighting, that they couldn't fight it.

As a result, they listened and read the things that were given and they formed their own rebuttals in their minds, carrying these thoughts and also expressing these thoughts, as was also my case. The result of all the things that I have brought out resulted in a chaotic mind in most POW'S.

The initial phase, total starvation (as many of us expressed our opinions, that if they would only have fed the first group better during the first year, as well as they fed during the second year, everyone would have been alive). In my opinion almost every man would have survived had a semblance of decency been followed during the first year.

The Chinese contended that, had we not been as they classified, the aggressors, who came into North Korea threatening their boundaries, that we would not have this lack of food, because it was our own bombers that were bombing their lines and bombing their barges and bombing the planes. It was extremely difficult for us to contain ourselves during this time, because we knew the fallacy of it. They were so close to

China, that is would have been quite simple to get enough staple foods over to feed the men and keep them alive. I can say that at times the food was comparatively good. There was always a reason behind it other than humanitarian, in order to extract or gain something from us for their propaganda machine.

I have been told many times by the Chinese, Comrades, volunteers, Chinese communists or whatever they classified themselves as, that the persons who were not or did not believe in the communist party were not more than animals. As a result one could expect such treatment as would be given an animal.

Long association with the Orientals has proven to me that an animal to them has no feelings and torture and starvation or death means nothing to them in any instance. They are quite child-like in their approach to life and mentally immature. As long as one stayed with a very soft disposition he was more or less left alone, but when one showed any belligerence, they having the gun so to speak, would immediately be made to suffer.

As a result, I believe it can be broken down quite easily: the first year was the most extreme and bitter and most atrocious. The second year, up to half of the second year, July and August, indoctrination had ceased completely and a general attitude of trying to grant our desires in normal living were given. At the last month, they finally erected beds in the compound so that we could get off the floor, which we had been sleeping on for the past two years.

Their methods seemed to be to try to break a man's mind so that he would become a puppet for them. Not being able to do that, to try to belittle him in the eyes of his country. Try to bring out something that might have happened to him in camp, which would embarrass him here, in America, which would be carrying on their schemes and designs. Also the facts that they have complete cooperation with the communists who are in America, under the protection of our American Flag makes their attempts bear fruit.

It is just as much, in my estimation, as if the actual enemy who we were fighting in the front lines in Korea, exists and is allowed to exist here in our Country, a thing I am in total disharmony with. Also, there are numerous cases of informers, persons who have signed things which have embarrassed our country and so-called opportunists who got along a little better than the other ones in camp.

All of these things are coming to light at the present time. In my opinion, the guilty should be punished, but in the same token that is exactly what the communists planned. As I was told many times in the camp, they would keep us under their thumbs for the rest of our lives.

It is my opinion that all personnel should either be taught one of the other:

(1) That under no circumstances to ever become a prisoner, to commit suicide first

(2) Or to have a method of procedure which would allow a certain amount of expression of opinion
when and if a man or officer becomes a prisoner
so that he at least would know what he is doing.

The communists have proven too, I believe, to the
majority of their prisoners that your name, rank and
serial number are not enough, nor will they accept
it, nor will you live if you adhere to it. I have
heard of two isolated cases in which supposedly was
given nothing but name, rank and serial number. In
one instance I know very well that more than name,
rank and serial number were given. It was no reflection against the man because he was very strong
and courageous. He spent about 2 or 2 ½ years at
least, in total solitary confinement in room barely
big enough to turn around it.

UNITED STATES MARINE CORPS

SUPPLY DEPARTMENT

Depot of Supplies

San Francisco 6, California

28 December 1953

From: Commissioned Warrant Officer Felix J. McCool
049274 USMC

To: Commandant of the Marine Corps

Ref: Via (1) Commanding Officer, Marine Corps Depot
of Supplies,

100 Harrison Street, San Francisco, California

(2) Commanding General, Department of Pacific

Subj: Report on period of captivity

Ref: (a) CMC ltr DP-1828-ls-23 of 18 Nov 53

Encl: (1) Copy of CWO McCool's ltr to Lt. Col Gay
Thrash USMC (avn)

(2) Copy of CWO McCool's ltr to Lt. Col John N.
McLaughlin USMC

(3) Copy of CWO McCool's ltr to Maj. Gerald Fink USMC (avn)

1. In compliance with reference (a) the following narrative is submitted:

On the 29th of November 1950, I attached myself to a convoy moving to Haggeru-ri, North Korea from Koto-ri, North Korea. With me were my driver, Private First Class Leon Roebuck 608320 USMC Motor Platoon, First Battalion and one Marine Sergeant whose name I do not recall. My mission was to contact the Commanding Officer of First Service battalion who was at Haggeru-ri, North Korea and deliver Service reports to him for his personal endorsement and return to Hamhung, North Korea and deliver these reports to the First Battalion Executive Officer by 30th November 1950. The finished copy was to be sent to Headquarters First Marine Division by the 1st of December 1950. I made the trip upon orders from the Executive Officer, First Service Battalion who informed me that I would have to penetrate three enemy-held road blocks. Events are as described below:

I left Hamhung, North Korea the morning of 28 November and arrived at Koto-ri, North Korea the afternoon of the same day. I was not permitted to continue on that date. The order holding me was given to me by the Commanding Officer of the First Regiment of the First Marine Division.

I attempted to contact the forward position of the First Service Battalion, and also to contact the First

Service Battalion (rear). The lines were jammed and I could get no contact.

On the early afternoon of 29 November 1950, I was allowed to proceed toward Haggeru-ri, North Korea from Koto-ri, North Korea. I pulled into a convoy which was opening through the enemy to Haggeru-ri, North Korea. We were under constant small arms and mortar fire from the enemy. I was able to penetrate through for about five miles at which time a truck, three vehicles ahead of me, was blown up and blocked the frozen road. Trucks and jeeps piled up at this place and we were forced down into a ditch by sustained fire. My vehicle was rendered useless. Lieutenant Colonel Arthur Adolph Chidister 05234 USMC, Major James K. Hagan 17760 USMC and First Lieutenant Herbert Barrow Turner 039278 USMC were also at this point and we attempted to turn the convoy back. At this point, the push of the convoy from the rear and constant firing made this attempt useless. Lieutenant Colonel Chidister and Major Eagan were wounded soon after that, about 300 yards from me. Lieutenant Turner and I jumped into a ditch which was manned by U.S. Forces. A Major John N. McLaughlin 08433 USMC was the Senior Officer present and had assumed command. We fought until dawn and were captured at that time. I destroyed all papers in my possession by burning. The captors-Chinese Communists- had previously promised to release the wounded and not to annihilate the remaining upon an immediate surrender. Major McLaughlin assumed responsibility for the surrender. We were moved from that spot to a place in the hills. In my opinion, the enemy concentrated upon this group and some elements of the convoy were given an opportunity to escape due to this concentration.

We were moved into the hills and put into Korean mud huts. A few hours later, a Chinese interpreter came into the hut and asked for volunteer truck drivers. Mr. Frank Noel, Associated Press Photographer who was covering the British Commandos prior to capture, I, and Private First Class Roebuck volunteered as drivers, as we intended to attempt escape during the lull. We marched to the road under guard and attempted to start any vehicle which was not hit. All vehicles were frozen with the exception of one jeep. We started the jeep and saw a moving wounded man on the road. It was Commissioned Warrant Officer Donald Meek USMCR. We put him in the jeep and Private First Class Roebuck drove; there were two guards present and enemy on both sides of the road. We then picked up two wounded army men and one South Korean. Mr. Noel and I dismounted from the jeep and pushed it. The jeep started and left under orders of the Chinese. We were taken back to the hut by guards along the road. We left the hut the next day with a group who were being collected along the way and marched over a hill for about eight miles. Colonel Chidister and Major Eagan were carried by litter and placed in a mud hut there. This hut was presumable a field hospital.

We were kept there and marched to an area about fifty (50) to one hundred (100) miles away. We were kept off the roads most of the time and had to beat trails through the snow in the mountains. We spent about fourteen (14) days in the place that we had marched to, and were given an Introduction to Communist's Indoctrination. There were about 30 to 40 POW'S present in this place, both Officers and Enlisted.

We then were marched to Kanggye, North Korea, close to the Manchurian border, arriving 26 December 1950 after about 350 miles of marching. We were given an extended indoctrination into the Communist Principles which we combated by argumentation. We were fed about 500 grams of grain per day and about two (2) ounces of a vegetable or protein daily. We had no sanitation and could leave our room only to answer the calls of nature. The temperature was about forty (40) degrees below zero. We had one blanket between two men.

Of the men who were wounded and had been frozen on the, I estimated that approximately forty (40) perished at Kanggye.

We left Kanggye for the central part of the Peninsula the middle of March 1951. The Marine Corps Officers present at Kanggye were Major John N. McLaughlin USMC, Captain Robert C. Messman USMC, First Lieutenant Herbert B. Turner USMCR, First Lieutenant Ernest H. Reid USMCR, First Lieutenant Allan Lloyd USMCR, First Lieutenant Frank E. Cold USMCR, and myself.

Upon leaving Kanggye, we were placed in cattle cars and taken to the center of the Peninsula to an unidentified spot. One (1) officer, First Lieutenant Frank E. Cold USMCR and eighteen (18) enlisted were separated from us at this point. The Communists told us later they were released.

We were told that we would have to return north to be "re-educated" and that our attitudes were still "wrong". We then marched to Pyockdong, North Korea, later named Camp # 5.

Lieutenant Colonel Gerald Brown 9625A USAF was the Senior Officer present.

I personally witnessed the death of over thirty U.N. personnel, Officers and Enlisted combined, in one month because of starvation. I was told there had been 1,600 deaths in that compound prior to the time of our arrival. The new Officers Compound was opened at Pingchong-ri, North Korea approximately 10 miles away from Camp # 5 on or about October 1951. This new camp contained officers from all of the countries of the U.N.

Letters to be written home were required to contain some manner of compliment to the enemy; otherwise no correspondence could be sent. It was the general consensus of opinion that "to get your name out" was an intelligent thing to do. "Get your name out" referred to allowing someone in the U.S. to know you were alive, so that you would not be shipped to the Russian Interior.

During my period of captivity, I was interrogated about five or six times a year. At the onset, I was made to realize that giving only name, rank and serial number was NOT acceptable to the Chinese Communists.

They gave me to understand that I would very likely sicken and die. I tried to devise a plan of half-truths and succeeded in giving them information of no value. This was discovered at a later date and I was put into a place called by them the "quiet reflection room". The room was a hole in the ground about 3 feet long by 3 feet wide and 3 ½ feet high. It was wet and I estimated about twenty or thirty rats were in the hole with me. I stayed there for 80 hours, at which time I confessed to hating Communism, being an aggressor and a "tool of the Wall Street Aggressors". I was expected to inform upon my fellow Officers, which I flatly refused to do. I was again forced to re-enter the hole. I persisted in refusing to inform, so they put me on probation and sent me back to the compound that evening. If I broke probation, I would be sentenced to three months in the hole. I was called in for interrogation at one time and told of experiences in my past life in America, and of one of the schools that I had attended. I realized that there was no other way for them to have that information than contact with Communists in America.

On or about 6 May 1953, while a prisoner of the Communists in North Korea; I was called out by a Platoon Leader "Wong" who informed me that I was to carry rocks from the mountain behind the camp. I was given two baskets and one pole, called "Yaho", for carrying. A guard took me out of camp. I loaded the baskets with a load that I could carry with comparative ease and made two (2) trips. On the third trip, the guards made me, at the point of a bayonet, load the baskets extremely heavy. I remonstrated but it was useless. I tried to lift the heavy baskets and finally succeeded, but while coming down the path I stepped upon a round rock. The baskets jerked up and down and I caught the full weight of them on my back. I felt a pull in my spinal cord and set the baskets down. The guards made me load it upon my back again and forced me to continue into camp. Upon my arrival, I fell to my knees and had to be carried into the school house where we were living.

Two American doctors, Dr. C.L. Anderson (Captain) and Dr. Bill Shaddish (First Lieutenant), both of the U.S. Army, inspected me and told me that a "ruptured disc" in the spine was indicated, but with lack of facilities they could not determine proper diagnosis. They advised me to lie on my back for 6 weeks. The Chinese Platoon Leader tried to make me stand but I was paralyzed at that time. He left and I was left alone.

I lay for two months on my back in an isolated area and recovered. During this period, I was fed by Communists.

I do not know the address of the two Doctors, but feel that they are still members of the U.S. Army.

During this time and until the last 8 months of captivity, we were constantly subjected to Communist Indoctrination. They used "Lenient Policy" which was "permission to live", increased food allowance, entertainment, and sports. However, the "Lenient Policy" failed to impress nearly all of the prisoners, and failed to impress 100% of the Marines.

2. The following Officers were the Senior Armed Officers present during the times indicated:

Lieutenant Colonel Gerald Brown, USAF, October 1951–February 1952

Lieutenant Colonel Alarich L. E. Zacherle 0-42817, U.S. Army, February 1952–May 1952

Lieutenant Colonel William Gay Thrash 06141, USMC (avn), May 1952–November 1952

Major Andrew Fedennts 0-1175433, U.S, Army (FA), November 1952–August 1953

3. I was repatriated at Kaesong, North Korea 0905 6 September 1953.

4. Copies of my letters to Officer fellow prisoners regarding my conduct, manner of performance of duty and all other matters bearing upon my fitness report as an Officer while confined as a prisoner of war are submitted as Enclosures (1), (2) and (3).

5. Happenings enumerated have caused as aggression in my mind against the persons in America who hide under the guise of Communism and I find it extremely difficult to contain that feeling.

FELIX J. MC COOL

Another statement-

There were numerous South Korean wounded, American Army Forces and a few Marines also wounded. Enlisted and officers were put into a room about ten by ten foot square. There were fifteen to twenty men in this on room now wounded. In the other room, which was slightly larger and contained about thirty men of which numerous were badly wounded. The ones becoming infected were subjected to a total lack of sanitation facilities. They crawled from the room to the door to relieve themselves. At this place we were interrogated to a small degree. About two days prior to leaving some of the wounded men were taken away and we never saw them again.

It was impossible to actually ascertain the amount of neglectful deaths. I remember on place that the officers were finally put into was a room eight by ten feet. There were fifteen of us in this room and in an adjoining shed there were numerous American GI clothes which were covered with blood spots. They appeared to have been taken from the bodies of American GI's who had been wounded or died; they were marched to this place without aid. I'm quite sure that this room we were in had been one of the chambers where they kept sick men until they died. There were buried on the side of a hill. We noticed the ground being burned off at a certain point which was the only indication that might be had as to what was going on. I would ascertain that about forty men had died through neglect of wounds and improper feeding and housing. The names of the men were impossible to ascertain as they were from various units of the

Army, Marine Corps and South Korean Army. At this place in Kanggye the food was two very small bowls of Kooleang, which is a rice type of food and an ounce or two of a protein substance twice a day. A small Chinese boy used to come around occasionally with the Red Cross bandage on his arm and snip off the putrefied flies of the men whose feet had been frozen. It could not be classified as adequate medical treatment.

I saw at least twenty-five or thirty men who had frozen to death overnight who could have quite easily been either housed by the Communist forces or taken back to a spot close to the lines and released, or at least allowed to be picked up by our own forces. In my estimation there was a total lack of humanitarian attitude, although the Chinese manifested that they worked under a policy called the "Lenient Policy". My first talk with any Chinese was with a young man by the name of Fong from Peking, China. He told me that the Chinese had no desire to take any of our personal belongings, however I saw looting going on of prisoners both wounded and well.

We left Kanggye, North Korea for the center part of Korea at about the fifteenth or twentieth of March 1951. We were placed in cattle cars and taken to an unidentified spot at which place they separated one officer and about eighteen enlisted and took them to another point. They told us there were going to be released.

We stayed at this place about two days and were put on a train. The Communists told us were going to return north because we had showed a belligerent attitude

and should be given more education. I gathered from
this the fact that we had refused to sign leaflets to
be dropped to our troops was the case. We also refused to take any such literature back with us.

We listened to their indoctrination until such times
as we became thoroughly disgusted and then we offered
an argumentation and rebuttal. For this our food
supply would immediately be cut and as inadequate as
it was at the time it became worse. The cutting of
it had serious consequences in the health of the men,
many died. We rode the train for possibly a day and
were taken off and marched for about fifty to one hundred miles to a place called Pyockdong-ri in North
Korea which was called camp five. We arrived there
in the latter part of the march. Upon arriving it
was quite obvious that this was a death camp. There
were living skeletons starved emaciated (UN) personnel walking and dead lying in two houses.

I estimated twenty to thirty persons died daily in
this camp from nothing but lack of food and improper
medication and sanitation for the first six months.

At this place I would say we were guarded by about a
battalion of Chinese volunteers. In the hills surrounding the camp there were possibly a company of
guerrilla volunteers and the local security policy of
the North Korean Army.

As I said before it was very difficult to know whom we
could trust. However, we officers in the Marines knew
each other pretty well and began to form a Marine

clique.   The senior man at the time was Major John
N. McLaughlin.   His instructions were that we should
not accept or do anything which would jeopardize our
country in anyway, nor any of the UN Forces.   We knew
what we signed was a blank sheet of paper and that
they had out signatures before and could apply them
to anything which they wished and they did.

Upon going on work details I noticed throughout the
camp there would be quite a few enlisted personnel scattered from the upper part of the valley at
Pyockdong down to the estuary or lake which let into
the Yalu River.   Pyockdong was adjacent to the Yalu
River.   These men would be sitting around emaciated
and starving.   This was the first year after the conditions began to improve.

We left this place in the latter part of October and
went to a place called camp two at Ping Chong Nee,
Korea.   This camp was located ten miles away from
Pyockdong, southwest.

I would approximate that at Pyockdong there must have
been over sixteen hundred to two thousand personnel
who died from starvation and lack of proper care of
their wounds.

Upon the move from Pyockdong to Pinghongne food improved to a certain degree.   An increase of grain was
given and our sanitation was increased greatly.

We were still sleeping on the floors but we were allowed to go to the river for our bath and given quite

a bit more of some type of grain or flour, in some instances one pig. Sometimes it was every two weeks sometimes it was once a week. That was our protein for two hundred to three hundred men.

No men died in this camp; however that does not say that any man who came to this camp and through this camp did not, because they were never heard from again. Numerous young aviators who were shot down after January 1952 were not seen or heard from again although they came through the camp for interrogation.

He knew I had been a Japanese prisoner of war and he said "what do you suggest we do about it?" I told him to increase the protein diet, give oils, salts and bulk to fill the stomach and he said he would agree to do such if I would show in my attitude that I realized the aid that we were being given. He also promised the six to eight Dyazine pills.

I asked him what was it he wanted me to say. He told me he wanted me to write home and tell the people as he called them, that the men were weak and the condition whey were in was due to the fact of their way of life in America and that if they would accept Communism and follow the rigid routine of Communism they would not be that way.

At the same time he was promising pills. I told them that I did not believe this to be fact and I believed American youth and men at pioneers still and that if there is any reason for the numerous deaths, one of them was the two discussed previously, the treatment and the association they had with the Chinese. I was denied pills!

I received a black mark in my book that they on my action but I noticed about two weeks later that the bulk did not increase in the camp. I recovered fortunately from the effects of dysentery.

The next year I had another attack, which was in Pingchong-Ni. While there I was put into a hospital and met what I would consider a complete reversal of treatment. There was a Sunyen, a Chinese nurse, who was very kindly disposed and who got additional food stuffs, sulfa pills and some other form of medicine which completely cured me of this disease I was having at the time.

I found soon after that the reason for the same was that the doctor expected me to write big treatise on the treatment so that it could be published in the Shanghai News.

I believe that in the same column was a Lt. Colonel Dunn of the US Army. He told me there were numerous women and children; one woman was carrying a small baby. These people did not make it through on the long march up north. These were nuns, priests and ministers on this march.

At Kanggye I would say there was about three hundred men captured, prisoners rather. At Pyockdong it appeared to be five thousand or so. At Pingchong-Ni I believe there were at one time around three hundred fifty officers. The senior Air Corps enlisted men the Chinese explained they were taking them and isolating them with the officers. They felt that the Air Corps had a higher caliber of enlisted men and that they would also be capable of influencing the lower ranking enlisted men away from the breakdown that the Communists were working on in trying to indoctrinate these enlisted men into Communism, a thing which they attempted to do with us for about a year and a half but finally gave up in the end.

Long association with the Orientals has proven to me that an animal to them has no feelings, torture, starvation or death mean nothing to them in any instance. They are quite childlike in their approach to life and mentally immature.

A long as one stayed with a very soft disposition he was more or less left alone. But when one showed any belligerence they have the gun so to speak and would immediately made him suffer.

As a result I believe it can be broken down quite easily: the first year was the most extreme, bitter and most atrocious. The second, up to half of the second year, July to August, indoctrination had ceased completely, a general attitude of trying to grant our desires in normal living were given.

At the last month they finally erected beds in the compound so that we could get off the floor, which had been sleeping on for the past two years.

Their methods seemed to be to try to break a man's mind so that he could become a puppet for them. Not being able to do that they tried to belittle him in the eyes of his country. Try to bring out something that might have happened to him in camp which would embarrass him here in America which would be carrying on their schemes and designs. The fact that they have complete cooperation with the communists who are in America under the American flag makes their attempts bear fruit.

KOTO RI — HAGGERU —RI ROAD BLOCK

The 14 day place- (a) Place in North Korea for collection point so named due to 14 days spent there.
(b) Kanggye, Korea Dec. 1950 — March 1951. (c)
Pyockdong NI Korea (Camp 5) March 51 — Oct (?) 51 (d)
Pingchong NI, (Camp 2 Officers) Oct (/) 51 — Aug 53.
(e) Panmungong Korea Aug. 53- 6 Sep 53 (at which time
repatriated at Exchange Center).

30 Nov 50 6 Sept 53

Initially was confined to 1 room with 15 men for 1st
phase, some attempt to indoctrinate these men was
attempted from my observation not effective (this is
Kangaye) — March 51 at Pyocktong in Camp 5 voluntary
chopped wood for kitchen, carried rations, these became an involved problem due to lack of handles for
axe. Temper of the steel in the axe, and distance
carrying wood and rations plus extreme cold of early
spring. Forced to stay in room at times and listen
to Communist indoctrination. Tried to devise scheme
of letter writing that would get my name out plus
let family know actual conditions and contact Marine
Corps plus FBI, using UNCLE FRANK, COUSINS BEATRICE
AND INEZ as imaginary persons whom I would send messages to such as Personnel, Place, where located,
Weather, and type of indoctrination.

FOOD- (re food; referred to my dog Pete and Red Heart
dog food as ideal Chow). Many such devised letters
were sent home. I have had no assurance that any
other than letters wherein I praised the captors were

kept by my headquarters. The _praise_ was used for one purpose, to assure letters getting out, but would be followed by a negation: "I am being treated fine, etc., please see that my last will and testament are up to date and in a safe place etc.

I had hoped to establish enough intelligent cross letters that the actual conditions and type indoctrination would be divulged to our Country without endangering the POWs. Many times lethargy would overcome me and I would vegetate. At various times I agitated by inference to other POWs that the Communists were stupid fools but always with a vague fear that some, whoever they were, would inform on my actions. I cursed the Communists; favorite expression was SON OF A BITCH. When going to forced classes I let off as many of the interrogators or guards as I could LIT OFF! Use, of a hot coal on the cheap cotton clothes, setting them afire.

Periods of ennui, then began a study of American Government, Chemistry, Algebra, Plane and Spherical Trigonometry, Spanish, learned to read, write and speak Spanish. Studied Artillery Sensing. Public Speaking, this was done by picking the brains of fellow POW's who had the advantage of a more formal education. It was effective in that I have a better education background than when captured as I have carried on since release for 2 years straight in Golden Gate College of Traffic with a "B" average.

The last two months of captivity I was on my back with a slipped disc in the Spine, caused by carrying heavy loads on a YOHO POLE, of dirt off a mountain. HAHO POLE: Bamboo flat stick with two cams balanced on rope from each end. A chant of "ya ho" "ya ho" used in rhythmic monitory while trotting with the load gives the name.

The most important thing was a constant search for food.

Initially starved systematically. Numerous attempts to extract information, I rebuffed the initial attempts but began to realize that I would probably not go home. I attempted to devise half-truths to some of the questions; believe this a wrong choice now as the more you say the more they find out there is only one way you must KEEP SILTENT give no information. I believe although you might be brutally treated, you would be respected in the long run; or DEAD either would be a better choice than aid to an enemy. I will cite specific incidents.

1. I was taken out of camp one day in Camp #5 at which time I had dysentery. The Chinese Captor showed me some surphur pills on a table which I would get if I would write an article stating the reason that American youth were weak and why so many were dying. I refused to do same and was denied the pills; but not obviously punished. Sent back to Camp.

2. It was wet cold, lice infested, and rats were present. I was told that if I would write on the fact that I was a trouble maker and inform on fellow officers I would be released from the hole. (I was

230

originally put in the hole for cursing an interpreter and spitting on a guard) I refused to inform but had to compromise by confessing my wrong actions. I continued in my refusal to inform and was released from the hole and sent back to the compound with other officers…again I insist that an adamant attitude is the best! DON"T TALK!

3. at one time at Ping Chong MI (2) I was told that I must write about my outfit. I refused but extreme cold and cramped space changed my mind. I began to write trying to tell about laundry equipment and PX rations (50 in 1 boxes) this gave them an in for further questions and the more I tried to evade the more they entangled me. I finally, after a few days shut up and by continuing to shut up was left alone. I reiterate DON'T TALK! It is impossible for a man to outwit better fed, better rested persons who have no fear of death. It is best to give only name, rank and serial number.

The Code of Conduct would have indeed been a wonderful thing to bolster the morale of a man or officer. While we of the Marine Corps have a belief in each other which is much greater than the other services, circumstances arose being in an isolated spot away from fellow Marines who although a few in number by their actions did not inspire confidence in their superior rank or did not divulge their intent to the lesser minions as myself even though a few in number their intent to the lesser minions or myself even though I had a great amount of respect for most all Marines still felt a vague fear that all was not well with "Semper Fidelis". If I had been indoctrinated with this CODE as set down I believe I as well as all others whether they be Marine, Army, or Navy or Air Force would then have a "Hard Core" beyond our individual services which we could have drawn upon. I believe this Code is good with one exception un- der no circumstances should you ever give more than Name, Rank and Serial Number. (a) I would then have determined whether I should surrender even though an Officer of Superior Rank had surrendered the command. A mixed group Army, Korean & Marine. I accepted this without question and in all fairness to the man I was damn well ready to. We had no ammunition- dead and wounded were around us, the wounded pleading that we not desert them. Exhaustion after about 10 to 12 hours of fighting also determined this.

(b) When interrogated I was cursed with a vague fear that if I refused I was only a fool as the others had been talking (I had a suspicion they had) but they as I were probably being cagy, again I say if a man set mute with exception of Name, Rank, and Serial number the entire group would be respected for that one man, and one doing that would add strength to others who were vacillating. A gnawing doubt of fear that I was the only fool present caused me to say more than my name, rank, and serial number. I, with this Code would have had the strength to carry on my initial belief.

© At all times during interment I respected strength integrity and good intent. I recognized fear- cow- ardice — and cunning. I knew fear and cunning but I needed a thing material, this Code is! My strength if

232

only was spiritual. I prayed for aid, but often God moves in strange ways, my strength were not always what I admire in men of courage. The Code of "Semper Fidelis".

Principle II, whether or not a man may determine that his Superior is surrendering without exhausting all other efforts and what to do about it.

Adhere to the hard Core of the Code — do not even whisper that any circumstances exists where he may accede to his captors — other than in routine of POW camp life. It is unrealistic to say you may never be captured. I said that I would never be again as I had been on Corregidor with the 4th Marines who were taken by the Japanese, - we had no (see attached sheet [editor's note-no sheet attached, sentence left hanging]

Due to my experience, my education and my background in Public Speaking (Semper Fidelis Toastmasters International) (Charter member) I volunteer my services to and in actual instruction. There is only one way for a Marine — Name, Rank and Serial number and no other. It is often more simple to die than to compromise with integrity. The Marine Corps has a motto, it should be all "Semper Fidelis".

3. Other way. I was wound there. I was not wounded in my battle with the Chinese and at about 0330 in the morning I decided that the time to escape was at hand or I would be a prisoner again. I listened to wounded calling for aid and in the shambles of this last ditch

stand I accepted that it was my duty to stay there. I was a free agent on a delivery mission to the front — in a jeep with a driver and one man, there were my responsibilities. My moral responsibilities reached to each man who was in this road block battle. I chose to stay and at daylight the position was surrendered by the Senior Officer present. I chose to follow the old principle learned in Boot Camp "Obey the last order given by a Superior Officer". I obeyed. From then on my confusion as to loyalty began. No one could and no one did give any concrete orders. A POW was on his own for about 15 days at which time the Senior Marine Officer rejoined us and we patterned ourselves after him. Overall commendatory action was not by me but more should have been done. I insist nothing should be said but NAME, RANK AND SERIAL NUMBER.

Code of Conduct Speech

Commanders should be counseled chiefly by persons of
known talent, by those who have made the art of war
their particular study, and whose knowledge is de-
rived from experience, by those who are present at
the SECENE OF ACTION, who see the enemy, who see the
advantages that occasions offer, and who like people
embarked in the same ship, are sharers of danger. If,
therefore, anyone thinks himself qualified to give
ADVICE respecting the war, which I am to conduct—let
him not refuse the assistance to the State, but let
him COME WITH ME INTO MACEDONIA". Thus spoke PALUS of
ancient ROME concerning the conduct of his mission.

WHY DO I QUOTE AN ANCIENT ROMAN? (Editor's note-the next sentence was lined out but I believe it was because Felix used this speech more than once.) Because I have been invited to speak about the Code of Conduct to you sojourners and Marines. I have seen the enemy, I have been behind his lines, I have lived with him! Tonight I will talk of experiences, responsibilities, and decisions, my experiences, my responsibilities and my decisions. Two times a Prisoner of War.

The last a prisoner of the communists.

"THE CODE OF CONDUCT".

I AM AN AMERICAN FIGHTING MAN! I AM TO TALK ABOUT IT!

Talks are made by people who are generally expected to have something to say—They may be impromptu talks, memorized, written and read or extemporaneous (that is prepared in content and structure but not completely filled in with the words(this is my choice, because each audience is different.

When (several names written and scratched out) asked me to talk I was pleased and proud. To be considered by such a dedicated group as you with your theme of better citizenship, honored me. As my theme of life is democracy in action, I believe in the United States of America. The Constitution, the Bill of Rights and the poetry of man's rights to "Life, Liberty, and the Pursuit of Happiness," I may emphasize happiness as a pursuit as happiness is a relative thing and man pursues it in many ways.

I know in the preparation of this talk that the subject was controversial, pros and cons have come about, due to too little information, or too much of the wrong kind.

So I decided to tell my story the way it happened, personally as observed, an opinion from my point of view.

I learned about my country not academically, as my education was spotty in my early youth, but on the edge of my bunk, in a tent, on guard duty reciting, drilling troops, acting as an education counselor, fighting in two wars, and later when faced with communistic indoctrination as a POW in the schools of the communists, and lastly upon arrival home in a relentless search from the tomb of the POW camp to the schools of the United States since 1953, night colleges in San Francisco while I was a Dept of Pacific, and here in the night extension of East Carolina College, History, Government, Geography, Humanities, Arts and Why? Because I saw the results of ignorance when young men couldn't counter with knowledge the attack of the communistic trained educations in POW camp.

I believe my reason for being pleased to speak to you is now more apparent!

THE CODE OF CONDUCT!

I AM AN American fighting man! A United States Marine!

I have a code to follow, in life! As in battle! In circumstances over which I have no control—to death's door or the bleakness of a POW cell!

I am an American Fighting man!

These are fine words, but what do they mean to the individual? Moments of decision, the difference between fear and cowardice, running or facing it.

Moments of decision

When the island of Corregidor, Philippines fell to the Japanese in World War II. I was a machine gunner of the U. S. 4th Marines out of Shanghai, China. We had been on half rations for a long time, and there was no possibility of any assistance. I was wounded and took a last ditch at Monkey Point on Corregidor! What happened after that is history, we all know of the death march, Bilibid prison, Lipa Batangas, punishment slave labor and final death or the ship to Japan and the mines.

In Cabanatuan POW Camp I herded Caraboa (water buffalo) and in that way was able to get out of camp, contact the underground brought in medicine, food and money to sick POWs. Many were beheaded for this type of aid. I wasn't, my decision was to wreck the enemy in any way I could, the way to do it in the mines get a job that had to do with dynamite, so Jack Ritter, a Marine, and I because the dynamiters, we caused fake blasts, tore up track, drilled into underground waters and rivers, flooding laterals! <u>The war continues even if I am a prisoner of war, I will carry on the fight</u>.

The Japanese were brutal at times and simple and childish at others, when I was operated on by Dr. Sarwald, a U.S. doctor who was cutting out some old shrapnel or fragments, and the only anesthesia was someone to hold me down, and the blessed relief of passing out, a Japanese gave me some candy and a cigarette when it was over, and the same man two weeks later clubbed me to the ground on a working party because I couldn't keep up due to my slowly healing wounds. We learned to take beatings in their stride.

The shock of the blow and you don't feel it anymore. Till you started to feel again, but there had been an intermission, you learned to savor the flavor of NOW, and no more.

At the end of WWII 3 of we Marines, 2 Navy men, and 1 soldier, kicked through the walls of Futase city jail in Kyushu and made our way to Kanoye, where the airborne troops were coming in they flew us back to Manila and further to freedom in the good old U.S.A. Convalescence, home, San Diego, San Francisco, Dept of Pacific, then back to Honolulu and the Philippines PX work and courts again in 48-49 in Subic Bay. Back to Hawaii, Lualualie where I was under the command of (then Major) Low.

There I learned troop movements, guard, drill, courts martial, and control of explosives. My past caught up with me there and I developed a skin eruption caused by nerves, so I was sent to Mare Island. Upon discharge from there I went to Camp Pendleton, 1st Service Battalion. Korea was boiling then early 1950, so I volunteered to go over with the 1st Marine Brigade; Colonel Klyme told me that there was one billet open, the Laundry Officer, so I became the Brigade Laundry officer. We had a good crew about 30 men who were qualified, and when the Division joined up with us before Inchon, I took over the rest of the crew and became the 1st Marine Division Laundry Officer. No heroics here, from machine guns to laundry man!

Well the Brigade went to Korea and we were in it from the first dragging the laundry machines around, with any prime mover we could hitch a ride with. MYRANG, TEGU, MASON, INCHON, SOUEL, and finally Hamhung and Hungnam, and winter coming on, water freezing. I took my unit Haggeru-ri, just before the big freeze it worked for a while. My crew finally joined the front line troops there.

Battle.

HMMMBMMRMMBMMRMMMR!!

I was on my way back to Hamhung from Haggeru-ri about 27 November with an empty truck convoy, and we stopped and picked up a woman who was freezing, my lead truck master didn't think we should but we did anyway and got her back to Hamhung. Just after arriving at

Hamhung where the balance of my units were operating, I was requested to go back up again, so 28 November I took off with the words, "there are three road blocks to run before you get to the Headquarters." I had some papers for the Colonel to look over and OK, something about the Inchon Seoul. Well I made it through two of the road blocks and stopped at Colonel Puller's outfit at Koto-Ri or thereabout, and joined a column of Britishers, MP Marines, some Army stragglers, and some ROKs. We got about 5 miles up the road when the Chinese communists blew up one of the trucks just three ahead of my jeep, it spun around in the road and blocked us. Colonel Chidister, USMC Division Supply Officer, came up and said "MAC, it looks like were in a hell of a hole, let's get these vehicles turned around and go back to Koto Ri. We tried but the rear had been hit and confusion, lack of space trapped us. Colonel Chidister was hit soon after that as was Major Eagan. My decision had to be this: to either crawl away from the little Custer's last stand, or stay and fight, I decided to stay. My carbine was good, I had ammunition and hoped that we'd be able to fight our way out of the mess, it started to get dark and the light of the burning vehicles made sitting ducks out of us. Probably about 30 or 40 people, I don't know the count.

I remembered boot camp when Jimmie Brandt, the DI, told us you'll get a chance to fight, don't run stay there and fight; the other guy is as scared as you are. So this laundry boy dug in to the frozen ground! The battle lasted all night; I knew when dawn approached that capture was coming for the few who

241

were left fighting. I remembered Bilibid Prison, the death march, beatings, beheadings, so I made another decision.

Stand up and fire off hand, I did, you know those curved clips which hold about 30 rounds, I had two taped together almost a TSMG, so I called out "wonbadusa" (son of a turtle) to the Chinese. The picture you all have seen many times, men dying, screaming white phosphorous burning, ice and snow and frozen blood, dawn came, we were surrendered, I wasn't even hit, just had holes in my clothes from bullets. Man proposes and God disposes. The enemy spoke English. Well here I was a prisoner again, and my spirit was low but I remembered there is always a tomorrow. The training in my past and the experience of one camp helped me!

Code. <u>I AM PREPARED TO GIVE MY LIFE FOR MY COUNTRY, I WILL NEVER SURRENDER OF MY OWN FREE WILL</u>.

I never accepted that anyone else surrendered the group or that I was a part of the group, it was just a drifting into the capture. All at once you are captured, wounded, dead, or escape, the line is a fine one at this time. Life or death!

The captured group were the remnants of some ROKs, a few Britishers, Colonel Chidister, Colonel Eagan, USMC, both badly wounded, presumed to have died a few days after, Colonel McLaughlin, Reid, Llyod (USMC), Noel (AP Correspondent). I told the group around me to gather anything that they could as what you got from now on was scrounged. Things began to take on significance, like a small pack of salt, canned meat, a pack of cigarettes, these were all that you had and would have until some better day in the distant future. Precious commodities. I remember a small tin of jelly saved for one year we were going to open it for Christmas and during a search a communist took it saying it was a bomb, yes, a jelly bomb!

We were marched off after the usual shake down, to a place called the 14 day place, interrogated, told to write home and the letters were thrown back at us two days later because they hadn't said the truth, "the truth we found out was something of a propaganda value to give them a chance to publish what an American prisoner had said. We had to start caging.

CODE

I will continue to resist with all means available. I will make every means to escape. I will never accept neither parole nor special favors.

We were marched 30 to 40 miles a day through the mountain regions to the Yalu River area close to Manchuria 26 December 1950 we arrived at the camp. From then on it was daily indoctrination of Communist propaganda from about three or four months trying to break into our minds, to accept their doctrine. I remember the Sergeant who had been the truck master on the trip back to Hamhung, the frozen woman and who mentioned it to me while we were in a large building icy cold, he said, "You know gunner I respected you for your decision way back then, what do we do now, is any of this stuff they are telling us any good?" I told him it was junk and to disregard, he was lucky and broke out of camp a few months later and got back with another group who came out in early 1951.

We POWs had learned by now that a chance word dropped around the interrogators got a working over and parts would be put into print with your name on it. The best thing was to be dumb as long as you could be and take it. The indoctrination was in Chinese and then translated into English. So if a harangue lasted for five hours in Chinese, it took about the same time to translate, it multiply this by a dirt floor bitter cold, lice, and guards who would poke you with a bayonet to listen made the time a bad one. And it was so idiotic, they would tell us about America as though we hadn't come from there, that we didn't have the things which our wallet pictures showed, "Dirty Pictures Wong" (got his name from looking for nudes in our wallets) used to try to tell us that we didn't have anything in America and I think the dope believed it. He was a brutal man and would kick at the slightest provocation. Our rooms were small 10X10X10 approximately 15 men at a time, lice, rats, and general filth prevailed, no baths for a solid year-no shaves, no tooth brush, just animal existence, food in a large bowl in the middle of the floor, one of the boys, black Jack Caldwell, said we were gentlemen the first year we ate with our hats off, someone else said, "yeah, Black Jack! We ate out of our hats!" And that was the way you would do, just scrape some of the gruel into your hat and sop it up with your fingers. I fashioned some chopsticks later on we used them then. Later it got better at another camp. The big cry was space, man needs air, water, food, and space, you can drive him crazy with too little space for his body, take a baby in your hands and hold it's arms and feet so that it can't move and you'll have a screaming idiot in a few minutes, we lived like that for days, months, each man came to hate the man pressing on his side. Then the political indoctrination, the gutted candle light the pressure of the bodies, loud speakers sending in thoughts, thoughts, and sometimes in the middle of the night when you'd slip into an exhausted slumber, music would come into the speaker and list for the balance of the night, got to the point when you'd say, "it the music on?" We began to suspect each other as a man would come back into camp smoking a cigarette, or eating something you could hear him in the dark, wondering if he'd been an informer. Do a good act or help your fellow man! And then the exact opposite would make a believer of you again. Like when Colonel McLaughlin swiped an apple from the Chinese and split it 15 ways in the dark, used my knife, which I kept hidden from my escape, if ever. Germ warfare came into being as a word; we saw pictures of President Truman with a Brigade of rats lined up with germs to invade the peasants. Ridiculous things of this nature kept the humor of the thing for us. Slogans banners, "Down with the Wall Street aggressors" and life became a misshape and horrible thing, lice running over your collar, Pellagra sores, swellings in the joints, then a promise of food, you could even smell it good food, if you'd be a turn coat, an informer, "say something about your country". Yes, this was indeed a new kind of enemy!

We fought them with the knowledge that we had trying to argue on points, but argument against a well
fed, well rested and unstressed individual was not so
easy, when you just climbed out of an ice chamber or
lice straw bed with one meal a day of soggy rice and
fish heads, it's a different kind of man unless he has
his own CODE!

At first many men were dupes but as time wore on and
the senior officers began to gather their own around
them, we set up our resistance, or escape plans, then
we had a new enemy, informers! You didn't know which
way to turn; someone had been broken and made to
talk. Many an escape plot was nipped in the bud; some
made it out of camp but never got far, Bob Gilette,
Marine aviator, stayed away for three weeks and came
or was brought back after a run in with some bears in
China. The Chinese knew so much about us that they
would tell it to us over the loud speaker. We organized hell week to harass, calling out in the night,
"this is cell block 1, where in hell is #2", then
back and forth the guards would scream out at us,
then we'd change rooms, and the assigned indoctrina-
tor would come into his room and his men wouldn't be
there, he'd run out for advice and then we'd change
back again. It sounds like kid stuff, but the harassment kept them occupied.

CODE:

If I become a POW I will keep faith with fellow POWs,
an informer was the worst of the lot, and they were
continuously trying for new informers by fear and

246

punishment. How? Well, the hole was one method, 12 span by 12 spans by 12 spans of my hand was the measurement. I took when it cams my time in the hole, it was filled with rats, feces, urine, and pounding on the outside to deafen you, it was dark and miserable, when they tried it on me I decided that it was time to die before I could be broken, and I made up my mind that I'd die first so when they finally took me out and thought I was softened up they wanted me to be an informer, as many men were in my confidence and I was trusted, so I told them I'd die first. They dumped me back in, and then released me, you couldn't figure them out. Some men broke in that hole, another one of the holes was a circular one where you were cramped down with an iron lid on top with a hole in the middle they pissed in that hole for a week. A man in there wasn't in too good shape when he came out. One cracked up and died another well he told us to watch him.

CODE:

If I am senior I will take command:

Gentlemen this is a thing to reflect upon as the minute you showed a force of character you were taken away, cleverly it has to be done and more clever than the enemy. One Major was hanged by his arms which were tied up his back behind him, feet tied with a rope pulled around his neck so when he tried to ease the pain on the arms he choked himself. He was finished this was by plain torture; just a threat in the future broke him into a slobbering mess.

There were men in our camps, Colonel Gay Thrash, USMC, Col McLaughlin who spent more time in solitary than any other way in POW camp, they had us Marines in line, and we sang the Marine hymn weekly and God Bless America too!

I was the Adjutant, advisor, confessor, poet and got all the brains to start up a study group in camp. We had Spanish, German, French, math all the way to spherical trig, Trig, Turkish, History, Public Speaking, that was Col Mac's job, and when the communists were trying to feed us dialectical materialism which we titled diabolical materialism we were attending our own little university at Pyockdong Ni. Major Gerry Fink, USMC, Bob Howell, Captain, AUS, Rotor head Thornton, USN made up a crazy week and every one had to do the thing that he'd done as a civilian acting it out, no speaking we went around for a week like that "rotor head" hung up a rat on the fence with a handkerchief parachute and we all point to the germ warfare. We contaminated their drinking water, guess how? Pulled up all their vegetables and put the tops back in again, the next morning when they were pulling the garden the tops started coming loose in their hands, and "rotor head" sat on a rain barrel saying "what's up doc?" The gardener went crazy. We dug a hole to bury ourselves in they said then they buried vegetables. Our diet consisted mainly of a little vegetable, rice or Kaolang, or potatoes, never all together, a little bit of salt, and the squeal of the pig.

<u>CODE</u>:

I am bound to give only name, rank, service and date of birth!

We had to fill out life history blanks and if you did then it was checked later, most everyone did, some for us fought it for a while but when the man kneeled you down with a pistol at the back of your head you changed your mind. We made mistakes, too much information about yourself on the paper verbal diahorrea, probably slightly cracked up from low protein diet and filth, I don't know, the yard stick is what condition the man was in not whether he was a POW, that is a relative thing what, when, and where and under what conditions? We need a code, many had stood up but could have better stood up with a firm grip on a single thing the code of conduct it would even more a different story. Officers make the code live.

<u>CODE</u>:

I will never forget that I am an American fighting man responsible for my actions.

We were never sent nor were we ever given any kind of a contact by our own or our allies, but I don't think that any man ever forgot that we was an American. Some slipped, the 21 did, they may have been criminal anyway, or just uninformed kids in the hands of a clever enemy.

<u>CODE</u>:

I will trust in my God and my fellow man.

We prayed nightly aloud and when the good Father Kapaun died Major Mac kept up the our Father, which art in heaven, then other took it up Jerry Fink carved a cross which was brought back from camp.

Now what can we do! What can we do about it, we can take heed from what happened, we can remember that an educated man is an armed man, we have a code, and we need to give it some meaning other than words on a bulletin board with the menu for the day or the theater program. We need to assist the teachers of America to impart the knowledge of freedom under our constitution.

FOR LIFE, LIBERTY AND THE PURSUIT OF HAPPINESS. END.

SECOND DENTAL COMPANY FLEET MARINE FORCES

CAMP LE JEUNE, N.C. 15 FEB 60

1800 Monday 15 February, 60 "No Host" Cocktail and
Dinner

Party of all dental officers and their wives at the
Commissioned Officer's mess Paradise Point (River
Room)

Topic

"Twice I was born and twice I have Died"

Survival as a POW of the Japanese and also Korean
Communist Chinese PW

"This Is Your Life" film 25 minutes

Brief introduction   C.W.O. McCool

Talk: Competition of Ralph Edwards show

The movie you have just seen was unrehearsed by me
and when I walked out on that stage I felt like the
little boy who described his appendectomy operation
like this: "They told me it wouldn't hurt and then
they stuck a needle in my arm and I disappeared." I
wanted to disappear, then I remembered that my wife
Marion would be there and everything would be O.K.
because all through those black years of prison camp
I could remember her, back there somewhere…waiting.

But let's go back to the men on the show: Navy, Marines and Army. How did I meet all those wonderful people? Each had a story of his own. Col. Mack, Curly Reid, Allen Lloyd met in a last ditch stand between Koto-ri and Hageru-ri, Frozen Chosen wastes. Too far into enemy territory, surrounded, fought all night, out of ammo, dead and wounded. A man had to make a decision: Captivity—it was made!

Another Officer, Doctor Anderson, stayed back when his outfit pulled out. He deliberately stayed to care for his wounded.

Jimmie Tighe, Marine, a sergeant of the Philippine Scouts, on Corregidor had gone to China to keep books for Col Sam Howards-4th Marines.

Civilian, Miss Utenski, a civilian who helped all PWs in Japanese Prison Camp and last but not least Lt. Commander John Thornton, stout fellow! Helicopter pilot, Korea. "Rotor Head" 40 miles behind enemy lines to help a man who was shot down, and then he was shot down himself.

I was with both groups, the first on Corregidor. "Twice I was born, twice I have died." My first death, prison camp Bilibid, Lipa, Cabanatuan, Coal Mines, then freedom a few years later penetrating through 3 road blocks, got through the first two and surrounded in 3rd. There I met Col Mack, Reid and Allen Lloyd. A sort of bridge to San Luis Rey! My second death in Prison Camp! All at 1 common meeting point one thing captivity.

What is a camp like? (Tell #5 and Cabanatuan)

Moments of Truth: Barbed wire, hell hole Korea

When man is faced with the utter desolation of the truth: of captivity, starvation, brutality and last, the horror of the Communist ideology. During the moment of truth all your faith, training, discipline, background, carry you through or you collapse into a wretched animal.

Twice I was born, twice died

On Corregidor when all men in my machine gun section, dead and with my broken ear drums and shrapnel cuts, I knelt in the middle of the road, waiting for death and shells burst all around but not for me and I realized that life can be death when there is no relief or your brain burst with concussion into a terror of sound and exploding light.

OR 2nd time

On a Frozen waste where spouting blood of wounded men freezes on their garments making a bright red shield and they freeze in the position they were hit (wax museum). God gives us courage to carry on with, then:

But you live each second,

Minute,

Hour,

Day,

Week,

Month

Year,

Into an eternity!

In a cell block, then a man goes back in memory

Remembering back the little things of life. "Remembering sounds"

An opening screen door, the sound of the refrigerator, a beer can's spew, the soft sound of your mother's voice under a lighted door—All's well!

One boy in PW Camp said his mother always quoted this one, "The joy of motherhood is what women experience when all the children are in bed."

A remembered kiss. And the man sitting, in squalor, filthy with lice, unwashed, unshaven, hungry, minds probed by daily interrogation on dialectical materialism of Communism.

What was the difference in treatment in each camp?

Japanese PW with Communist PW:

JAP: Brutal

COMMUNIST: Brutal ideology, lack of thought freedom which we have-Constitution

On stark starving brutality a man's eyes gouged out of his head, heads rolling, clubs descending on bared backs, agony of labor coal mines, black pit of depression, chattering bits of steel into a vein of coal. Men's bodies weighing 100 lbs., 120 lbs. torn, emaciated, sores and a prayer for quick death, self-injury.

Pain, tooth aches, men searching for silver or gold scraps to give a dentist who had for his tools a pair of pliers and his lecture on oral hygiene, like this; "Take the outer bark off of a tree, skin back the cambium layer, cut into strips, chew daily and massage gums and teeth with the residual. And a man would laugh remembering tooth brushes, paste, and the very nice dentist who put that needle into your jaw before he worked and you disappeared like the little boy who described his appendectomy. No pain there but in PW camp pain-yes.

Yes, man looks, looks and searches for the hidden truth which makes for the hidden truth which makes him WILL to survive because at these times your will and God's help are the only reason for survival and where does the will come from? IT comes from memories of that person waiting. The good you know exists in man, and while you munch on a piece of dried corn kernel, yes, kernel, because you learn to make each kernel, each morsel of food saturates and grind into a paste which loses nothing in digestion. You learn that while eating a handful of grass or dry millet seed, grasshoppers, snails, the memory of a martini and steak with a piece of cake stuck somewhere in your conscience mind that all the good comes to you.

Incidentally toasted grasshoppers and boiled black snake are good too!

Black Joe Caldwell's men were gentlemen, ate with hats off. Hea, yeah, we ate out of hats. Pig trough, Christmas, Allen Lloyd and I, bucket, pig.

Humor: Rotor Head Thornton demanded an egg. When he had dysentery, big hullabaloo, his logic was irrefutable, "You say the little man is of the masses, well I'm a little man and I want an egg. You eat eggs. You are the masses. Why didn't I have one. Next day he had an egg!

We drove a few of them crazy with the work details.

WE WORKED ON A GARDEN then weren't going to be given any of the vegetables. So we sneaked out at night. Pulled the turnips and took their tops off—MAKE TEARING OFF GESTURE—put them back into the ground—and when cook came with the guard to pull up veg-etables we'd be sitting on the porch of the hut and rotor head chomping would say, "WHAT'S UP, DOC? HE HE WHATS UP?"

Cook took a flip and went crazy and the guard begins to stir us all up with a bayonet calling out

"Wombazuza, Woed Butze doy." Meaning, you animals, I don't understand you, and then he went nuts later on that day we saw them carrying the cook down the path in a strait jacket still yelling and hollering out.

At night we'd yell out between the cell block rooms where we slept about thirty to a room, "THIS IS CELL BLOCK NUMBER 10 WHERE IN HELL IS 2, then Two WOULD CRY OUT THIS IS CELL BLOCK #2 where is in HELL IS EIGHT? AND THE GUARDS WOULD BE RUNNING UP AND DOWN THE CORRIDOR GIBBEING IN CHINESE TO TRY AND SHUT US UP.

We were allowed to sit and talk together so we devised a study system.

Any man who had a degree and some who didn't but had specific knowledge about anything would set up lesson plans and then teach a little group, I learned to speak, read and write Spanish and many times in the communist class rooms when they would be lecturing on dialectical materialism I'd be giving out Spanish verbs to Hector Cordero, a Captain from San Juan, a fellow POW. It worked the commies thought we were deep in Marx, and we'd be declining the verb Quiero, Yo te Quiero mucho o' digan acerca la muhera, besa me mucho, OR SOMETHING LIKE THAT—

ESCAPES WERE NIPPED IN THE BUD IN THE commie camps mainly because of the informer system they had pretty good knowledge of our group attempts, some men escaped singularly, but were caught and brought back.

In Japanese camp they killed ten men if one escaped, this was a deterrent. I got out of the Jap camp at the last and backed a train into Kacukoka, then a group of us took a truck into Kanoya to meet the first airborne troops coming in after the cease fire. All of this has pointed for a definite need, that of a code, a way to go, some men are well oriented in all situations others are not, it depends on the background, but we have laws all over the land and man is used to law, and here you are in a camp, where rank has gone in the first insulting blow in the face of a Captain or senior man, and all become the same lice eaten, dirty hungry prisoner, then a man needs a way, a direction, and we can't keep putting our heads in the sand, becoming a PW is a possibility of any man who is close to the front line just as in death or injury it is a casualty of war. SO THIS CODE WAS DEVISED: IT IS CALLED THE CODE OF CONDUCT, AND I HOPE THAT YOU NEVER HAVE TO USE IT IN THE CONDITIONS THAT I HAVE BUT IT EXISTS AND IT IS A WAY TO GO AND GIVES THE MISDIRECTED A GUIDING HAND WHEN THEIR SENSES ARE TAKEN UP IN PLAIN SURVIVAL. Like I said some of us need guidance more than other, we won't go into the way of this now but there are mother's here, have any of you taught your sons how to face death, how to stand up to ridicule, to face hunger, to DIE LIKE A MAN and not be a sodden little TURN COAT? IT REALLY ISN'T NECESSARY, JUST LOVE THEM GUIDE THEM IN HONESTY, INTEGRITY, AND TELL THEM ABOUT THIS WONDERFUL COUNTRY OF OURS. HISTORY. Reminds me of this joke: KID CRYING, MAN: "WHAT'S THE TROUBLE SONNY?" AMONG SOBS, LITTLE BOY ANSWERS "MY MOTHER LOST HER PSYCHOLGY BOOK AND SHE'S USING HER OWN JUDGEMENT NOW? OWW OWW OHH!

LET'S INSPECT THIS CODE OF CONDUT FOR FIGHTING MEN.

—HERE HOLD THE RED BOOK "CODE OF CONDUCT" UP IN RIGHT HAND

—-this book tells it in brief.

    I.   I am an American fighting man, to guard the USA

    II. Never surrender while a means to resist is there

    III.Continue to resist the enemy in different ways if captured

    IV. Keep faith with fellow POW

       —Here tell in brief about the incident in the hole—

    V.   To give only name rank and serial number

They have many methods to extract information from you, casual questions about your fellow pow, the letter home where you show your anxieties, over your wife, son, daughter, home etc.

Perhaps in this final summation I can say here is the time for a man to face the final truth the MOMENT OF TRUTH, we all die someday

MAKE IT AN HONORABLE ONE.

VI. Never forget that I am an American fighting man, that I am an American responsible for my actions.

TO TRUST IN GOD AND IN THE UNITED STATES OF AMERICA.

REMEMBER SOCRATES SAID. "There is only one good, namely, knowledge, and one evil, namely ignorance!

THIS IS MY STORY MY DEATH AND REBIRTH AND EACH TIME I TELL IT I DIE A LITTLE.

(Editor's note-Evening of Inspiration was written and published following the previous speech.)

Evening of Inspiration by Ginger Wright

The gentleman who rose to talk was no Adonis, he looked like what he is, an officer in the Marine Corps of middle age, even features and military bearing. When he talked he used neither grandiose language nor grandiloquent gestures; his was a not the trained voce of an orator. Moments after he began to speak, however, his audience of over a hundred were spellbound; as one lady said, "Not only was there no fidgeting, reaching for a cigarette or coughing, but one realized later that one had even been holding the head in an almost frozen position, so great was the interest and concentration on the words he was saying."

THIS IS YOUR LIFE

The occasion was the dinner meeting of the 2nd Dental Co., Monday, February 15, in the River Room of the Paradise Point club. In addition to the Naval Dentists and their wives, invited guests of the evening included Maj General and Mrs. J.P. Berkeley; Brig General and Mrs. O.M. Conoley; and dentists and their wives from the surrounding areas. After a social hour around the fireplace in the River Room, a delicious buffet was served featuring chicken curry, with accompanying conditions, and chocolate éclairs. The guests were seated at beautifully appointed tables; green cloths with delicate pink satin runners, accented the stunning roseate arrangements of spring flowers. Following the dinner, Capt (USN) H. McInurff, CO, of the 2nd Dental Co. welcomed General Berkeley and the other guests. Gen. Berkeley's reply was most appropriate when he said, "In a group like this, I don't dare open my mouth—". And briefly told the group how delighted he was to be there. Capt McInturff then called on Capt (USN) R.F. Huebsch, who was in charge of the arrangements for the evening, who introduced CWO McCool. Mr. McCool has the distinction of being a prisoner of war longer than any other living American. Before the talk, a film of the TV show, "This is Your Life," was shown from when Mr. McCool was the 'star' last April. This furnished a visual background for his speech which followed.

YEARS IN PRISON

CWO McCool, then a Sgt. In the Marine Corps, was captured by the Japanese on Corregidor in the opening days of World War II; he was part of the infamous Death March, and spent four torturous years in Japanese prison camps. Again, when fighting broke out in Korea, he was with the Marines, was captured by the Chinese Communists in Northern Korea, and spent two and a half years in prison camps in China. Any talk on such dramatic experiences would undoubtedly hold the attention of an audience, but the talk of Mr. McCool deeper than that. He not only painted vivid word-pictures of humor, pathos and tragedy, but the feeling was general that here was a man of overwhelming personal courage, and a message of far reaching impact. Over and over again, Mr. McCool emphasized the importance of strong religious faith, a well-adjusted home life, and adequate education in the importance of our own history and government. To him the Code of Conduct, or Ethics, is all important, not only for the military, but for every American. "Many of the boys who capitulated to the Japanese or Communists," he said, "did so because they didn't know what they believed in." He went on to say that where the Japanese captors were more cruel in their treatment of prisoners, it was the insidious tactics of 'reasoning' that the Communists used that were actually more difficult to bear.

"ROTOR-HEAD"

One of the warmest incidents he related concerned one "Rotor-head" Thornton, a Navy flier who attempted a daring rescue by helicopter, and was shot down and imprisoned. "Rotor-head" (so called not only because he was a helicopter pilot, but also because his head gear all during his time in prison camp was a 'beanie' with a propeller he'd found somewhere) brought to the prisoners that all-important characteristic, a genuine and courageous sense of humor. When starving men, with bodies racked by disease are still able to laugh at ridiculous situations, there is still something to live for. "Rotor-head" provided this laughter, and by it often saved the crumbling morale and confounded his captors…

CWO McCool also told of the way the men shared with one another, not only their scraps of food, but also their intellect. Not having any reading material (except the Communist propaganda), those that knew language taught language; those with historical or mathematical backgrounds gave instructions in those subjects.

MAN OF STEEL

The talk, which was scheduled to last for thirty or forty minutes, was continued by the importuning of the audience, and the many questions asked by member of the audience. One remark, which seemed to voice the opinion of all who were there was, "It was the most interesting and inspiring evening I've had for a long long time, the talk was not only informative, but there was a message there for everyone. I consider it a privilege to have heard Mr. McCool—who is truly a man of steel."

BASIC SCHOOL

JNM:vk

MARINE CORPS SCHOOLS

08733

QUANTICO, VIRGINIA

7 Jan 1954

From: Lieutenant Colonel John N. McLaughlin 18433/
      0302/0130/0306 USMC

To: Commandant of the Marine Corps

Via: Commissioned Warrant Officer Felix J. McCool
049274 USMC

Subj: Report on period of captivity, case of
      Commissioned Warrant Officer Felix J. McCool
      049274,

      USMC

Ref: CMC ltr, DF-1828-1s-35, of 18 Nov 1953

   1. Commissioned Warrant Officer McCool was captured
      0530, 30 November 1950 near Koto-ri, North
      Korea.

2. I was with Commissioned Warrant Officer McCool for the major portion of his approximately thirty-three months of captivity.

3. During a long march through snow covered mountains from the place of capture to the vicinity of Kanggye in the winter of 1950-1951, Commissioned Warrant Officer McCool conducted himself in a soldierly manner and was an example to the less experienced United Nations personnel associated with him. He assisted men in weaker physical condition.

4. Possessed of outstanding loyalty to the U.S. Marine Corps and to his country, Commissioned Warrant Officer McCool exhibited throughout his captivity a strong personal animosity toward Communism and to the efforts of his captors to sway his allegiance to his country. To my personal knowledge he strongly resented and rebuffed attempts to get military information from him. He eagerly and enthusiastically supported attempts to oppose and abolish the indoctrination program of the camp authorities.

5. It is my opinion that Commissioned Warrant Officer McCool is a man of strong moral character and that his actions reflected favorably on the service of which he is a member.

JOHN N. MC LAUGHLIN

MARINE INSTRUMENT TRAINING SQUADRON 10

MARINE TRAINING GROUP 10

Aircraft, Fleet Marine Force, Pacific

Marine Corps Air Station

El Toro (Santa Ana), California   11
Feb 1954

From: Major Gerald (n) Fink 023889/7302 USMCR

To: Commandant of the Marine Corps

Subj: Fitness report in the case of Commissioned
Warrant Officer Felix J. McCool 049274 USMC

Ref: (a) CMC ltr DF-1828-ls of 18 Nov 1953

1. This is a narrative in the nature of a fitness
report on the above mentioned officer while confined as a prisoner of war. This narrative is
addenda to any other fitness reports of senior
Marine officers at Camp 2. The report covered in
this narrative is from October 1952 to August
1953 as observed.

2. It is this officer's privilege to submit this
report on Commissioned Warrant Officer Felix J.
McCool for the aforementioned period. Gunner

McCool in the face of the enemy while a prisoner of was outstanding in his conduct, his loyalty, and appearance during the period observed. Despite infirmities and disabilities arising from his imprisonment and due to the early treatment in the hands of the Chinese, Gunner McCool exhibited a coolness and conduct I have come to expect of all Marines. He steadfastly resisted all communist efforts to propagandize him and to cause him to turn his loyalty. His experience as a prisoner of war of the Japanese and his ability to confront the problems that faced him in Camp 2 were very outstanding. We relied on Gunner McCool's judgment and cool head when many problems arose in camp. He served in an unofficial capacity as our Adjutant. He busied himself in camp by furthering his professional knowledge. He studied mathematics, psychology, humanities, history of music, chemistry and advanced mathematical theories from those people in camp who were professional. In doing so he kept his mind active and kept his own morale and that of the officers who taught him in a high state. He was always the Marine. Whenever our group assembled to sing The Star Spangled Banner and The Marine Corps Hymn, Gunner McCool's voice was raised the highest. These were forbidden songs by the Chinese.

3. He was subjected to solitary confinement by the Chinese for his so-called "hostile attitude". It was his job in many cases to bolster the morale of the so-called "weaker sisters" that

were there in Camp 2. Gunner McCool, because of
his steadfastness and his military bearing was
an extremely valuable man in camp. I would be
proud to have Gunner McCool in my organization.
I would be proud to serve alongside him. I am
proud that he is a Marine.

Gerald Fink

ANNEX – 3

JAPAN/WW II

This annex contains reports and affidavits about Felix's time during World War II. They include a summary of a letter home from Shanghai, China and an article published in the Saturday Evening Post.

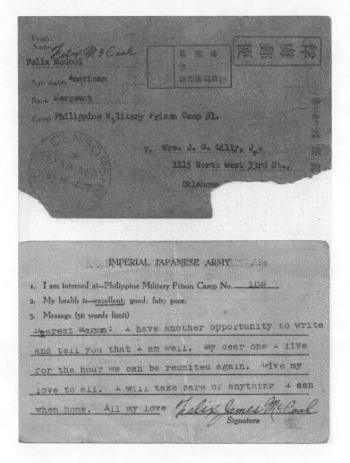

*"Felix with James Tye and Margaret Utinsky. Miss Utinsky (Miss U)
helped run the underground in the Philippines during World War II."*

AFFIDAVIT OF FELIX JAMES McCOOL

Sergeant, United States Marine Corps

Serial Number 242-450

STATE OF CALIFORNIA

COUNTY OF LOS ANGELES

FELIX JAMES MC COOL, FIRST BEING DULY SWORN ON HIS OATH, DEPOSES AND SAYS:

On board the ISHI MARU, which took me to Japan, there were nine hundred fifty (950) prisoners crammed into the hold amidships. We were jammed in like cord-wood and we couldn't sleep or sit comfortably. There were no toilet facilities, and men got sick and lay in their own filth. There wasn't anything else to do. The Nips sent down a bucket on a rope through the hatch. It was lowered by one of the prisoners from topside. This bucket was used as a toilet. When it was full it was hoisted aloft but before it could reach the deck the Nip guard would lunge with naked bayonet at the prisoner holding the rope causing the man to flinch and the bucket would jerk and spill the contents all over the men down below.

Water was lowered once a day in a bucket. This water was not fresh. It was kept in old rice barrels which had been left in the sun, and the water was putrid and stinking. Usually the Nips pulled the same stunt on the prisoner who was lowering the water pail as they did on the man lowering the slop bucket. It took a man with steel nerves not to flinch when a Nip jabbed at his belly with a bayonet. As a result, the water was usually spilled and we went without. The Nips said it was our daily ration and if we spilled it, it was our own fault. It was just plain hell in the hold of that ship.

The Japanese whom we held mainly responsible for our misery was a Taiwanese guard known as an ITO HAY — we called him "The Snake". He had been in charge of our detail in CABANATUAN and had been very cruel on the island. His favorite punishment for the slightest offense was to place a man with his bare hands and feet in an ant heap. "The Snake" was about five feet on inch (5'1") in height and weighed between one hundred thirty-five (135) and one hundred forty (140) pounds. He did not speak English. He was an energetic guy, but he was an excellent soldier and was very neat in his appearance. He liked to eat snakes, and whenever a prisoner caught one in the field and gave it to him, he would allow the prisoner to rest an hour or so. He made the men work in a bent-over position for six hours at a stretch, and if a man straightened up a guard beat him with a big club. During the so-called "rest periods" the men were forced to do gymnastic exercises with their digging tools.

AFFIDAVIT OF FELIX JAMES McCOOL

Sergeant, United States Marine Corps

Serial Number 242-450

STATE OF CALIFORNIA

COUNTY OF LOS ANGELES

FELIX JAMES MC COOL, FIRST BEING DULY SWORN ON HIS OATH, DEPOSES AND SAYS:

At Cabanatuan Camp No. 1 one evening in the later part of 1942, a big, tall kid who worked on the farm detail went AWOL from the working party and remained behind to pick up a small pumpkin to eat. The Nips noticed his absence when we fell in for roll call as we were about to leave the field. We knew he was absent, but didn't say anything. Then we saw the Nip guards fanning out in a large circle, pretending to be very busy doing something else. Finally they closed in on the kid and we didn't see him anymore. We were too far off at the other side of the field to see what happened, but all of us saw his body the next day. The Nips had used him for bayonet practice. One eye had been gouged out, his throat had been slit, and his body was slashed up and down. The corpse was laid out in the carabao corral for a whole day and all the prisoners had to walk by and see it.

It was supposed to be a lesson to us not to steal or try to escape.

This killing occurred in a plot close to the Navy and Marine group, away from the main road and about one and a half (1 ½) blocks from the rear of the camp. I didn't know the boy, or where he was from. I did see his body in the carabao corral.

AFFIDAVIT OF FELIX JAMES MC COOL

Sergeant, United States Marine Corps

Serial Number 242-450

STATE OF CALIFORNIA

COUNTY OF LOS ANGELES

FELIX JAMES MC COOL, FIRST BEING DULY SWORN ON HIS OATH, DEPOSES AND SAYS;

In Japan I was beaten nearly every day for some infraction of the rules. As you probably know, a rice diet causes weak kidneys and all of us were afflicted in this way. They had a tag system for us when we left our bunks at night to go to the head. As we left the room, we were supposed to take the tag with our number on it and transfer it from a nail on one side of the room to an "out" nail on the other side. One night I was in such a hurry to get to the head that I failed to put my tag on the nail and laid it on the window sill. When I returned, a small Nip by the name of SUGI, a doctor's helper (called an Ishi hay) was waiting for me. He asked me why I hadn't placed my tag on the nail — I explained I was in a hurry. He just smiled and slashed me across the face with a riding crop. Then he got a jiu-jitsu hold on me and slammed me against the wall. In so doing, I pulled a muscle on my back. After I was down he stamped on my stomach. This injury was very painful, but I was forced to work just the same.

In October, 1944, my foot was broken by a cave-in in the HONKO MINE. I was a driller and had to drill holes for the dynamite. Usually, we waited sometime after an explosion to allow the loose chunks to flake off before we returned to work. On this occasion, a civilian Jap miner, by the name off ISHIDA, forced me back into the galley before the yellow powder fumes had cleared away. The ceiling was still flaking and a big chunk fell on my left foot and crushed my toes. I had to walk out of the mine as best I could and a Nip guard we called "Bluebeard" made me run. Then I had to walk back to camp, which was on a hill about three city-blocks distant from the mine. When I reached the camp the guards made me stand at attention, and pressed on my foot to torture me. SUGI came up and stamped on my foot and then made me stand at at-tention. The Nip doctor, by the name of SUENAGA, wouldn't allow my foot to be bandaged, but that night a Navy corpsman in camp put a makeshift splint on it and bound my foot with a piece of mosquito netting.

Dr. SUENAGA was a civilian doctor employed by the coal company. He was a slight man with a light com-plexion and a small black mustache. He spoke some English and was always smiling. He claimed my foot was not broken and sent me back to work. I had some old shrapnel wounds on my left shoulder which had never healed well, as well as a number of deep, raw ulcers on my back. The doctor delighted in poking these open wounds with his finger and then asking me in Japanese if it hurt. If my face showed the slightest reaction to the pain he pushed his finger in deeper and harder — I think he was a sadist in this respect. He showed me a list of medicines, bandages, etc. which he had supposedly issued to me, but in reality I never received any of the things on the list. It was just a damned lie, and he was covering up. He wasn't a good doctor, and as far as I know he gave all of the prisoners the same, poor treatment. The only prisoners who received any deference at all were those who were demented. The Nips marked such men with a black cross and gave them good treatment. One of our men working in the coal mine pretended to go crazy. He went through the motions of catching fish and the guards sent him out. Doctor SUENAGA made a pet of him. Every day he would ask this man how many fish he had caught, and the prisoner would describe in pantomime the big ones he had caught. The doctor tried to catch this man off-guard to see if he was pretending. He would rush up and flash a light in the prisoner's eyes, but the prisoner just gave him a blank stare and went on fishing. After the war ended the prisoner recovered his sanity in a hurry, much to Doctor SUENAGA's mystification. At the end of the war Dr. SUENAGA brought an old phonograph and some records into the sick bay and played them for the boys by the hour. I guess he hoped to make us forget the mean things he had done. We finally told an officer in charge that they had better keep the doctor out of the hospital or something might happen to him.

279

One of the lowest type Nip guards at the camp in FUKUOKA was called "Joto Nye". He was about five feet three inches (5' 3") tall and weighed about one hundred fifty (150) pounds. His eyes slanted more obliquely than any Nip I ever saw, and the eyeballs were a peculiar greenish-yellow. He had been an athlete - a track man and I believe he lived in FUTASI CITY. "Joto Nye" beat the prisoners at the slightest provocation or would knee a man in the groin. He would hammer a man over the kidneys or beat in a prisoner's face with a wooden sandal. As soon as the war was over "Joto Nye" left camp almost immediately; so did some of the other guards. They knew we'd probably kill some of them. In fact, several of our boys left the camp in search of ''Nye" and some of the meaner guards. If they had found them they would have killed them.

FJM

AFFIDAVIT OF FELIX JAMES MC COOL

SERGEANT, UNITED STATES MARINE CORPS

SERIAL NUMBER 242-450

STATE OF CALIFORNIA

COUNTY OF LOS ANGELES

FELIX JAMES MC COOL, FIRST BEING SWORN ON HIS OATH, DEPOSES AND SAYS;

EXECUTIONS

In CAMP CABANATUAN NO. 3, I witnessed the torture and execution of four United States Army men who were caught trying to buy food from the Filipinos. These men had Filipino pesos on them when detected by the Nips. This was early in November, 1942, about three or four days after my arrival. At first the Nips made the men kneel in the sun for forty-eight hours without water. The prisoners were bound with their hands behind their backs and a noose around their necks. This torture was so severe that the men begged to be killed. The man responsible for this was a Colonel MORI, in command of CAMP NO. 3, CABANATUAN. I stood about five feet from those men when they were kneeling in the sun. These men were in Group No. 2; I was on a wood-chopping detail near the galley in Group No. 2 and was forced by the Japs to witness the torture.

The men were dragged through the camp on ropes — a rope was tied to each arm and the Nips took the free ends of the ropes and held them taut so that the men hung from the ropes. They were so exhausted they couldn't stand. Their heads rolled from side to side and they smiled as they passed us. These prisoners were taken to a spot about two hundred (200) meters distant in the rear of the camp toward the river. This place was on a direct line and even with the galley of Group #2. The shallow graves 18" to 24" deep were previously dug. The Nips then stood these men in the graves and shot them to death with a squad of ten or twelve riflemen. I think they used .27 caliber rifles. After the execution, which we were forced to witness, the graves were filled in and all traces obliterated. One of the victims, a tall red-headed soldier, wasn't killed on the first fire, and he tried to claw his way out of the grave to get at his executioner. He was shot again in the head and fell back into the grave.

Although these graves were unmarked, there another grave nearby which contained the body of a prisoner who had died of disease. This grave was marked by a small, wooden cross and it was about four feet to the left of the four graves of the murdered men, on the side away from the camp, toward the river. In time, the grass grew over the four unmarked graves, and unless the small marked graves could be found there would be no evidence of the other graves visible.

CAMP NO. 3 was in the BONGA BONG Stock Farm district between CABANATUAN and the town of LAUR.

I saw one Filipino woman and four Filipino men killed in about July, 1942. These people were caught by the Japs when the Filipinos tried to pass food through the fence to the American prisoners. I was working near the galley when the Filipinos were dragged into camp at the end of ropes and tied to four upright stakes. The Japanese guards used knives on these people. They were a long time dying. During the torture, the Jap guards laughed at their victims and prolonged their misery by walking into the galley and resting, then returning to their task of mutilating the Filipinos. The men and the woman were stuck repeatedly with knives and bayonets, and the Nips were careful not to drive their knives into the bodies in vital spots. Each time they pierced the flesh two or three inches, the Filipinos would scream. This seemed to give the Nips a lot of pleasure. Finally, they gave each one the death flow and slit their throats. The last I saw of them, the bodies were hanging on the posts.

FJM

AFFIDAVIT OF FELIX JAMES MC COOL

Sergeant, United States Marine Corps

Serial Number 242-450

STATE OF CALIFORNIA

COUNTY OF LOS ANGELES

FELIX JAMES MC COOL, FIRST BEING DULY SWORN ON HIS OATH, DEPOSES AND SAYS:

1. I am thirty-three (33) years old and my permanent home address is 129 Carr Drive, Glendale, California. I am and at all times hereinafter mentioned was a member of the armed forces of the United States and I now am a Sergeant in the United States Marine Corps, Serial Number 242-450.

2. I was taken prisoner on CORREGIDOR 6 May 1942 while serving with the Fourth Marines. I was on CORREGIDOR ISLAND about two weeks after being captured, and was then removed to BILIBID Prison in MANILA where I remained about three days. I was then taken to CABANATUAN CAMP No. 3 also in CAMP No. 1 CABANATUAN, where I stayed for six months. In November, 1942, I was transferred to CAMP LIPA No. 10B in BATANGAS Province where I remained until March, 1943. In this month I was

sent to CAMP MURPHY at ZEBBLIN FIELD just outside MANILA. I was in bad physical condition at this time and I stayed here but a few weeks and was returned once more to BILIBID Prison inside MANILA. I remained in BILIBID a short time and was sent to CABANATUAN Camp No. 1.

In August, 1944, I was shipped on board the Japanese steamer, ISHU MARU, to the Island of KYUSHU where I was placed in Camp No. 10, FUTASI CITY, FUKUOKA District. Later I was one of five prisoners who left this camp on foot at the end of the war, and made my way to KAGOSHIMA and KANOYA where I contacted the Americans.

3.TORTUE - PUNISHMENT

In the camp at LIPA I was put to work with other prisoners building an airfield. Here the prisoners were assigned a certain amount of work to do, and when a prisoner failed to fulfill his daily 'contract' he was punished. I received this punishment every two or three days. It was impossible for me to remove the four to five meters of earth assigned to me with the flimsy galvanized shovels supplied by the Nips. These shovels bent and made digging in the hard ground almost impossible.

The punishment consisted of being forced to kneel upon narrow iron rails which were used in the push-cart railway for removing earth from the airfield. These rails were only an inch or so wide. The Nips placed four-by-four (4 x 4) timbers, or round, bamboo poles about three to four inches in diameter, back of my knees and forced me to kneel upon the iron rails. Sometimes they put a noose around my neck and drew this down my back and tied it to my hands which were tied behind my back. I was made to kneel for three to four hours in this strained position, and if I leaned forward or tried to alter my position, I was strangled by the noose around my neck. Some of the men had to kneel for as long as seven days at a time, being allowed time off only to go to the head. This treatment caused our ankles to swell so badly that we could barely walk. This punishment took place in an enclosure outside the airfield. This place was the 'tinko' ground, or assembly area.

During the day we were allowed only one canteen of water. Often the Nips brought water carts on the field where we were working in the hot sun, and then they would turn on the spigots and let the water run slowly onto the ground in front of us. Sometimes they gave us empty canteens and allowed us to reach the water; then they knocked the canteens out of our hands and splashed the water on the ground in front of us. This water was drawn from a well dug alongside the head, and all the filth drained into the well. As a result we had amoebic dysentery very badly.

We were beaten at the slightest pretext. We were supposed to push the cars on the railway at a dead run; if we slacked up we were beaten. These beatings were done with two by four inch (2"x4") clubs or heavy bamboo sticks which we called "Vitamin Sticks" because they put new energy into us. One specific instance I remember was the terrible beating administered to a Lieutenant WANDEL of the U.S. Army — I don't know his first name or his outfit. He was taken on BATAAN. Later he was put in charge of a fifty-man work detail at CAMP LIPA, 10-B-BATANGAS Province, where we were building a Nip airfield. Lieutenant WANDEL rode across the airfield in the cab of a work truck. He was beaten for this because the Japs said he should have ridden on the rear of the truck. The beating was done by the worst Jap in LIPA camp, an interpreter whom we knew by the name of "Carabao". He was a heavy-set, barrel-chested man about five feet four inches (5'4") in height. We didn't know his Nip name. He was a "Hacho" or squad leader. He was one of the camp guards. He spoke good English, and the scuttlebutt was that he had lived in the United States, but this was never confirmed. "Carabao" ordered Lieutenant WANDEL into a horizontal, push up position and made him hold an absolutely rigid position. Then "Carabao" proceeded to beat the Lieutenant with a bamboo club about four feet (4') long and four inches (4") in diameter. He made the rest of us watch and put guards around us with fixed bayonets to see that we didn't interfere. This beating took place one afternoon in February, 1943. "Carabao" beat the lieutenant for about forty minutes. The bamboo pole broke into shreds and "Carabao" ordered a Nip private to bring another club. This was a thick limb of a tree. To keep Lieutenant WANDEL from sagging, the Nip put a series of sharpened wooden stakes in the ground under Lieutenant WANDEL's belly. The lieutenant's back was beaten to a pulp. The Nip pounded him from the neck to ankles and paused only long enough to wipe the sweat from his face. When the lieutenant finally collapsed, the interpreter hauled off and kicked the lieutenant alongside the head, knocking off his glasses. Lieutenant WANDEL was myopic and had to wear special, thick lensed glasses, and he told me that if he ever lost those glasses he'd be as blind as a bat. This was the worst beating the lieutenant got, but he was beaten many times because the men under him failed to fulfill their work contracts. Lieutenant WANDEL knew we were sick and couldn't do the work laid out for us, but all he said was, "Do your best. I know you can't do all of it — I'll take the licking". I don't know what happened to Lieutenant WANDEL after I left.

Two men by the of STEELE and HOUSE, (I don't know their first names nor to what outfits they belonged) escaped from LIPA CAMP #10-B shortly after we had received our first Red Cross boxes early in January 1943. When the escape was discovered, the rest of us were taken out to the "tinko" field and made to stand in a cold, driving rain, clad only in our breech cloths or shorts for a stretch of four to five hours. Then we were returned to our barracks at about eleven o'clock at night and found

everything turned upside down. The Nip non-coms
had confiscated all of our Red Cross boxes as well
as our "dobe" food; that is what we called the stuff
we were able to get from the Filipinos to help
supplement our camp rations. We were always hungry. The Nips said they took our food to keep anyone else from escaping. The following day the Nip
privates came into our quarters and stole all our
remaining supplies, including our toilet articles,
extra blankets, etc. They even took a small straw
pillow I had. We now had but one blanket apiece,
and we had to huddle together at night to keep
warm. Three or four days after the escape of the
two men, the Nips selected eighteen (18) men from
our contingent and made them kneel on their bare
knees on the graveled ground for seven days and
seven nights. It was cold and rainy and these men
had very little clothes on. Later, these eighteen
men were taken out of camp and they never returned.
We never heard of them after that, and I don't know
definitely what happened to them.

Date of Statement

18 October 1945

FJM

STATE OF CALIFORNIA

COUNTY OF SAN DIEGO

14 September, 1946

AFFIDAVIT OF F. J. MC COOL, Gunnery Sergeant

U.S. Marine Corps Serial No. 242450

I, Felix James McCool, Gunnery Sergeant, U.S. Marine Corps, Serial No. 242450, presently stationed at Marine Corps Base (Base Troops), San Diego 40, California, being first duly sworn upon my oath depose and state:

I believe that I have just claims against the Japanese Government for the following reasons. During the first six month of my captivity by the Japanese Army, the dates being 6 May, 1942 to 6 November, 1942, inclusive, I was not given even the privileges of a prisoner of war at Cabanatuan Camp #3, P.I. the food was not enough to sustain life and I was forced to work with this food — rice in a small quantity and weed soup. If I had not begged, borrowed and stole (at the risk of my life) from the Japanese, I would not have existed. During that time there were over two thousand men who died from dysentery, beri-beri and primarily, malnutrition.

After 6 November, 1942 we were told that we were official prisoners of war and would fare better, which was true for a very short time. I was transferred to Cabanatuan Camp #2 where I worked on the farm, subjected to numerous beatings which have scarred me for life. These beatings, plus malnutrition, were the cause of numerous scars all over my back which now cause me pain and much embarrassment in public, bathing beaches, etc. This condition, which took place during those times, may be enumerated into five serious beatings, many of which were witnessed by our American officers, being subjected to the same treatment, were unable to do more than remonstrate and that at the risk of a serious beating by the Japanese. This lasted until I was transferred to Lipa Batangas Province, P.I. ; Where I was subjected to work on an air field in danger of being bombed by my own countrymen; beaten severely three different times; given only one canteen of water per day for two months. This water was to drink, bathe in and clean my mess gear, the latter, however, being unnecessary — I did that with my tongue! When I asked for more water with which to keep clean (working in the sun shoveling dirt for nine hours), I was allowed to use water which was from a well situated approximately eight feet from a Japanese "head" — toilet open this water was filthy, so was I! When at the same Camp #10, we received Christmas Red Packages. They were given to us along with some accumulated mail and, upon the escape of two American POW's, the Red Cross packages and mail was taken away from us. We were made to stand in a small enclosure with barbed wire entanglements around it and machine guns facing inboard. This, coupled with frequent jabs with a bayonet then, and now, caused and causes considerable mental anguish and nervousness.

Leaving Lip Batangas Provice #10, I went to Zebblin Air Field near Manila. There I was subjected to heavy labor on extremely light rations. By pretending a serious pain in my chest, which I convinced the Japanese was tuberculosis, I was sent to Bilibid Prison. The food there was about six to eight teaspoons of rice per meal and my weight then was one hundred pounds (my average weight is one hundred and seventy pounds). I was sent from there to Cabanatuan #1 and then to Japan early in 1944. I was packed in a ship with sixteen hundred other men. Our water ration was about six teaspoons per day and we spent seventeen days like that. We were put off at Kyushu, Japan, Fuokoa #10 coal mine. I was in the mines until October, 1945 — subjected to severe beatings, starvation, a broken foot and ulceration of my old wounds. Care was inadequate.

These statements are all true and not exaggerated. It would be impossible to tell completely the general mental attitude which this has caused me. I have given statements to the War Crimes Investigation special agent, Joseph Burwasser, CIC, 6th A . These statements parallel with the foregoing.

SWORN TO BEFORE ME AND SUBSCRIBED IN MY PRESENCE THIS 20th DAY OF SEPTEMBER, 1946 AT SAN DIEGO, CALIFORNIA.

From the Saturday Evening Post

We Were Saboteurs

By PL/SGT. Felix J. McCool, USMC,

As told to Edward A. Herron

One of the survivors of the 4th Marine Regiment tells
how, though prisoners, he and his buddies fought back
at the Japs.

We helped win the war by sabotage. We gloried in ab-
senteeism, broke down machinery, crippled electric
motors, and brought buildings tumbling down upon our
heads. We killed people and we maimed them, and at
night would sit huddled in little groups asking ourselves, "What did you do today to screw up things?"

It was a great game, and we didn't dare lose, for
losing meant our heads in the quick way, or our food
ration and slow starvation in the longer way.

Being a prisoner of war is a hard and cruel thing if
it means nothing but barbed wire and confinement, but
It means more than that if you are stripped down to a
G string, with a miner's lamp jammed upon your head,
and dropped sixteen hundred feet underground to grub
for coal. And a horde of little yellow men eager to
give you the club treatment, the vitamin pick-up, every time you lift your head.

You hang on to an air drill, have it chattering and kicking and screaming between your bare feet, biting into the white rock all about, supposedly seeking for the black streak of coal that will be lifted topside and sent to the far corners of Japan, where steel mills are turning out guns to kill American troops.

Your mind stops turning over and it becomes fixed on one point: "No matter how little it is I can do to cripple and halt this work, that much may save the life of an American, keep him from this hell that has hold upon me." So, leaning on the drill, you twist your head cautiously and see the Nip Honcho, the boss overseer underground, turn away for a moment. You throw all your weight on the drill.

The steel begins to falter under the weight of your body and the tough bite of the rock. It slows still more and labors, and a trickle of hot smoke curls out of the barrel resting against your thigh. Then the steel crystallizes; you give a forward shove and the piece snaps off, jammed irremovably into the face of the rock. Then you lean back and call for the Honcho, gesturing wearily at the snapped steel.

Your bit of sabotage for the day is done, and the Nips lose four hours of production while you go up to the surface, look around for new steel, and get on down again.

That night, over a mess of rice with a bit of mouse thrown in for flavor, you grunt out a story in the barracks to you pal, Ritter, and pull out a smile of appreciation.

Then he tells his deed for the day. He's smart with electricity, this guy Ritter, and when the holes are all loaded with dynamite, he breaks the wires, pulls out a fit of the copper, then rethreads the wires together neatly, so neatly that the stupid Nips cannot detect the break. They waste three hours looking for the cause of the fruitless down thrust of the blasting plunger.

Tricks? You got a hundred of them, and every one born of desperation and hate of the little men who herd you around like so much cattle. And in your mind is always the burning thought that the flow of coal from this mine in Futase will be hampered and slowed in every possible way, so you can hurt the Nips in your own slow way, and end the war that much sooner. The end of the war is freedom. It is a wild, burning thought, an impossible dream, but a man has to keep the dream alive or else die.

You've seen it happen. Guys who fold up quietly, lose all hope of ever seeing home and the people they love, and die very silently during the night. There's no movie play about it; the guys just die because they can't dream any more. You and Ritter can spot them. Slip them a bit of your food, kid them along a bit, throw an arm about their shoulders there in the darkness of the barracks and give them the old line about Come on, kid, we'll be walking together down Hollywood Boulevard someday. We'll drop in at the corner drugstore and grab a coke, and we'll pick us up a gal who'll knock your eyes out!" Some of them snap out of it, but lots of times they give that weak grin and turn away. And the next day you're stomping six inched of dirt down on their graves.

So you go back to your little game with the Nips. They were seeing how much of the vitally needed coal they could squeeze out of Futase, how many Americans they could kill in the process; and you fight them at every turn. You and all the other guys. Throw a false bottom of timbers into a mine car, fill it with a shallow load of coal, give the signal and let it go on out half empty; result lost coal, and steel never made, American lives never lost.

Pull links out of a conveyor belt, throw rocks into the pins and jam the belt as often as four times in a night. Derail a loaded train of coal cars, short a dangling wire. And the little yellow men come scurrying around, saying, "Why does this happen" Why does this happen?"

And you and the gang stand with modest, downcast eyes, bowing slight as you answer, "I do not understand. Something is wrong with the earth here. I do not understand."

Ritter is the guy. Ritter is the man who can cave in a whole section of tunnel, hundreds of yard of lateral tunnel, running and breaking away from it as fast as his thin legs can carry him, lest he be caught in his own destruction. The tunnels are lightly timbered, and Ritter takes his hook and slashes at the bottom timber and watches the roof cave. Then the weight of the falling rocks crashes the next timber and the next and next, so they are falling and caving like so many tenpins.

It is wonderful, marvelous, and we look on Ritter as the best of the saboteurs. Only once the cave-in comes too fast and Ritter is buried under tons of rock. But luck is with him — the luck that keeps a man alive through two years of enslavement in the Philippines, carries him through a "hell-ship" crossing, and dumps him down for a year in a coal mine in Japan. He is trapped near an air vent, and the guys dig down through the screen of rocks and get to him.

Ritter is rescued safely, but there is a pair of skinny Jap legs sticking out from under a glut of rocks. Knowing he is dead, you go back to work.

You had long, bitter training for the tricks being pulled in that mine in Japan. The bitterness started in Shanghai all during 1940 and '41 when a thousand American marines were surrounded by a half million Japs. You pulled out of Shanghai on November 27, 1941, and were sleeping in the marine barracks at Mariveles on Bataan Peninsula when the news of Pearl Harbor came through.

You lost the first men two weeks later, when the Nips strafed the base, and then pulled out for Corregidor, catching it every day during January, February, March and April, right on into the screaming crescendo of May fifth when the Japs landed on the Rock.

The gang you were in held on at Monkey Point, a place so hot even American artillery gave you up as lost and turned guns in the direction. Upon those that were left. You picked up some souvenirs, a piece of shrapnel in the back and a slug in the left leg. A five hundred pound bomb burst twenty yards away from your foxhole. In trees all about, birds swung around and hung limp, their rigid claws tight on bare branches. You come out with two shattered eardrums.

The stuff came so fast that it was unbelievable. You ran out of water to cool the machine gun jacket and used a pot of tea. The Nips lined up 320 cannons on the shore across the water and turned on a continuous fire so heavy it sounded like the rat-tat-tat of a machine gun. They'd turn big cannon on a single man. Those were the days when men learned to shed tears all over again.

A Plane in a Bear Trap

Anyway, you surrendered and started off with the Japs and started pulling tricks. The best was the time you were repairing an air strip and filled over a deep hole with bamboo strips, sprinkled a bit of rock above and started to pray a Nip plane would hit the soft spot. One of them did — a big passenger plane — and the wing was ripped off, there was a burst of flame, and afterward the Nips hauled off eight bodies.

When the Americans started to come close, there was one of these hell-ship trips to Japan. A hell ship is a freighter with 1600 men jammed down in the hold, body to body, one man sitting in another's crotch. And no sanitation. Stumbling off the ship onto the dock at Moji, in Japan, you were stinking and the Japs turned atomizers on the gang. Then you were herded into troop trains and dumped down at the camp in Futase.

Even then the Dutchmen who were already there said the smell was so bad they couldn't stand it. The Nips shaved your heads, rammed you full of Jap words, so you could understand commands underground, and sent you down into the hole.

There are some of the guys who can't take it after a while. If a man is rotten with dysentery and he can't eat, he knows that doing down into the hole for a twelve-hour stretch is a death sentence. So he deliberately breaks his foot or he pours acid over his legs, and he stumbles into the sick bay to stretch out on a bamboo mat for a couple of weeks and fight his way back to health and another go in the hole.

Some of the guys pretend to go crazy. They walk around underground with a long thin rod, like a fishing pole, in their hands, pretending to be fishing. And the Japs have one weakness — they have a great respect for crazy people — and they put the guys in the sick bay.

You have the Japs whipped mentally, and they know it. That's why they hate you so much.

In August you know the end is coming for the Nips. You can see them begin to ease up, start throwing a little more food your way. But the war for prisoners at Futase drags on right through the whole month, right on into September. American planes come over and drop food and medicine.

Take a last minute fling at crippling the mine, rip out wires wholesale while the Nips look around, dazed, afraid to move against an American. On the eleventh of September, with the Yanks not yet in sight, and the Nips not knowing whether to shoot you or open up the gates, you take off with five other guys, swing on board a train full of Nip soldiers and civilians, all of them hating you. Fingering the long knife tucked in your belt, you wonder if this is going to be the end of the trail after all the suffering. Then a Jap kid begins to cry, and you slip her a bit of chocolate bar dropped from one of the planes over the camp. Somebody cracks a smile. A Nip soldier wriggles up and offers a cigarette, and the tension is over.

You swing off the train, commandeer a Nip truck and start picking up guys who are breaking out of prison camps all over the country and heading down to the sea. Four hours later you see your first American soldier.

The war is finally over at that moment, but, given a mountain of sand, you'll stay in the cursed country long enough to sprinkle some for it into every electric motor still turning over in Japan.

18 JULY 1940

SHANGHAI, CHINA

Felix thanks Momma for the letter he received saying, "Just the kind of letter I want, ask lots of questions". He agrees the mail service is terrible but they will have to get used to it as it is better than none at all. He says that's the way it would be in they went into the interior. The men don't go to Chingwangtao due to the unsettled conditions.

He tells Momma that Antoinette and Aileen (sisters) hardly ever write and he'll return the same. It's hard to compose letters without questions and he likes lots of those.

Felix just finished reading ‹Each to the other' by Christopher Le Farge which he feels is a beautiful novel written in verse. He would like to have read some of it to Momma.

He still has the statue of Our Lady Queen of Peace —peace, he says, is a funny word right now. He feels it doesn't really matter, a few more to their just deserts prematurely.

Felix hopes Momma's heart isn't bothering her too much and tells her to be careful. He would like to get her a teakwood box but would be happy to purchase a gem for her. She just has to name what she would like.

The weather today is quite sultry and rainy, but won't rain. There was a nice lightning storm last night and you should have seen the Chinese scurry for cover as they do not like it.

Felix sees a dead person nearly every day. He doesn't know what hits them, whether they are beaten and robbed or starved to death. He saw three the other day and one was a young boy. It's best not to render aid if they are dying. According to the local custom, if they die they are your charge. A heartless country is how Felix describes it. He saw one of the upper lords beat a young coolie because a feather duster he was carrying brushed against the higher up's clothes. It was all Felix could do to keep from knocking his head into a brick wall. That would lead to international complications and that would be unacceptable.

Three new Officers joined this company today and they are all new to the Corps. He knows it will be a mad house for a few days with their writing letters, etc. They go letter crazy for a week or so then they simmer down.

Felix is going to take the NCO exams in October, asks Momma to pray that he will pass. Ratings are hard to get where he is, they don't just give them away.

Momma is thanked for the Holy Communion; Felix feels it has done him good. His next will be for her.

He doesn't want Momma to worry about the war, it's too bad but lots have gone before and more will follow. The end is what they all want and when you are ready, he feels it doesn't matter. Remember what Omar said he tells Momma, "Why, if the soul can fling the dust aside, and naked on the air of Heaven ride. Weren't not a shame — weren't it not a shame for him. In this clay concise crippled to abide?" He was a trifle violent but not too wrong. Hope this doesn't disturb you — I go thru different moods every day and this is one.

Felix took a girl to the Club show last night and then we had a banana split. We met up with the top Sgt and his wife who joined us.

He's signing off for now with all his love.

ANNEX – 4
MISC

This annex contains a press release upon Felix's retirement from the Marine Corps, a speech given to a local school (which includes one of the editor's favorite poems at the end), a recollection from Felix's niece (and co-editor), and a letter from President Truman. There is also a poem and military citation for Felix's unit at the Battle of Chosin.

FOR IMMEDIATE RELEASE

CAMP LEJEUNE, N.C., March 9- - Commissioned Warrant Officer Felix (incorrectly spelled Fein in official release) J. McCool, an instructor in the Freight Transportation section of Marine Corps supply schools, Camp Lejeune, N.C. has compiled an outstanding record during his 25 years of service in the Marine Corps.

He was a subject of the Ralph Edwards show; This is your Life, last April.

McCool, who enlisted in the Marine Corps in 1938, was appointed to the rank of Warrant Officer (WO-1) in 1945. He received his present rank that of Commissioned Warrant Officer, in April 1953, while a prisoner of war in Korea.

During World War II, Warrant Officer McCool saw service on Bataan and Corregidor before he was captured by the Japanese in May 1942. As a prisoner of war, he was made a slave laborer by the Japanese and was taken to Japan in 1943-1944 to work in the coal mines on Kyushu. After his liberation from prison camp, McCool was sent to California. He spent the period between World War II and the Korean Conflict stationed on the West Coast and in Hawaii as a member of the First Marine Division.

When the First Marine Division was called to Korea, McCool was with them. And he was with them when they made their historic march on the Inchon Seoul. He was with them at Seoul; at Wonson; at Hamhung; and at Koto-Ri — "Hell Fire Valley", where he was again taken prisoner, this time by the Reds.

After his release from Communist POW camp in 1953, McCool was stationed in the Oakland-San Francisco area where he attended the Navy Base Transportation School, and Golden Gate College, San Francisco, Cal., until 1956, when he was assigned to Freight Transportation Schools at Camp Lejeune, N.C.

His medal and decorations include: Purple Heart, Presidential Unit Citation, Army Distinguished Unit Citation w/cluster, the Good Conduct Medal (received six times), American Defense Service Medal, American Campaign, Asiatic-Pacific Campaign with 1 star, World War II victory Medal, National Defense Service, Korean Service with three stars, Marine Corps Reserve Ribbon, United Nations Medal, Philippine Presidential Unit Citation, Korean Presidential Unit Citation, and Philippine Defense. (Oklahoma Cross of Valor [hand written in])

McCool, a native of Oklahoma, has attended Golden Gate College in San Francisco, Calif., and is presently studying at Eastern Carolina College.

In addition to his military and scholarly activities, McCool, himself a former boy scout, is Public Relations Chairman for the Onslow County, N.C. Boy Scouts. He has also given talks on his wartime experiences to local high schools and fraternal organizations and has appeared on an East Carolina College Educational television program entitled, "History Alive".

Warrant Officer McCool and his wife, Marion, reside in Tarawa Terrace, Camp Lejeune.

The President of the United States take pleasure in presenting the PRESIDENTIAL UNIT CITATION to the

FIRST MARINE DIVISION, REINFORCED

For service as set forth in the following

CITATION:

"For extraordinary heroism and outstanding performance of duty in action against enemy aggressor forces in the Chosin Reservior and Koto-ri area of Korea from 27 November to 11 December 1950. When the full fury of the enemy counterattack struck both the Eighth Army and the Tenth Corps on 27 and 28 November 1950, the First Marine Division, Reinforced, operating as the left flank division of the Tenth Corps, launched a daring assault westward from Yudam-ni in an effort to cut the road and rail communications of hostile forces attacking the Eighth Army and at the same time, continued its mission of protecting a vital main supply route consisting of a tortuous mountain road running southward to Chinhung-ni, approximately 35 miles distant. Ordered to withdraw to Hamhung in company with attached army and other friendly units in the face of tremendous pressure in the Chosin Reservoir area, the Division began an epic battle against the bulk of the enemy Third Route Army and, while small intermediate garrisons at Hagaru-ri and Koto-ri held firmly against repeated and determined attacks by hostile forces, gallantly fought its way successively to Hagaru-ri, Koto-ri, Chinhung-ni and Hamhang over twisting, mountainous and icy roads in sub-zero temperatures. Battling desperately night and day in the face of almost insurmountable odds throughout a period of two weeks of intense and sustained combat, the First Marine Division, Reinforced, emerged from its ordeal as a fighting unit with its wounded, with its guns and equipment and with its prisoners, decisively defeating seven enemy divisions, together with elements of three others, and inflicting major losses which seriously impaired the military effectiveness of the hostile forces for a considerable period of time. The valiant fighting spirit, relentless perseverance and heroic fortitude of the officer and men of the First Marine Division, Reinforced, in battle against a vastly outnumbering enemy, were keeping with the highest traditions of the United States Naval Service."

The President of the United States take pleasure in presenting the PRESIDENTIAL UNIT CITATION to the

FIRST MARINE DIVISION, REINFORCED

For service as set forth in the following

CITATION:

"For extraordinary heroism and outstanding performance of duty in action against enemy aggressor forces in Korea from 15 September to 11 October 1950. In the face of a determined enemy and against almost insurmountable obstacles, including disadvantageous tidal and beach conditions on the western coast of Korea, the FIRST Marine Division Reinforced, rapidly and successfully effected the amphibious seizure of Inch'on in an operation without parallel in the history of amphibious warfare. Fully aware that the precarious situation of friendly ground forces fighting desperately against the continued heavy pressure of a numerically superior hostile force necessitated the planning and execution of this extremely hazardous operation within a period of less than thirty days, and cognizant of the military importance of its assigned target, the Division moved quickly into action and, on 15 September, by executing three well-coordinated attacks over highly treacherous beach approaches defended by resolute enemy troops, captured the island of Wolmi-do, the city of Inch'on and Kimp'o Airfield, and rendered invaluable assistance in the capture of Seoul. As a result of its aggressive attack, the Division drove the hostile forces in hasty retreat over thirty miles in the ensuing ten days, completely severed vital hostile communications and supply lines and greatly relieved enemy pressure on other friendly ground units, thereby permitting these units to break out from their Pusan beachhead and contributing materially to the total destruction of hostile ground forces in southern Korea. The havoc and destruction wrought on an enemy flushed with previous victories and the vast accomplishments in turning the tide of battle from a weakening defensive to a vigorous offensive action reflect the highest credit upon the officers and men of the FIRST Marine Division, Reinforced, and the United States Naval Service."

The President of the Unites States takes the pleasure in presenting the PRESIDENTIAL UNIT CITATION to the

FIRST PRVISIONAL MARINE BRIGADE, REINFORCED

For service as set forth in the following

CITATION:

"For extraordinary heroism in action against enemy aggressor forces in Korea from 7 August to 7 September 1950. Functioning as a mobile, self-contained, air-ground team, the FIRST Provisional Marine Brigade, Reinforced, rendered invaluable service during the fierce struggle to maintain the foothold established by friendly forces in the Pusan area during the early stages of the Korean conflict. Quickly moving into action as numerically superior enemy forces neared the Naktong River on the central front and penetrated to within thirty-five miles of Pusan in the southern sector, threatening the integrity of the entire defensive perimeter, this hard-hitting, indomitable team counterattacked serious enemy penetrations at three different points in rapid succession. Undeterred by road-blocks, heavy hostile automatic-weapons and highly effective artillery fire, extremely difficult terrain and intense heat, the Brigade met the invaders with relentless determination and, on each crucial occasion, hurled them back in disorderly retreat. By combining sheer resolution and esprit de corps with sound infantry tactics and splendid close air support, the Brigade was largely instrumental in restoring the line of defense, in inflicting thousands of casualties upon the enemy and in seizing large amounts of ammunition, equipment and other supplies. The brilliant record achieved by the unit during the critical early days of the Korean conflict attests to the individual valor and competence of the officers and men and reflects the highest credit upon the FIRST Provisional Marine Brigade, Reinforced, and the United States Naval Service."

THE WHITE HOUSE
WASHINGTON

26 November, 1945.

Dear Felix J. McCool,

It gives me special pleasure
to welcome you back to your native
shores, and to express, on behalf of
the people of the United States, the
joy we feel at your deliverance from
the hands of the enemy. It is a
source of profound satisfaction that
our efforts to accomplish your return
have been successful.

You have fought valiantly
and have suffered greatly. As your
Commander in Chief, I take pride in
your past achievements and express
the thanks of a grateful Nation for
your services in combat and your
steadfastness while a prisoner of war.

May God grant you happiness
and a successful future.

Harry Truman

YOUNG MEN AND WOMEN!

CONGRATULATIONS ON YOUR ACHIEVEMENT!

How would you like to climb to the top of PIKES PEAK?
Well, you couldn't do it all day one. You would have
to take it step by step and pause for rests to sort of
catch your breath. You would get to the top though.
WHY? BECAUSE YOU WANTED TO!

Each step up would lead to a plateau or flat spot
where you could rest up for the balance of the journey. Those stopping places are a lot like graduation
times. When you finish the 8th grade, for instance, you
stop for vacation and then you group your thoughts,
and continue on to HIGH SCHOOL and from there another
stop, and on up to COLLEGE.

Yes, it's like climbing a mountain and at each stop
you see things a little clearer and when you reach
the top YOU SEE ALL.

Do you know what I see tonight before me? I see another group, the group that I was with who graduated
from the 8th grade and I remember how we all felt,
that the world was opening up. It was opening up! But
that was only the first door opening to the light beyond. The first plateau, or flat place, the place where
the runner gets his second wind.

Have you ever run a long race? There must be some of
you here who have. Well, remember how it was when you
just felt you couldn't put another foot down or grab

313

another GASP of air. And then all of a sudden you got your second wind. New energy came to your muscles, and then it seemed as if you could go on forever. Well here again we can see that you doing that now, getting your second wind, reaching a rest spot preparing for BEYOND, THE PLACE BEYOND!

I told you that I sat as you are doing some years ago thinking of the future. And do you know I still think of the future. Just as I did then, but now with a little more understanding, a little more patience. And I know now that by education all of us can reach the very top, ONLY you must keep trying. What is the first step before doing something? Why, it's THINKING! You have a mind—you must always use it!

THINK!

Do you know what sharing is? Well, it's teaching you to think while on your feet in front of people, and also teaching you to speak out your truthful opinions. Never be afraid to speak the truth, or to voice an honest opinion. If I may be permitted to give you advice let me say this to you. Learn the tools of education then apply them, SOCIALLY. Learn civics, local town government, be a part of your community. Do not look down on a person who does not know, help him to know—Then you have a sharing, there is no fear when you share knowledge.

When I started talking to you this evening I said you could get to the top because you wanted to . That's true, but you must also have help. The teachers have given this help to you; they have guided you to this top! Take advantage of those helps. Look around you now: at the people you have associated with. Mr. Ruubelein's education background has been yours for these past few months. Mr. Bender, Mrs. Hudson, Miss Reeves, OUR TEACHERS. I say our as I feel part of them just as you do, Think of the care they have given to you morning, noon, and night and then some. Because when you were playing at home in the evenings they were preparing for the TOMORROWS in your life! How will you use all of the fine things you have been taught? The good friendships you have formed, HOW? By being successful, by using your God-given brains.

CONTINUE YOUR EDUCATION!

Be a success. What is success? Well, it is measured by many in different ways, not always money. True, success is an achievement, an inner feeling of a job well done. Always go ahead, and when you must stop, dig in and hold on to what you have achieved. During vacation read good books, look to tomorrow. Go to your future High School and talk with your future teachers, PLAN.

It is a wonderful thing to experience the success of completion. You are experiencing it tonight, the final act for you at BLUE CREEK SCHOOL. Others in High Schools and Universities are also having a complete experience tonight. You are the ones who direct your own paths. Others light and guide the way. But you and only you direct the way!

Wasn't this a wonderful school? Remember at the beginning of last year when you had to sit in at the high school for classes, this area was a vacant lot, then brick and mortar and man's will caused the building. Then the final and important choice the best trained brains were collected here and all for you!

And you have used the assistance that these people brought to you. You have used it well, you have studied, played, acted, developed your minds, your bodies, and your talents in the arts.

One time, a time and a half ago, I had to stop my education because a depression came. I stopped and worked awhile but I knew that a man does not live by bread alone, he must feed his mind. I joined the U.S. Marines for education and travel. But one thing that was a drive in my mind that education was the only answer to a better life, and continuance was the only way that it could be achieved. Soon I hope to have my degree and desire to join the honor roll of teachers of young men and women, that I too may light a light and guide someone to their fulfillment.

We here in America have so very much. Our history and our Constitution have made it so, remember this when you study on in high school, that everything you have in freedom and good living comes from THINKING PEOPLE, people who knew that there were troubled times ahead and prepared for it just as you must prepare for your future. All of the gifts of freedom are yours; continue on in school that you too may add to the good of everyone. Some people before you have not had the opportunities to educate themselves as you have today. But they know the value to you!

What can I leave to you now? May I tell you a story about a few Armed forces troops in the Korean War.? They were out too far in the front lines and were surrounded by the enemy, many were wounded and all became prisoners of the Communists. As prisoners they were indoctrinated by the Communists who tried to teach, them to hate our country, to be godless, but they had the heritage, the background that you have gained here in Blue Creek School by your education achievement. Why, even in prison camp they made their own secret schools to continue on in the seeking for knowledge and fight the communists. Each man taught what he knew best to his fellow prisoners of war. They continued to educate themselves just as you must do after tonight's graduation. You have reached a plateau, a place of second wind, a place to rest and think, NOW THEN GO ON TO HIGH SCHOOL (even though hardships are in the way).We all know that your parents will help you, won't Mother's and Father's help. They are the first to want you to have your heritage of education. Tell them what you want. Tell your teachers and then DIG IN, push forward to the very top and watch it blossom out into more knowledge. Find out what your future school stands for then work toward fulfill that policy. You will all have an opportunity to play sports; don't feel badly if you are not the 1st string, a morning team plays the same game as the starred evening team. The main thing is to play the game as best you can. Have a good attitude whether you win or lose and you'll develop a genuine

respect for the personality of others, KEEP TRYING
AND CONTINUE ON.

REMEMBER THIS!

Out of the world of yesterday the world of today has
grown; and out of the world of today will come the
world of tomorrow! YOUR TOMORROW: WORK FOR IT**STUDY
FOR IT**PRAY FOR IT**AND FIGHT FOR IT.

Good night, go in FREEDOM!

MY JOURNEY WITH MY UNCLE, FELIX J. MC COOL, 2

BY

AILEEN ANN (HISS) MARCKMANN

This story is dedicated to my brother, Michael, who was scheduled to take this trip with Felix. Due to an unforeseeable accident, Michael was unable to go and I was asked to take his place.

We left Burbank airport on October 5, 1953 at 11:36 p.m. headed to Chicago. We landed in Chicago at 8:00 a.m. on October 6, 1953 with weather at 50 degrees. Jerry Fink and his wife were there to meet us. Bobby Saksa and his mother, Larry Taft and his wife were also in the greeting party. The weather wasn't bad for 50 degrees. I learned the crucifix that was carved in the prison camp for Father Kapaun was now in Patterson, New Jersey. It was a very short visit as our next flight left Chicago at 8:52 a.m. We were traveling on a Convair with a speed of 240 miles and an altitude of 11,000 feet. The temperature outside the plane at 11,000 feet will be 25 degrees. Jerry sends regards to the family.

We had a 10 minute stop in Detroit and I'm feeling a little air sick. The weather is fine here. The stewardess is going to help me with the time changes. We are 3 hours ahead of Los Angeles, 2 hours ahead at Denver and 1 hour here in Detroit. Somehow that doesn't seem correct. Lt and Mrs. Miller met up with us at the airport where they were being held up for a flight to Albany. Eleanor Roosevelt was in Chicago at this same time.

We are off again and on the way to Niagara, airborne at 2:25 p.m. (our time, 11:25 a.m. at home). Just saw Lake Erie and Ontario while landing at Niagara at 3:42 p.m. I'm sitting on the plane looking at a sign pointing to Canada. The pilot took us once lightly over Niagara Falls and it's raining outside. The plane landed to let off some passengers and we took off again. Uncle Felix was sharing some photos with the stewardess.

We are airborne again at 3:58 bound for Buffalo. It feels really good to be so high in the air. It stopped raining as we landed in Buffalo at 4:04. There is a man outside filling the right wing with gas and it's freezing outside. One person boarded and there is a miscount so the flight was delayed for that. The plane was stopped to get a federal clearance due to the number of planes in the air between Buffalo and Rochester, which is about 30 minutes.

Airborne again at 5:13 p.m. bound for Rochester and it's still freezing outside. I just woke from a short nap as we landed in Rochester at 5:45 p.m. Left at 6:07, flying at 5,000 feet, and it's raining very hard and is very cold outside. Landing at Syracuse at 6:45 was very exciting for us as we were about to be fed. We changed planes there and headed straight for New York City. We're on our way at 7:32. On this part of the trip I met an Army Colonel on a government business trip.

When we arrived in New York City we took a taxi to another airport for the trip to Miami. We went to a restaurant for dinner. Uncle Felix couldn't wait to get a New York steak. I was still airsick and couldn't eat anything. I think Uncle Felix was very disappointed but I was very tired and upset. When we got to the airport, I slept on a bench until it was time to board the plane. The plane left at 1:00 a.m., east coast time, on October 7th and arrived in Miami at 6:00 a.m. I slept all the way down the east coast as Uncle Felix was pointing out and enjoying the landmarks. I noticed the change in weather immediately as we approached Miami. It was very warm.

Aunt Pat, Uncle Dick and Frances met us at the airport and took us to their home. After breakfast I took a nap. After lunch Frances and I went downtown and saw a movie, then went to the library and a record store to buy some new records. It was raining when we left the movie and the streets had completely flooded but it was still very warm.

The next day I spent helping Paul (Frances' boyfriend) paint model ships. Aunt Jean picked me up later that day and I went home with her and the twins, Charlie and Larry. They took me to see the Venetian Pools and we had dinner together. Aunt Ruby and the kids, David and Michele, Granddad and Grandmother came over later. I went home with Aunt Ruby for the night. The following day Aunt Jean, Aunt Ruby, Charlie, Larry and I went to Crandon Park and lunch at Howard Johnson's. I was supposed to spend the night with Aunt Jean but stayed with the Grandparents.

Granddad took me swimming at the Venetian Pools and I dove off a ledge at 24 feet. Later that night I had dinner with the Grandparents (the Hiss side of my family) and Uncle Don. Uncle Jimmy and Aunt Marilyn, Uncle Don and Aunt Sue with Grandparents took me back to Aunt Patricia's to meet Uncle Felix.

After Mass on Sunday we, Patsy and Bill Richardson and their kids, Aunt Pat and Uncle Dick, Frances and Paul, Felix and me, went to Miami Beach. The water was warm and the tide was out far which was very different from the Pacific Ocean. Paul, Francs and I went to a movie that night to see 'Return to Paradise'. Stopped for a soda while waiting for the bus and met up with a friend of Paul's. I got to bed/sleep that night around midnight.

The following morning we were up at 6:20 a.m. to pack for the next part of the journey. The plane left Miami at 8:30 a.m. for Tampa and the airline was National. I remember this because it was the most comfortable landing I had had so far. Next, we were on the way to New Orleans at 9:45 a.m., then airborne again for Dallas. Arrived in Dallas about 1:30 p.m. and were met by Curly Reid, his wife, son and mother. They took us out to Irving to see their home and back to the airport for the flight to Oklahoma City. It seems that there was a mix-up in reservations and we were a day late getting in to Oklahoma City.

Upon arriving in Oklahoma City it was 5:25 p.m. and we were met by Antoinette and Clara Cole. There was also a large number of people at the airport to see Felix. I met some cousins, Kathy and Rebecca. Antoinette took us to Mrs. Lilly's house (Gordon's mother) for a reception and we had a very nice time. When we arrived at Antoinette and Gordon's home we all said the rosary and got to bed at 2:00 a.m.

The next afternoon Antoinette, Uncle Felix, Cathy and I went to WKY TV because Uncle Felix was being interviewed. We met lots of the TV personalities. We all went out to Betty's cabin to go horseback riding and motor boating later that afternoon followed by dinner. Uncle Felix gave a speech that night at the XPWS regarding Father Kapaun. Cathy and I were to pull the car around front after the speech but had to go around the block 3 times and park in a 'No Parking' spot to wait for Uncle Felix. We made it to bed about 1:30 am.

The next day we were taking Kathy and Maggie back to Tulsa. We skipped breakfast and Antoinette gave us a glass of milk and said we would eat later. Hours later we stopped at Howard Johnson's and by then I was car sick. When we got out of the car and passed by the big window of the restaurant ,I lost that glass of milk in view of all the diners. After cleaning me up we all piled back in the car and went on to the next restaurant where we stopped to eat. In Tulsa, we had dinner at Anna Catherine's house. After dinner Cathy took me on a tour of the city and showed me Utica Square and St. John's Hospital. I spent that night at Katie's, the next day was packing. We met up with Jeanne Maxwell, Wanda and Peggy Young who took us to the airport. Betty, Ollie and Buddy were also at the airport.

We are on our way again at 6:38 to Tucson, looking at a beautiful sunset. Dinner will be served soon. At 8:45 p.m. we are flying over El Paso and the city is full of lights and it is a lovely sight. I think we passed over the Rio Grande River, too. I had a nice conversation with the lady across the aisle on this flight. Time changed an hour when we landed in Tucson and now we are just an hour ahead of home. It was 8:30 p.m. when we got off the plane to pick up some things to send to Patsy's kids.

We were airborne at 9:00 p.m. for Phoenix and looked back at the beautiful sight of the lights of Tucson. When we landed in Phoenix it was 9:30 p.m. and we were 45 to 50 minutes behind schedule. The weather in Phoenix was very nice. We were in the air again at 9:55 p.m. and Uncle Felix told me he was going back to Oklahoma City soon to receive the Medal of Honor from the Governor of Oklahoma.

Landed in San Diego at 10:10 and took off again for Los Angeles at 10:30 p.m. Uncle Felix and I arrived at Los Angeles International Airport at 11:10 p.m. We were met by Mommy, Daddy, Michael and Aunt Mary. We took Aunt Mary and Uncle Felix back to Glendale and went home. I got to bed at 2:30 a.m. I had a wonderful and exciting trip around the country and met many terrific people. It was good to be home with my family again.

Anecdotes that I want to add to my story as the memories flood back to me. It is now July 2010. In telling my story I am amazed about the difference in travel from 1953 to today. In 1953 it took us 2 to 3 days to cross the country and today it is done in hours. It was no wonder that the 12 year old girl got air sick and tired.

Felix's family and friends worried and prayed for his safe return for many years. Aunt Mary would get word thru military channels from time to time and would keep everyone informed. On a Saturday evening in the fall of 1953, my parents, Joe and Aileen Hiss, were in Glendale visiting with Aunt Mary and Uncle Louis. I was at home listening to the radio when an announcement came on with news of POW's that were being released. Several groups of POW's had already been released and this was to be the last group. As I listened I heard, all the POW's names were called off and the last one was Felix J. McCool. He was coming home. I quickly called my parents to tell them what I had heard and everyone was excited and crying.

We made plans to drive to San Francisco to meet the ship he would be on. Several family members were there and as the ship came into the dock, there he was, standing on the deck in his uniform. We all spent a few days at the Marine Club in San Francisco visiting.

Back home there were lots of family and friends gathering to visit with Uncle Felix and the stories he told of his experience's we heard many times. They were all written down by Uncle Felix in his poetry and his many short stories.

When Uncle Felix and I left Miami on the way to Oklahoma City, he asked me a question. He wanted to know what I thought about Marion Landers whom I had met in Miami. It seems that Marion and her family were part of the family thru marriage and close friends to the McCool's. Well, Uncle Felix told me then that he planned on marrying her. And that did happen in late 1953. During the time they lived in San Francisco I spent many vacations with them and became very close.

My favorite story from my trip was told to me by Aunt Marion. It seems that she was at the airport in Miami to meet her man and I got off the plane with him. She thought that Uncle Felix had brought along a girlfriend, she was upset, but somehow they got that cleared up because they married and spent many years together.

Copyright by Aileen Ann Marckmann

July 2010

"Felix post Korean War reunion with Miami family sister Patricia Swift, her husband Dick Swift, Frances Swift and Aileen Ann."

MARION

I have no lines to write

But only my heart to speak to you

Of feelings old but new

Please listen with your heart

And not with hearing confused

By the brassy tongue of hasty

Anger — Who tastes the fleshy

Fruit, digesting the pulp with

Ruminations and tosses away

The seed

But listen closely to my

Heart which only says

Love is my splendid thing

And only my love for you

FJM

June 7, 1959

"Felix and Marion Christmas 1954"

I, Felix McCool USMC, carried this throughout the battles while in the USMC.

From 1938 to 1956.

Whoever shall carry this prayer on their person shall not be drowned, nor die a bad death, nor suddenly. He shall be delivered from the plague, the pest and the lightning, in the house where this prayer is kept shall never happen any betrayal or mean thing of those who speak this prayer and heed it, will be pardoned of their sins. Even though they should be as many as the stars in the sky, says God, provided they fully repent.

"God who has left us a memorial of the passion in the Holy Shroud from the Cross, mercifully grant that by the death and burial we may reach a glorious Resurrection. Who liveth and reigneth one God, world without end. Amen!"

From the years 1934 to 1960 a member of the USMC 242450 enlisted officer 049270 USMC.

ACKNOWLEDGEMENTS

My mother and I would like to thank several people who helped, inspired and motivated us to complete this project. For their help typing and retyping from the original manuscript, thank you to Michael Hiss, Jerry Lilly, and Lori Marckmann . For technical assistance, Kathy Varney, Captain (Ret) Ed Hrivnak, Lieutenant Colonel (Ret) William Latham, and Gina M. DiNicolo. A thank you to Ken Marckmann, Donna Egeland, Trevor Marckmann, Terry Lowenstein, Dan Richard, Bob Simmons, and Major Alan Bevilaqua for their love, support and encouragement on this project. Mostly to Marion, who gave us encouragement as well as the original papers and more contained within this book.

There are many more stories behind every veteran and their family. We encourage all veterans to leave their legacy and story for future generations. There are also many organizations which support veterans and their families, we also encourage support of these organizations as another means to support those who defended our freedoms, the freedoms Felix remained faithful to during his captivity and cherished every day upon his repatriation. We intend on setting up a Facebook page with more of Felix's papers, stories and his television appearance on "This is Your Life."

Out of the world of yesterday the world of today has grown;
and out of the world of today will come the world of tomorrow!
YOUR TOMORROW:
WORK FOR IT
STUDY FOR IT
PRAY FOR IT
AND FIGHT FOR IT.

*"Marion and Aileen Ann. Aileen Marckmann grew up in the Southern
California area where she raised three children. She was active in
the children's schools and the church communities. She worked in the
banking industry for over 20 years prior to retiring and now resides in
Northern California. Marion is happily retired in the Miami area."*

"Marion and Scott. Scott Marckmann is a retired Air Force Lieutenant Colonel. He served thirty years Active Duty and Reserve. He was a command pilot, who also served in the Intelligence community and Headquarters Air Force Staff. He is a graduate of the Air War College and also a Captain with a major airline. Scott currently resides in the Seattle Washington area with his family."